CARL WELLMAN

challenge
and response

JUSTIFICATION IN ETHICS

southern illinois university press

Carbondale and Edwardsville

feffer & simons, inc.

London and Amsterdam

CONTENTS

Contents

I began work on this book at Oxford during the winter and spring terms of 1961. In addition to reading widely in the libraries, I enjoyed philosophical discussions with Elizabeth Anscombe, Philippa Foot, Mary Warnock, Gilbert Ryle, William Kneale, H. L. A. Hart, James Urmson, and especially Richard Hare. At that time I was trying to collect and organize my thoughts on justification in ethics. No matter how hard I tried I could find no neat classification of ethical theories (such as ethical naturalism, intuitionism, and noncognitivism) which would reveal the main alternatives among which one must choose. Gradually I came to realize that this was because any theory of justification must solve several relatively independent problems, so that any classification of answers to one question tends to be misleading with respect to other equally important questions.

One problem is "what makes some consideration a good reason in ethics?" John Wisdom and Jonathan Bennett stimulated my thinking on this question at Cambridge during the summer of 1961. It is not easy to determine, much less to explain, exactly what it is that distinguishes relevant from irrelevant considerations in ethics or in any other subject. Reflection on what we do when we give reasons for our ethical statements led me to believe that reasoning is somehow connected with persuading, but my conviction that ethical statements are objectively valid forced me to admit that it cannot be mere persuasion. My compromise has been to define validity in terms of what would be persuasive after criticism.

How many kinds of reasoning are there in ethics? I discussed this and other problems with Henry Aiken, Rogers Albritton, Raphael Demos, Abraham Edel, Paul Edwards, Roderick Firth, John Ladd, Morton White, and Donald Williams while spending a summer reading in Widener Library. My conclusion is that ethical statements can be established by three distinct kinds of logical arguments—deductive, inductive, and what I call conductive.

Preface

My central problem, of course, has been "what is justification?" At first I assumed, like most others, that to justify an ethical statement is simply to give good and sufficient reasons for it. But two things came to disturb me more and more. Even conclusive evidence for an ethical statement can sometimes leave room for doubt about its claim to truth because one may wonder whether it is as conclusive as it appears; and some of the things one says in defense of an ethical statement, such as "why do you think me mistaken?," do not seem to be reasons in any ordinary sense. Very slowly I came to conceive of justification in a very different way, in terms of challenges and responses. My present view is that to justify an ethical statement is to meet whatever challenges have actually been made to it. As I groped toward this view my efforts were assisted by William Boardman, John Dreher, Carl Hamburg, Leonard Pinsky, Herbert Spiegelberg, Stephen Barker, William Alston, and Phillips Griffiths, who have each criticized my early efforts to write down the ideas that were taking shape in my mind.

Can the challenge of ethical skepticism be met? In particular, does the existence of ethical disagreement force one to give up the objective validity of ethical statements? In the end I think not, provided one can explain precisely what it means to say that a statement is true, an argument valid, an ethical judge competent, and a response adequate. I have been forced toward greater precision in formulating these critical claims by the criticisms of almost every member of the Department of Philosophy of the University of Michigan, where I completely revised my manuscript during the academic year 1965–66. My debt is unusually great to Richard Brandt, Irving Copi, William Frankena, Alvin Goldman, Joseph Sneed, Charles Stevenson, and James Urmson, who have commented extensively on various chapters in rough draft.

I am also indebted to the American Council of Learned Societies, whose grant-in-aid in 1961 and fellowship in 1965–66 enabled me to take the time to think and write free from my regular academic duties. Finally, I must thank the secretary who transcribed the final draft into a finished manuscript and the press that transformed this into a book.

St. Louis, Missouri   *Carl Wellman*
December 1970

How can ethical statements be justified? Similar questions can be posed in many areas. How can ordinary factual statements be justified? How can the scientist justify his theories? How can the logician justify his logical principles? How can legal claims be justified? Each of these questions raises interesting philosophical problems. In the following pages I work out a theory of justification that applies to all these areas. But the question of justification seems particularly urgent in ethics because of the pervasiveness and persistence of ethical disagreement and doubt.

When one person asserts that a specified act is right, another is apt to declare it wrong; disputes about particular value judgments are so common that it is often said that good and bad are all a matter of taste. Even when philosophers agree that some object is good or some act a duty, they typically disagree about which theory correctly explains this value or obligation. Although ethical disagreements are sometimes resolved by rational discussion, even the most reasonable of men are often unable to reach agreement on ethical issues. Nor is this uncertainty over ethical statements limited to disagreement, to conflicting ethical claims made by different people; an individual is often his own severest critic. A man may sincerely believe that some act is right at the same time that he has serious reservations as to his own moral judgment; a philosopher may hold to an ethical theory, even state it publicly and in print, while being very much alive to strong arguments against his theory. Thus the claim that any ethical statement is true may be confronted with interpersonal disagreement and personal doubt, both of which frequently resist solution by factual inquiry and ethical reasoning.

In spite of this uncertainty, people continue to make ethical statements. All men assert, with varying degrees of confidence, particular judgments of obligation and value, while philosophers formulate and defend ethical theories. Not only do we make ethical statements, we try to justify the claim to truth implicit in them. Hard as we try, we all too often fall short of complete justification. For the sake of practical assurance as well as theoretical truth, we would like to do better. But how can we do better in justifying our ethical statements? How can anyone succeed? How can ethical statements be justified?

The most popular answer these days seems to be that one justifies an ethical statement by giving good reasons for it, but this reply is quite inadequate. For one thing, it raises as many questions as it answers. What distinguishes good from bad reasons in ethics? Are factual premises related logically or psychologically to ethical conclusions? If ethical arguments presuppose ethical principles, how are ethical principles in turn established? Must the premises of ethical reasoning be known to be true, or simply true, or only believed to be true, or what? More radically, it will not do to say that justifying an ethical statement consists in giving good reasons for it because giving even the best of reasons may be insufficient to justify fully any ethical statement. Imagine that I have given a sound argument for some ethical conclusion, that I have defended it with a deductive argument that is logically valid and whose premises are all true. By hypothesis, the premises of my argument are true; but it is still possible for someone, even myself, to doubt their truth. And if their claim to truth is questioned, then I must go beyond my original argument to produce evidence in support of its premises. Again, my argument is, by hypothesis, logically valid; but someone may not recognize or acknowledge its validity. If its validity is challenged, then merely repeating my original argument is hardly enough to justify the ethical statement it is intended to establish. Before I can use my argument to justify its conclusion I must somehow establish its claim to logical validity. Giving good reasons for an ethical statement is not the end of justification because both the truth of these reasons and their relevance to the ethical conclusion can be questioned in any given case. Not only is giving good reasons not always the end of the matter, it is sometimes not even the beginning. To assert seriously an ethical statement is to claim that it is true. This claim to truth has been challenged wholesale by some emotivists. Ayer, for example, has argued in *Language, Truth, and Logic* that ethical sentences merely express and evoke emotions; they assert or deny nothing. To try to meet this challenge by giving good reasons for one's ethical statement would be to beg the question, for Ayer is claiming that ethical statements are the sort of sentence for which it is entirely out of place to give reasons. If one is to continue to claim truth for one's utterance, one must meet Ayer's challenge in some other way. Most recent attempts to answer the question "how can ethical statements be justified?" have been both incomplete and misleading because they have mistakenly assumed that to justify is simply to give good reasons.

In this way, the question "how can ethical statements be justified?" gives rise to the more basic question "what is justification?" Surprisingly enough, this is a question that is seldom explicitly raised. When it is raised, it is seldom discussed at any length. My guess is that the current neglect of this central philosophical question and the many philosophical issues it poses is caused by the uncritical assumption that to justify is simply to give good reasons or adequate evidence for one's assertions. Since this presupposition is false, there is a vital need for a new and more prolonged look at the nature of justification. Part One of this study explains and defends a conception of justification that is broader than the good-reasons conception but not so broad as to imply that persuasion by any means, fair or foul, is genuine justification.

The starting place is deductivism, the view that all valid ethical reasoning is deductive in form. Granted that many ethical arguments are deductive, I argue that many others are nondeductive yet logically valid. Some of these are inductive arguments of the same logical type as those by which scientific theories are confirmed or disconfirmed. By an examination of thought experiments in ethics, I show that ethical theories are verified or falsified by something analogous to the scientific method. Other nondeductive ethical arguments infer some evaluative or deontic conclusion about a particular case from factual information about that case. I argue at some length that these arguments are a genuine form of reasoning, that they are logically valid in spite of being neither deductive nor inductive. One result of extending the domain of logical argument beyond the bounds of deduction and induction is the need for a broader conception of reasoning. I suggest that "valid" be defined as "persuasive after indefinite criticism." To many this definition will seem so preposterous that it may be rejected out of hand. It does, however, have the advantage of defining the word "valid" in terms of empirical language. Unless one wishes to claim that logical validity is experienced in something like the way that yellowness, tiredness, or fear are, anyone who wishes to hold to empiricism as a general epistemological position is confronted with the necessity of defining our basic logical vocabulary in empirical terms. And if the appropriate terms are not psychological in the main, what are they? Moreover, my definition has the additional advantage of explaining how reasoning is so closely tied to persuasion without reducing reasoning to mere persuasion. Anyone who has pondered the pages of Stevenson's writings in which he discusses the role of persuasion in ethical argument will realize that some such approach is at least worth a try. I then go on to develop a challenge-response model of justification along the same lines. It is my contention that to justify a statement, ethical or nonethical, is to meet all the challenges actually made to it. Although the notion that justification consists in meeting challenges is hardly novel, the way in which I define the crucial expressions "a challenge," "a response," and "meeting" is original. One obvious objection to my view that to justify a statement is to meet those challenges actually made to it is that this is not sufficient; to justify fully one must meet all possible challenges. I argue that this is not so and that the data of ethical justification are simply any premises, arguments, or moves that are in fact accepted.

Now that the nature of justification has been explained, it is possible to return to the original question, "*how* can ethical statements be justified?" On the challenge-response model of justification, this question becomes "how can all the challenges to any ethical statement be met?" Part Two of this study surveys the methodology of ethics. It defines the various dimensions of challenge and response, and it gives enough examples of each to illuminate the nature of the dimension. A review of the complexities of ethical discussion and reflection has convinced me that there are only seven dimensions of justification in ethics, seven fundamentally distinct sorts of challenge that may need to be met to justify any ethical statement. The claim to truth implicit in the ethical statement can be challenged. More radically, one can challenge the claim to truth-value; one may suggest that the ethical sentence is not really a statement at all. One can even challenge the meaning-fulness of the statement, challenge its right to be considered a significant part of language. One can challenge the claim to logical validity implicit in any argument used to defend the ethical state-ment. More radically, one can challenge the claim of any such argu-ment to be a genuine argument; one may insinuate that it is mere persuasion to which the valid-invalid distinction does not apply at all. One can challenge the competence of the speaker to assert the statement seriously. Finally, there is the traditional challenge of ethical skepticism, the suggestion that although the ethical state-ment might be true, no human being can ever be in a position justifiably to claim to know its truth. In each case I give examples of challenges that fall on the dimension and discuss ways in which such challenges might be met. Obviously I cannot discuss every possible challenge and response; I can and do, however, describe the sorts of challenge and response that can be made in ethics. To do this is to explain how ethical statements can, and typically are, justified.

What about the question "*can* ethical statements be justified?" Some of the grounds for doubting that ethical statements can be rationally justified are discussed in Part Two of this study. The contention that ethical sentences are neither true nor false because they are not empirically verifiable is discussed at length in the chapter dealing with truth-value challenges and responses. Steven-son's argument in chapter 7 of *Ethics and Language*, intended to prove that ultimate ethical arguments are not a genuine form of logical reasoning, is considered in its proper place as a validity-value challenge. To be sure, no complete and conclusive proof that ethical statements can be justified is given. But if my conception of justification is correct, no such proof is either possible or necessary. It is not possible because, wherever one rests one's case, new chal-lenges can always arise; it is not necessary because justification can be quite sufficient without meeting all possible challenges. Therefore, I have structured my systematic account of justification in ethics around the two questions "what is justification?" and "how can ethical statements be justified?"

one

WHAT IS
JUSTIFICATION ?

1. deduction

WHAT is justification? Precisely what is it to justify any statement, ethical or nonethical? Surprisingly, there is very little explicit discussion of the nature of justification in the philosophical literature. The literature is, however, full of implicit treatments of justification. An examination of what philosophers have to say about related topics, like good reasons in ethics, knowledge of moral principles, and ethical skepticism indicates that most philosophers take it for granted that justifying is deducing. Justifying any statement consists in, or at least always includes, deducing it from one or more premises; the attempt to justify succeeds only if it takes the form of or can be reconstructed as a valid deductive inference. Thus all justifying is deducing.

The converse is not true, however. To deduce a statement from purely arbitrary premises or from one or more statements known to be false is not to justify the conclusion at all. Only if the premises of the reasoning are acceptable does deduction justify the conclusion. Exactly what is required to make a premise acceptable is open to debate. Some demand that the premise be true; others insist that it be known to be true; still others ask only that it be believed. I shall postpone this large and important issue until chapter 6, dealing with the problem of the infinite regress in ethical reasoning.

At the moment, I am interested in another aspect of this commonly accepted notion of justification. Those who hold, usually without argument, that justification is deduction probably do so because they assume that the only way to justify any statement is by giving good reasons for it and that all genuine reasoning is deductive. It is this latter assumption, which I shall label "deductivism," that I wish to examine right now.

Deduction is that form of reasoning in which the claim is made that the conclusion follows necessarily from the premises. If it is possible for all the premises to be true and the conclusion false, then the argument is invalid; if the truth of the premises is a sufficient condition for the truth of the conclusion, then the argument is valid. It is deductive reasoning that has been the traditional subject matter of logic. Deductivism is the view that this is the only form of reasoning. If so, and if only reasoning can justify any statement, then clearly all justification is deduction. The obvious question to ask is what reason there is to accept deductivism.

Arguments for deductivism

There are many strong arguments to support deductivism, at least in the area of ethics. One is that it would be more convenient if deductivism were true. If all ethical arguments were deductive, it would be relatively easy to distinguish between valid and invalid ones; one could simply employ the powerful techniques of deductive logic. And if there are ethical arguments to which the rules and test procedures of deductive logic do not apply, how is one to decide whether or not a given argument is really valid? Certainly there exists no logic of ethics in the sense that there is a logic of deduction, and I doubt whether there can be such a logic. Unfortunately, to accept the legitimacy of arguments that need not conform to any logical standards is to make it difficult, if not impossible, to tell the difference between mere propaganda and cogent reasoning.

The power and precision of modern logic cannot be denied. If it is possible to interpret ethical arguments in such a way that the techniques of symbolic logic are applicable, this should be done. No one who values responsible and exact thinking will leave the arena of deductive reasoning gladly. Nevertheless other considerations may force the candid philosopher to admit that not all ethical arguments are deductive. Such an admission involves a real loss of logical rigor, but not all is lost. There may still be other ways, less easy and decisive to be sure, to distinguish between valid and invalid ethical arguments. If so, we must accept the inconvenient consequence that it is harder than one might hope to tell the difference between logical argument and mere propaganda.

Another argument in favor of deductivism is that it is the simpler of the two hypotheses. If all valid arguments are deductive, one need recognize only one kind of reasoning and one body of logical rules. But if some ethical reasoning is once admitted to be essentially different, then it is hard to imagine on what grounds religious, political, economic, legal, and historical reasoning could be denied an equal autonomy. Nor would the proliferation of kinds of reasoning stop there. Surely we do not argue for judgments of obligation in the same way we argue for evaluations or ascriptions of responsibility. We do not even argue for judgments of moral obligation in the way we argue for judgments of legal or political obligation. There is no telling how many kinds of reasoning we will have to accept in the end. To reject deductivism seems to complicate our theory of reasoning unnecessarily.

This appeal to Ockham's razor is quite legitimate. Logical rules should not be multiplied beyond necessity, and the number of kinds of reasoning should be kept to a minimum. Still, the facts of the case may not allow the highest degree of theoretical simplicity. If deductivism can explain all the aspects of ethical reasoning, it is the preferable hypothesis; but if there are some ethical arguments it cannot explain satisfactorily, then we must accept the complications inherent in any theory that can give a better explanation.

The third argument for deductivism is that the very nature of reasoning rules out the possibility of nondeductive reasoning. Reasoning, it is often claimed, is simply making explicit what is contained in one or more premises. Since the conclusion of any valid argument is already implicit in the premises, it always follows necessarily, that is deductively, from them. Put otherwise, to claim that one is reasoning is to claim that one is simply making explicit what is implicit in one or more premises. If this claim is correct, then clearly it would be impossible for the premises to be true and the conclusion, which is already contained in these premises, false. Hence, all reasoning is deductive.

The advantage of this conception of reasoning is that it explains how the premises of an argument justify its conclusion. If the conclusion is contained in the premises, then clearly the truth of those premises does guarantee the truth of the conclusion. The difficulty with this conception is in explaining clearly just what it means to say that the premises "contain" the conclusion. If no adequate interpretation of this spatial metaphor can be found, then this conception of reasoning must be rejected.

In the old-fashioned interpretation of this metaphor, meanings are ideas in the mind, usually thought of as images or at least introspectable contents. One discovers what is contained in some meaning by looking at the meaning, a sort of mental picture, with the mind's eye. Just as the painting of a house on a hill contains a painting of a house as a part, so my idea of a bird contains the idea of two wings (or two ideas of one wing) as a part. Philosophers from Locke to Wittgenstein have rehearsed the difficulties in the notion that ideas are images; to my mind these difficulties cannot be met. I do not find these little pictures in my mind when I reason, nor could they perform the function of ideas if they were there.

More recent empiricists are more hardheaded. They speak of words instead of ideas and interpret containment in terms of definitions. The meaning of "sister" contains the meaning of "female" in the sense that the definition of the word "sister" would literally contain the word "female." In this view analysis becomes a matter of formulating definitions rather than introspecting images. One wonders, however, whether this view will account even for all deductive arguments. We argue "red therefore not green" and "sweet therefore not sour," but these inferences cannot depend upon definitions because we are unable to define empirical qualities like redness and sweetness. Moreover, one can often recognize the validity of an argument without being able to formulate any explicit definitions of the key terms. Although symbolic logic may be regarded as having defined the words "all" and "some" in terms of the quantifiers and their mutual relations, Aristotelian logic had recognized the validity of syllogistic arguments long before these definitions were proposed. Apparently our knowledge of validity, even in deduction, does not depend upon explicit definition.

A third notion of containment is harder to refute, perhaps because it is harder to make precise. The meaning of "sister" contains femininity in the sense that teaching the meaning of "sister" includes explaining its logical connection with "female." In the process of teaching someone the meaning of the word "sister," one does, and must, include in the lesson things like "this girl is a sister because she is a female child of the same parents" and "that can't be a sister because he isn't female." Again, "not green" follows from the very meaning of "red" because part of what it is to teach a person the meaning of the word "red" is to correct him when he applies the word to a green apple.

Why must one include lessons in logic in teaching the meaning of our language? Probably because, to use Carnapian terms, the meaning of a word consists of or is determined by syntactical rules as well as semantical rules, rules governing the relation of the word to other words as well as rules governing the relation of the word to objects in the world. But to put the matter in this way suggests a difficulty. How are the syntactical rules related to the semantical rules? Even granted that the distinction between syntactical and semantical rules is a tenable one, it might be that one teaches only the semantical rules which then necessarily determine the syntactical ones. Granted that we say things like "that can't be red because it is green" in teaching the word "red." It might be that we are *using* logic *to* teach the meaning of the word rather than *teaching* logic *in* teaching that meaning. In fact, it is very hard to imagine how teaching the meaning of a word could possibly consist of two independent lessons—teaching the semantical rules and teaching the syntactical rules. If these were really two lessons, it should be possible to introduce a word with the same semantical rules as "red" but with different syntactical rules. But what on earth would it be like to teach a word that referred to all and only those things to which we now apply the word "red" but which was not governed by the rule "if red then not green"?

If it is granted that weighing the pros and cons is genuine reasoning, a further difficulty emerges. Various considerations occur in different combinations and in different degrees. Do we teach *how much* each consideration counts as well as *that* it counts in teaching the meaning of our language? We could hardly teach in advance the weight of every consideration in every possible situation. My conclusion is that none of the usual interpretations of containment is adequate. Therefore, it is unhelpful to say that the premises of a valid argument contain its conclusion. To provide a more helpful conception of the nature of reasoning, to be sure, will not be easy.

Although these first three arguments are insufficient to establish deductivism, they do show that nondeductive ethical arguments would be inconvenient to handle in practice and difficult to explain in theory. At this point the deductivist might argue that it is unnecessary to accept any such troublesome arguments. Granted that many ethical arguments are stated nondeductively, it is always possible to interpret these as deductive but enthymematic arguments. If it is possible to transform every valid ethical argument into deductive form, then one need not grant the existence of nondeductive reasoning at all.

One difficulty with the view that what appear to be nondeductive arguments are really deductive but enthymematic arguments is that the notion of an enthymeme is far from clear. Just what is one supposed to be doing when he supplies a missing premise? *1*) One might be making explicit what the speaker meant. On this view the speaker intended his argument to contain the missing premise. Although he had this premise in mind when he uttered his argument, he did not express it in so many words either because he assumed that the hearer would realize that it was involved or because he thought that it would not be in question or because he was afraid that it would be questioned. Thus it turns out that when everything the arguer has in mind is put into words, every valid ethical argument is really deductive. It is not so easy to show, however, that the speaker really did have in mind the premise required to put his argument into deductive form. Supose that the speaker does not mention this premise when pressed to explain his argument. Suppose he refuses to withdraw his argument even after someone gets him to deny the allegedly missing premise. Suppose that he answers in the negative when asked whether the reformulated argument is the one he intended to use. All of these things are quite possible. Are we still to say that this premise is part of the argument he intended to propound? No doubt many ethical arguments are enthymematic, but I doubt whether it can be held that when a speaker advances a valid ethical argument in nondeductive form he *always* has in mind additional premises that make the argument deductive.

2) When a person supplies a missing premise, he might be logically completing the argument. Whereas the first view depends upon what the speaker has in mind, this one depends upon what is logically required. Whatever the speaker may have intended, his argument as stated is logically incomplete; that is, the premises, as they stand, are not reasons for the conclusion. The missing premise is the minimum assumption that can be added to make the argument valid. In this view arguments that seem to be both nondeductive and valid are nondeductive, but they are not valid. They seem to be valid only because they are fragments of deductive arguments that really are valid. But how do we know that every nondeductive argument is logically incomplete? Whether or not one must add a premise to make the nondeductive argument valid is precisely the question at issue. The fact that one can produce an additional premise that will transform the argument into deductive form does not prove that one needs to do so.

3) When a person supplies an additional premise, he might be producing a substitute argument. In this view there is no need to claim that the nondeductive argument the speaker put into words is only part of what he had in mind or of a logically complete argument. Let us assume that the argument he enunciated is just what it seemed to be. Still, it is hard to know what to make of such arguments. Fortunately we can dispense with such troublesome bits of reasoning, for there is

a respectable deductive argument to correspond to every disreputable nondeductive one. Let us, therefore, write off these dubious nondeductive arguments as invalid since we can justify all our conclusions by using deductive arguments alone. The person who adopts this view is proposing a change in the way we justify ethical statements, a change that would make ethical reasoning less vulnerable to the validity challenge.

Before we adopt this attractive proposal, let us consider a second, and more serious, difficulty with the argument that every valid ethical argument can always be reformulated in deductive form. Is it true that one can always find one or more premises to transform a nondeductive argument into a deductive one? If one is allowed to pull any old premise out of his hat, there is no doubt that the trick can be done. (Awkwardly enough, one can even transform every invalid argument into a valid one by adding the appropriate premise. This is one reason why the deductivist must either explain clearly his conception of an enthymeme or reduce his position to absurdity.) The trouble with adding premises to an argument is that a false or doubtful premise is of no help in establishing a conclusion. If ethical arguments are to be of any use in justifying ethical conclusions, the arguer must be able to justify his premises as well as the logic of his argument. To save the validity of the argument by adding unjustifiable premises is to make the argument useless for justifying ethical statements. This is too high a price to pay.

Unfortunately, I can think of no way of transforming conductive ethical arguments into deductive ones that does not pay this price. Let us try out a few of the more obvious alternatives. The usual procedure is to add an ethical principle to the argument. This principle serves to relate the factual premises to the ethical predicate and so allow one to deduce an ethical conclusion from the facts of the case. Consider this variant on a traditional example: You ought to return my book by Sunday because you promised to do so. Although this is not a deductive argument as it stands, it could be made into one by adding the premise "you ought always to do what you promise to do." Unfortunately, this premise is unjustifiable, for it implies that if I have promised to meet my friend for golf at noon sharp, then I ought not to delay my arrival at the golf course by stopping on the way merely to save a drowning man or give first aid to the victim of a hit-and-run driver. The obvious reply is that I have simply added the wrong premise. No doubt there are exceptions to the rule that one ought always to keep his promises, but if the exceptions are just built into the rule, then the resulting ethical principle will never be false. I agree. In principle it is always possible to reformulate our moral rules so that they are true without exception. I do not think that in practice, however, we are ever able to do this. In the case at hand, we are not much nearer the truth if we say "you ought always to do what you promise except when keeping that promise would prevent you from saving a human life." For one thing, there are many other situations in which one ought to break a promise; for another, each of the considerations that define such situations is a matter of degree. It would be necessary to specify in the rule what degree of danger to life or limb outweighs what degree of solemnity in promising, etc., etc. For my part, I find myself unable to formulate any ethical generalizations that seem to me true universally, and I can always think of exceptions to the principles asserted by my friends. Until we can actually formulate such principles, I do not see how we can use them to justify our ethical conclusions. Therefore, the mere fact that ethical principles are possible in principle does nothing to show that we do or could justify our ethical statements by deductive reasoning from such principles.

Perhaps I have been slightly less than honest. I have not quite abandoned all hope of formulating ethical principles. For example, I still hope someday to reformulate "the principle of utility" in a tenable form. Suppose that something like "one ought always to do that act which produces the greatest amount of good" is universally true. Then surely one could deduce particular obligations from this rule. Yes, indeed. But notice that this rule does not connect obligation with a *description* of those acts that ought to be done but with their *value*. Therefore this rule will not do what the rules we were just discussing were called upon to do—namely, allow one to deduce an obligation statement from the facts of the case. In no way does this rule help to solve the problem of how factual premises can be relevant to ethical conclusions; this problem is simply moved to a new location. Before one can use this premise to draw any conclusions about what he ought to do in any particular situation, he must be able to establish a minor premise to the effect that this or that act actually produces the greatest amount of good. Now I suggest that, since value words cannot be defined in purely empirical terms, the reasoning from the various descriptive characteristics of the act to its value requires the same sort of nondeductive reasoning that before was needed to go from a description of the act to its obligatoriness. This new reasoning could be deductive only if we could formulate ethical principles that connect the empirically discoverable descriptive characteristics of the act with the degree of its value, and these will have to specify how each degree of each descriptive feature is correlated with each degree of value. Here we are right back at the specific rules relating descriptive and ethical terms that we momentarily escaped by trying to appeal directly to the principle of utility. In the end, then, I was not as dishonest as I seemed. Granted that some ethical principles can be formulated by philosophers, no mere human is in a position to formulate the kind of ethical principle that would be needed to make all ethical reasoning deductive.

Many will think my pessimism premature. There are other ways of trying to save the principle that promises ought to be kept besides writing in all the exceptions. Although it may not be true that one ought always to keep his promises, it is universally true that one ought to keep his promises other things being equal. Or, to take another suggestion, it is universally true that one has a prima facie obligation to keep his promises. I shall consider these two alternatives together since they seem to amount to the same thing in the end. What is it for other things to be equal? Others things are equal if and only if there are no other features of the situation that make a difference, if and only if the act has no other morally relevant characteristics. What is a prima facie obligation? It is an actual obligation provided it is not outweighed by stronger contrary prima facie obligations; it is what would be an actual obligation if and only if it is not outweighed by contrary moral reasons. Both ways of lookng at moral principles invite the same replies. *a*) One cannot transform the original argument into deductive form simply by adding such a moral principle. From the fact that you promised to do something together with the principle that you ought to do what you promised other things being equal, it does not follow that you ought to keep this promise unless it is also assumed that in this case other things are equal. Similarly, a principle about prima facie obligations does not allow one to deduce **any** actual obligations unless it is also assumed that in the case at hand there are no more stringent contrary prima facie obligations. It is not easy, I think, in many particular cases to be sure that other things are equal or that there are no more stringent contrary prima facie obligations. In fact, does not a judgment on this point amount to an ethical judgment of this particular case? Thus this gambit only seems to be drawing a conclusion about this case by appealing to a universal principle about all similar cases. The deductive reasoning is an empty show because before one can use it one must have already made a judgment of the case at hand. It is not just that one has implicitly prejudged the case as Mill argued that one has prejudged the morality of Socrates in asserting that all men are mortal. No, one must explicitly decide what one ought to do in this case in order to know that in this case other things are equal or that in this case no stronger contrary prima facie obligation does exist.   *b*) This interpretation of ethical principles really concedes what it is trying to deny. "Other things being equal" really means "provided there are no other relevant characteristics" and "prima facie obligation" really means "actual obligation unless there are other relevant characteristics that outweigh this one." Intuitionists like Ross try to avoid this interpretation by talking of "tendencies" and thinking of ought-making characteristics as ontologically determining the nonnatural characteristic of oughtness.[1] Not only do I reject this analysis of ethical language and deny that any nonnatural realm of ethical characteristics exists, I suggest that the way Ross is forced to talk of ethical characteristics as resultant or derivative or ought-making reveals the truth—that the facts are reasons for the ethical conclusions drawn from them. Take away the notion of relevance and it is impossible to make any sense of the notions of other things being equal or prima facie obligation. To interpret relevance as an ontological relation is to obscure and falsify its logical status. And the kind of relevance required by these ethical principles cannot be interpreted as deductive, for it is presupposed in stating the very principles needed to make the ethical reasoning deductive. What this appeal to obligations other things being equal or prima facie obligations has really done is to build the nondeductive reasoning into the premises needed to make the original argument deductive in form. To do this is not to save deductivism but to abandon it.   c) What forced the deductivist into this subterfuge? Because deductive arguments are so obviously respectable that he wants to be able to justify all of his ethical arguments by making them deductive. But deduction requires the very strong logical relation of entailment by which it is impossible for the premises to be true and the conclusion false. In order to make his premises entail his conclusion he is forced to strengthen his premises by adding to them, most obviously by adding an ethical principle to them. If this is the route into this hopeless search for ethical principles, the way out would seem to be to allow a weaker logical relation between the premises and the conclusion in ethical reasoning. This is precisely why I argue for a nondeductive form of reasoning.

There might seem to be a way to have one's cake and eat it too. Suppose we try using a probability syllogism, for example: Most promises ought to be kept, you promised to return my book by Sunday; therefore, you probably ought to return my book by Sunday. Since the major premise asserts only that most, not all, promises ought to be kept, it is very likely justifiable; and with a suitable definition of probability in terms of frequency, the argument is deductively valid. The trouble is that the conclusion does not, as it stands, say anything about what one ought to do. It might seem that to assert (with conviction) "probably you ought to return the book" simply amounts to asserting (more tentatively) "you ought to return the book." In some interpretations of the word "probably" this is so. But in these interpretations the argument given above is nondeductive. The argument can be deductively valid only if "probably" means something like "in most cases," but then the conclusion of the argument really asserts something about the odds that you ought to return the book. One might still try to deduce "you ought to return the book" from "probably you ought to return the book" by introducing one more premise, the premise that one ought to do what one probably ought to do. This premise, alas, is simply not true. It is precisely because one ought not always keep his promises in spite of the fact that he usually ought to do so that we got into this mess in the first place. Therefore, I venture to predict that it will be impossible to discover any true principle that will enable one to deduce what one ought to do in this case from what one ought to do most of the time.

One last expedient remains. The usual attempts to save deductivism depend upon appealing to some ethical principle, some universal generalization about obligation, that can then be applied to the case at hand. From a merely logical standpoint there is no need for any such generalization. One can always turn any nondeductive inference from factual reasons R to ethical conclusion C into a valid deductive argument by adding a premise "if R then C." Since the premise is tailor-made to fit this particular case, it raises none of the problems that arise when one tries to generalize beyond a single instance. In the example we have been considering the resulting argument would be this: If you promised to return my book by Sunday then you ought to return it, you did promise to return my book by Sunday; therefore, you ought to return my book by Sunday. The first premise is a remarkably modest one. It says nothing about what everyone ought to do about returning every book on all appointed days; it simply asserts that you, one particular individual, ought to return my book, the one you borrowed, by this coming Sunday, no other day. Modest as this assertion is, I wonder how it can be known to be true. If it is known a priori by recognizing the relevance of "you promised" to "you ought," then it presupposes the nondeductive reasoning it is trying to avoid. If it is known by judging what ought to be done in this particular case, then it can hardly be used to justify any conclusion about what ought to be done in this case. In fact, precisely the advantage of this premise, that it is tailor-made, makes it impossible to justify the premise without justifying the conclusion it is advanced to justify. Therefore, this way of saving deductivism gains nothing for one who wishes to use ethical reasoning to justify his conclusions, for the old problems now arise in trying to justify the premise "if you promised to return my book by Sunday then you ought to return it."

There are, no doubt, other premises that could be used to transform nondeductive ethical arguments into deductive ones. That such transformation is always possible and in many different ways I would be the last to deny. What I do deny is that such reformulated arguments can be used to justify ethical conclusions in the way that their originals can. This is because one is often not in a position to justify the premises that must be added to make the arguments deductive in form. Since I believe that arguments really do, at least in some cases, justify the conclusions drawn from them, I conclude that it is a mistake to try to save deductivism by trying to find additional premises.

One could, of course, draw the opposite conclusion. If in fact we are unable to formulate moral principles, then we must give up the claim to justifying our ethical conclusions, at least those that are specifically moral. Hare has argued[2] that to justify any particular judgment of obligation one *must* appeal to a moral principle because this universalizability is built into the very meaning of the word "moral." This is almost, but not quite, true. As Kant showed, our conception of obligation is such that if one person ought to do some act on a given occasion, then everyone ought to do the same kind of act in the same circumstances. While this in principle requires that there be moral principles, universal generalizations to the effect that acts of this kind ought always to be done in similar circumstances, this does not imply that we can actually formulate these principles or that we must do so to justify our moral conclusions. Hare thinks that these principles are implied because he recognizes that judgments of obligation can be justified only by reasoning and he assumes that all reasoning is deductive. This last assumption is just the point at issue. He cannot assume it in proving that moral judgments can be justified only by appeal to moral principles and then go on to argue that because this is so deductivism is true. Baier has also argued that there must be moral principles because adopting the moral point of view involves acting on principle.[3] Presumably if we cannot formulate moral principles we can accept, then we cannot act on them. But why must one act on principle? Surely a person is acting and judging morally if he acts and judges in the light of the relevant considerations whether or not he can formulate a moral principle to fit every case. Granted that a specifically moral judgment must be supported with specifically moral reasons, I can see nothing in the nature of a moral judgment that requires that these reasons include a moral principle. The necessity for appealing to moral principles is not built into our conception of morality.

But might it not be built into the nature of reasoning? I have admitted that ethical statements can be justified only if they can be supported with reasons. Clearly only relevant facts really justify any given conclusion. Now what makes the facts of the case relevant to the ethical conclusion? The attractiveness of deductivism lies in the fact that it seems to answer this question so easily. The facts are linked to the ethical conclusion through the ethical principle that asserts a universal connection between certain descriptive characteristics and value or obligation. That there must be some such principle is built into the conception of a reason. Surely the facts cannot be a reason for this ethical conclusion in this case unless the same facts would be a reason for the same conclusion in every case! Quite true. But the universality of reasoning is quite different from the universality of any premise. If any argument is valid, then any argument from logically similar premises to a logically similar conclusion is also valid; this is as true of nondeductive reasoning as it is of deductive reasoning. But there is nothing in this to require that all reasoning be deductive. What it does require is that the relevance be universal. It is a mistake to imagine that we recognize the relevance of the facts to the ethical conclusion only by means of an ethical principle. In fact quite the reverse is true. My ability to formulate such principles presupposes my sense of relevance, for it is this that tells me what I must include in my principle. This last point is a crucial one. The various attempts to save moral principles by building in the exceptions or by making them principles of prima facie obligation or by making them probability generalizations all begin with the recognition that the principles that first come to mind are false to certain actual or imaginary cases. But to recognize that these cases force one to modify his original principle is to recognize that certain features of these cases have a relevance for ethics that had not been suspected. Here one sees most clearly that a recognition of relevance is presupposed by and not a result of adopting or discovering ethical generalizations. It is just not true that all ethical reasoning can be made deductive. Before deduction can get started, one must do some ethical reasoning about particular cases in order to justify the premises one needs to use in deducing anything about further cases.

A fifth argument for deductivism is in the form of a dilemma facing anyone who wishes to claim that some valid ethical arguments are nondeductive. Either one must hold that these arguments obey discoverable rules of nondeductive inference or one must hold that they do not obey any such rules. But if one holds that there are such rules, he can be forced to accept deductivism; while if he denies that there are such rules, he can be forced to give up his claim that these arguments are valid. Therefore, anyone who tries to hold that some ethical arguments are both nondeductive and valid can be forced to admit that these arguments are either deductive or invalid.

Consider our familiar example: You ought to return my book by Sunday because you promised to do so. How is one supposed to know whether this is a valid argument or only a plausible but fallacious inference? The nondeductivist might try to defend his claim that this argument is really valid by appealing to a rule like "from a statement asserting that someone promised to do an act one may infer that that person ought to do that act." This looks like a rule of inference, a rule in a special logic of ethics. But the deductivist like Hare [4] will counter that this appearance is misleading. The marks of a genuine rule of inference are that it can be established by analyzing the meanings of the logical words involved and that it is empty. For example, the rules of the syllogism depend only

upon the meaning of the words "all," "some," "no," and "is" or
"are"; and these rules tell one nothing about what the world is
or ought to be. The alleged rule of ethical inference fails on
both counts. Its correctness hinges on the meaning of the nonlogical words "promised" and "ought." Therefore, it really
amounts to the moral principle "one ought to keep one's promises" in disguise. It is not a tautological logical principle, but a
substantial moral principle. If so, in defending his claim that
the argument is valid by appealing to a rule the would-be nondeductivist has turned his argument into deductive form without realizing it.

This horn of the dilemma does not impale one quite so
firmly as it might appear. It is doubtful that the rules of the
syllogism are established by an analysis of the meaning of the
logical words involved. Boolean algebra did not depart from
traditional logic because it was discovered one day that the
words "all" and "some" had been previously misunderstood;
rather modern logicians have changed the meaning of these
words, to the extent that they still use them, in order to save
certain rules of inference they accepted on other grounds.
Moreover, what is a logical word? One would like to hold that
the logical words are those that determine the form of the argument, while any word that fills in the subject matter is nonlogical. But even within deduction there are nonformal inferences. Examples might be "John is a father therefore he is a
male" or "it is colored therefore it is extended." Are we to class
words like "father" and "male" as logical words on the grounds
that they determine the validity of these logical arguments?
The precise sense in which rules of inference are empty also
requires clarification. Certainly they need not be trivial or unimportant. A rule of inference is not merely verbal in the sense
that we could choose to make a conflicting rule valid by choosing to speak another language. Logical rules are probably
empty in the sense that experiences neither confirm nor refute
them, but it is equally hard to see how the connection between
promising and obligation is empirically verifiable. It has not
really been proved that the alleged rules of ethical inference
cannot properly be said to be logical rules.

On the other hand, what is gained by such an allegation?

These rules lack two great advantages of the rules of deduction; they are not formal and they are not neutral. Their validity depends upon their content or subject matter. For this reason they cannot be applied to a variety of arguments dealing with different subjects. Even if such rules exist, they necessarily lack the logical power of the rules of formal logic. Moreover, there is no common set of rules of ethical inference acceptable to arguers holding different ethical theories. This means that the logic of ethics could not be used to settle disagreements about which ethical theory is true. And to the degree that a person's individual ethical judgments depend upon which ethical theory he accepts, the logic of ethics would be inapplicable to any particular ethical problem as well. Although this does not prove that there is no logic of ethics, it does severely limit its usefulness for the purposes of justifying ethical statements.

Let us, therefore, explore the other horn of the dilemma. Perhaps the argument "you ought to return my book by Sunday because you promised to do so" is not to be shown valid by appealing to any rule of inference at all. How, then, is its validity to be established? If there is no procedure to show that the argument is valid, then the claim that it is valid becomes meaningless. But how on earth would one establish validity except by appealing to a rule of inference? This question is intended to be rhetorical because it is taken for granted that the only way to justify the claim to validity is by a rule of inference, but this is just not so. Quite apart from the appeal to test procedures, like Venn diagrams or truth tables, one can show that an argument is valid by reformulating it or by explaining its point. Far from its being true that the claim to validity in particular cases depends upon the existence of a rule of valid inference, the rules are derived by induction from particular cases. We decide which logical principles to accept by discovering the principles implicit in the arguments we find acceptable prior to any appeal to logic. The absence of a rule of inference, therefore, is not necessarily fatal to the claim that a given argument is valid. This horn of the dilemma forces one to accept deductivism no more than the other.

Arguments against deductivism

Are the arguments against deductivism any stronger? The most obvious argument against the view that all genuine reasoning is deductive is the existence of inductive arguments. Consider this example: I have eaten at Barney's ten times and have enjoyed nine delicious meals; therefore, if I eat at Barney's again tonight, I will enjoy another delicious meal. Although the conclusion of this argument does not follow necessarily from its premises, as would be the case in any valid deductive inference, its premises certainly seem to be good reasons for its conclusion. Therefore, it would appear that inductive arguments are both valid and nondeductive. If so, deductivism is false.

Some philosophers rule out the possibility of a valid nondeductive argument by definition. They point out that most logicians define the word "valid" to mean such that it is impossible for the premises of the argument to be true and the conclusion false. Obviously, according to this definition every valid argument is deductive, for its conclusion follows necessarily from its premises. There is nothing wrong with this technical use of the word "valid," but I am not using the word in this special logical sense. By a valid argument, I mean one that is logically correct, one that, leaving aside the truth of its premises, at least offers premises that would be, if true, good reasons for its conclusion. It would be a mistake to brand this use of the term as an abuse of language simply because it is different from that found in textbooks on logic. Surely one has the right to use the word as one wishes provided that one explains what one means by it. I have given a brief explanation here and will give a more extended one in chapter 4. Moreover, in ordinary English, the word "valid" is frequently used in a much wider sense than that coined by the logician. It is in this sense that it is quite meaningful to claim that inductive arguments are both valid and nondeductive.

Unfortunately, the meaningfulness of this claim does not guarantee its truth. There have been many attempts to reduce inductive inferences to deductive form. Traditionally, the usual move has been to introduce some additional premise, such as the uniformity of nature or the similarity of unexperienced cases to those which have been experienced. More recently, Popper has tried to show that the only genuine reasoning in induction is falsification of hypotheses, which is deductively valid.[5] Williams has introduced a probability syllogism using Bayes' theorem.[6] Finally, it is often thought that the calculus of probability, which can be worked out as a purely deductive system, is sufficient to reveal the logical structure of induction. This is not the place to introduce a long and technical discussion of the logic of induction. Let me simply go on record as asserting that, after examining a good many attempts to reduce induction to deduction, I have come to the conclusion that all such attempts must fail. Those readers who have come to the same conclusion will agree with me that the existence of inductive reasoning refutes the view that all genuine reasoning is deductive. Readers who believe that inductive arguments can be reduced to deductive form will, of course, see no incompatibility between deductivism and the existence of valid inductive arguments. Let me simply remind them that those who specialize in this very technical field offer very different interpretations of inductive reasoning and that all such interpretations present generally recognized difficulties. In time some deductive model may be able to handle all these difficulties. Meanwhile, it can hardly be assumed without some argument that inductive arguments are really deductive. If they turn out to be nondeductive and yet genuine reasoning, as they certainly appear to be, then deductivism is, in the end, mistaken.

Whether or not the problem of induction can be solved, the existence of ethical arguments that *appear* to be both valid and nondeductive is also an argument against deductivism. A person often gives what seem to be good reasons for or against the assertion that some act ought or ought not to be done even though his conclusion does not follow necessarily from the reasons he gives. For example, "I ought to go home now because we are expecting company in half an hour" or "you ought not to have hit that boy because he is much smaller than you." If the proper function of a hypothesis is to save the appearances, it would appear that deductivism should be rejected.

Appearances may, of course, be deceiving. What appear to be nondeductive arguments may really be deductive enthymemes. In the previous section I have argued in detail that such is not always the case. To try to force all arguments into deductive form may well be to sacrifice appearances to a preconceived theory. The dangers in this sort of attempt become clearer if we look at a controversy that is no longer a live issue. Before Descartes and Hobbes it was commonly assumed that all valid arguments were syllogistic. From our vantage point it is obvious that a great many arguments were tortured and misinterpreted in order to reduce them to syllogistic form. Our deductive logic is far removed from the traditional logic of the syllogism, but it would be a more sophisticated form of the same sort of mistake simply to assume that any argument that fails to fit our logic must be invalid. Logic has advanced since the time of Descartes because logicians have been willing to modify their theory to fit more adequately the arguments that seemed to them, quite apart from any theory, to be valid. This does not imply that every argument that seems at first glance to be valid really is valid, but it does imply that the burden of proof is on anyone who would deny the validity of any argument that retains its appearance of validity upon reflection. Whatever the reality, all the appearances are against deductivism.

A third argument against deductivism is that many ethical arguments are inconclusive even granted the truth of their premises. It is essential to a valid deductive argument that its premises give conclusive evidence for its conclusion. By this I mean that, *if* its premises are true, then its conclusion *must* be true, that it is impossible for its premises to be true and its conclusion false. It may be this feature of entailment that gives rise to the notion of logical necessity, for the premises of a valid deductive argument necessitate its conclusion. This is frequently not the case in ethical arguments. Consider this example: You ought not to stick that needle into my arm because it causes avoidable pain. It is quite possible for this conclusion to be false even though the premise is true. Nevertheless, this inconclusiveness does not rob the argument of all logical force. The fact that a penetrating needle causes pain is a good reason not to stick it into someone's arm. It is not a conclusive reason, even granted its truth, because it can be outweighed by other reasons, such as the need to make a blood test or to inject a serum. But it remains a valid reason against jabbing with a needle even in those situations where the doctor will reluctantly conclude that he ought to stick the needle into me.

The deductivist wants to make the reasoning an all-or-none affair. He insists that, as they stand, the premises of an ethical argument are either conclusive evidence for its conclusion or entirely irrelevant. It seems to me that this dichotomy is quite false to our actual situation in justifying ethical conclusions in particular cases. It is almost never true that mentioning a few salient facts of the case either completely settles the question of what one ought to do or leaves the question entirely open. Such facts usually provide a more or less strong reason for a certain conclusion. Ethical reasoning can be genuine even though it is inconclusive.

The obvious move of the deductivist is to try to transfer the inconclusiveness from the reasoning to the premises. The different degrees of strength possessed by different ethical arguments simply reflect the varying amounts of evidence for their premises. Deductive arguments vary greatly in their probative force, their power of rationally showing that conclusions which had been in doubt are indeed true, although in all arguments the implicative link between premises and conclusion is absolutely strict in the sense that the premises necessitate the conclusion. A valid deductive argument will have more or less probative force depending upon the degree to which its premises are less open to doubt than its conclusion. The deductivist's move is a good one as far as it goes. It is indeed true that even a valid deductive argument does not completely justify its conclusion because it is always possible to challenge its premises. But this move still does not save deductivism because it is not this sort of inconclusiveness to which I refer. As I have defined the terms "conclusive" and "inconclusive," the difference lies within the implicative link.

The point is this. One cannot (logically) deny the truth of the conclusion of a deductive argument once one has granted the truth of its premises and the validity of the reasoning. But one may (logically) disagree with the conclusion of an ethical argument at the same time one admits the truth of its premises and the validity of its reasoning. This alternative exists whenever it is possible to bring forth additional evidence that might outweigh the facts contained in the original premises. This alternative is never possible in deduction because it is impossible for the conclusion of a deductive argument to be false while its premises are true and its logic valid. Therefore, the model of deductive reasoning can never explain the importance of the reply "yes, but . . ." in the give-and-take of ethical discussion.

A fourth, but closely related, argument against deductivism is that it leaves no room for the weighing of pros and cons. In deductive reasoning all the evidence is on one side of the fence, at least as long as all the premises are true. If a set of premises seems to entail both a conclusion and its contrary, this would show that there is some hidden inconsistency in the premises or unrecognized error in the reasoning. Therefore Euclid had no need to weigh the evidence for and against the hypothesis that the interior angles of a plane triangle equal one straight angle. He could deduce this theorem from his axioms, postulates, and definitions confident that, as long as these were granted, nothing could be said against his conclusion.

But in judging an ethical issue, as in establishing a scientific hypothesis, there are usually two sides to be considered. Suppose that nurse White is trying to decide whether to give patient Brown a strong barbiturate. Brown is unable to sleep because he is worried about the major surgery he will undergo the next day, and he will need all his strength to enable him to endure this ordeal. On the other hand, the doctor has prescribed only a mild sedative. Perhaps he intends to use an anesthetic that cannot be given soon after barbiturates have been taken, although this particular anesthetic is seldom used in heart surgery. The doctor has asked to be consulted if the patient becomes restless; but when Miss White calls his home, she discovers that he is on a prolonged emergency call. What ought she to do? Coming to any reasonable decision or judging its rightness afterward would seem to require weighing the pros and cons, the reasons for and against administering a barbiturate. At this point deductive reason is inadequate to justify ethical decisions, for it has no place for a balancing of reasons for and reasons against.

One could, of course, construct a valid deductive argument whose premises would include all the reasons for and against the conclusion. One would simply have to add a premise to the effect that the reasons for outweighed the reasons against, or vice versa. But, as a way of showing that ethical conclusions can be rationally justified by deductive arguments, this seems a peculiar subterfuge. How is this additional premise itself to be rationally justified? I do not see how it could be known to be true except by the weighing of pros and cons, but then this bit of reasoning cannot be deductive. Therefore, the difficulty has simply been pushed back one stage in the process of justification. Moreover, the additional premise seems to presuppose what it is intended to avoid. The other premises do not become deductively relevant until this new premise is added to the argument; that is precisely the point of adding this premise about the relative weight of the factual considerations. But the premise is about the *logical* weight of the factual *reasons*. There would be nothing to assert in this new premise unless the factual considerations were already logically relevant before the premise is assumed. Therefore, the premise needed to turn the argument into a deductive one presupposes a kind of nondeductive relevance which it attempts to assess and summarize.

There is another way of deducing a judgment of obligation from the conflicting facts of the case that does not use any premise about the relative weight of these facts. This argument begins with an ethical principle that incorporates the various pros and cons. In this case the principle would be something like "whenever a patient who needs to conserve his strength for a serious operation the next day cannot sleep without being given a barbiturate and the doctor cannot be contacted, then, even though there is a slight chance that this will conflict with the doctor's choice of an anesthetic and the doctor has left orders that he is to be consulted if the patient is restless, the nurse ought to administer a barbiturate." I have already explained at some length my main objection to this interpretation of ethical reasoning; usually we cannot justify individual judgments of obligation by appealing to ethical principle because we are unable to put justifiable ethical principles into words. Fortunately, even when I am unable to subsume the particular case under a universal principle, I can still recognize that this or that feature of the given situation is relevant to what ought to be done. In fact, it is only by such a recognition of nondeductive relevance that I can know what needs to be packed into my ethical principles. A second objection to this interpretation is that it makes it hard to see just how the major premise is to be rationally justified. My own view is that ethical principles, to the extent that they can be formulated and justified, are inductive conclusions from particular cases. If so, there must be some way of reasoning out the ethical status of particular cases prior to any appeal to such ethical principles. This means that nondeductive ethical reasoning is required to justify the principles one would use in deductive ethical reasoning. However one might justify such an ethical premise, such reasoning would seem to require a weighing of the pros and cons. Therefore, the nondeductive reasoning simply occurs one step further back in the process of justifying.

Hare can admit this limitation in deductive reasoning without abandoning his deductivism. What this shows, he thinks, is not that ethical reasoning is nondeductive at some stage, but that there is more to deciding an ethical question than reasoning. In particular, it is a mistake to think that one does or can weigh reasons against one another; the weighing is prior to the reasoning. When one tries to find some ethical principle that includes all the important features of the situation, he often finds himself undecided between several conflicting principles, for example the principle mentioned in the previous paragraph and its contraries. One weighs principles rather than reasons, and this weighing is only in part reasoning. Deciding which principle to accept is partly a matter of reasoning out the implications of each principle and partly a matter of deciding what one is willing to accept in the way of implications. It follows that, although reasoning can force a man either to reject some principle or to stop denying some implication of it, reasoning can never establish any ethical principle at all. In the end this view forces one to give up the claim that ethical statements can be rationally justified, for there is no way to meet the challenge of the man who asks for some reason to accept the ethical principles to which one appeals in justifying particular judgments of obligation. Perhaps I will be forced to give up this claim in the end. But unless the truth of deductivism is assumed, which would be to beg the question, I do not see why one cannot hold that we can and do establish ethical principles by reasoning. If we do, this reasoning is clearly not deductive, for at some point or other it requires a balancing of pros and cons that has no place in deduction.

A final argument against deductivism is that it cannot explain the convergence of evidence in ethical reasoning. Leaving aside the weighing of pros and cons, there is the fact that there are several of each. Thus it is frequently possible to appeal to several reasons to justify an ethical statement. For example, I ought to pay my income tax in full because I have an obligation to my country, I will be fined or jailed if my cheating is discovered, and I promised my wife to be honest from now on. This sort of accumulation of reasons is not possible in deduction.

It is true that there are usually several premises in a deductive argument, but there is no accumulation here. Each individual premise does not add to the support provided by the others because no individual premise lends any support to the conclusion. Although the premises together, if true, constitute conclusive evidence for the conclusion, no single premise taken by itself has any logical force. The situation is quite different where there is a convergence of the evidence. In the argument mentioned in the previous paragraph each of the premises has some logical force quite apart from the others so that each adds its bit to the total force of the argument. In effect, three valid arguments are combined into one.

This suggests a different comparison with deduction. It is often possible to deduce a given conclusion from several different sets of premises. Considering each set of premises as a complex reason, we now have several reasons for the conclusion such that each reason by itself does have logical force. The trouble now is just the reverse of the former situation; instead of having too little logical force, each reason now has too much. Because each set of premises, if true, constitutes a conclusive reason for the conclusion, adding other sets of premises does nothing to add to the logical force of the argument. It does not follow that there is no point in defending a given conclusion by several deductive arguments. Because the truth of any set of premises can be challenged, there is a real advantage in appealing to several sets of premises. It is less likely that several sets will be challenged or, if so, that the several challenges can be made good. Therefore, an argument consisting of several deductive arguments often has more probative force than any of its constituent arguments. In this sense one argument supports another, but this is not the sort of accumulation to which I refer here. I have in mind the strengthening of one premise with another when the truth of these premises is not in question. Where there is a genuine convergence of evidence it is the logical force, not the probative force, of the argument that is increased with the addition of each new premise. Many ethical arguments are such that adding a premise to them will increase their *logical* strength, that is the strength of their implicative link. It is this feature of certain ethical arguments that the deductive model cannot explain.

CONCLUSION

It is too often assumed that all genuine reasoning is deductive. This deductivism, assuming also that justification is reasoning, suggests that to justify an ethical statement is to deduce it from one or more acceptable premises. I have begun my attack on this conception of justification by arguing that deductivism is false. Not all reasoning, ethical or nonethical, is deductive.

This does not imply, of course, that no ethical arguments are deductive. The most obvious use of deduction in ethics is to support a particular judgment of value or obligation by subsuming it under an ethical principle. The hedonist may well argue that, leaving aside any extrinsic value or disvalue, the experience of eating the meal before me will be good on the grounds that eating when one is hungry is pleasant and that all pleasures are intrinsically good. Pacifists often argue that it is wrong to fight in a given war because fighting in this war would involve killing human beings and it is wrong to kill any human being. How frequently such arguments constitute an adequate justification for their conclusions depends in large measure upon our ability to formulate ethical principles that do not turn out to be untenable upon further reflection. My own conviction is that the formulation of general principles that allow no exception is so very difficult that it is seldom possible to use this form of argument to justify any serious moral decision. Still, there is no need to deny that such arguments are widely used in ethical discourse.

A second use of deductive reasoning is to support an ethical principle by deriving it from a higher ethical principle. One might, for example, justify "every citizen has an obligation to vote" by appealing to the more general principle "every citizen has an obligation to do those actions required to make his government effective." The obvious limitation of this type of justification is our ability to frame tenable principles that are very general without being empty of practical consequences. To the extent that it is possible to have an ethical system, as opposed to a mere collection of unconnected principles or a set of fairly specific rules of thumb, this sort of justification can be effective.

The third use of deduction, and probably the most important, is to test an ethical principle. Instead of deducing the principle from some more general one, one here deduces the consequences of the principle. In this context deduction is used to discover what one is committed to if one accepts some suggested ethical principle. This use of deduction to refute some tempting generalization goes back at least to Plato, who refuted the suggestion that justice is telling the truth and paying one's debts by pointing out that this implies that one ought to return a dangerous weapon to the owner even though he may have gone insane since he entrusted it to one's care. In such cases deduction is used to show that some principle must be rejected because it has unacceptable consequences.

But this same sort of argument can be used in the process of confirming an ethical principle by showing that it implies many ethical truths. Ironically, it turns out that this use of deduction to establish the principles so much desired by the deductivist occurs within the framework of a nondeductive form of reasoning. In ethics, as in science, the confirmation of a hypothesis often uses deduction within a total argument that is inductive. Therefore, the obvious subject to consider next is the role of induction in ethical reasoning.

2. induction

THE most obvious view as to the nature of justification is that to justify a statement is to deduce it from one or more acceptable premises. But if it is recognized that not all genuine reasoning is deductive and still maintained that all reasoning from acceptable premises justifies, then one is forced to broaden his conception of justification. Since the most plausible candidates for nondeductive inferences are inductive arguments, the most natural move is to suggest that justification consists in reasoning, either deductive or inductive, from acceptable premises.

One way of showing that this modest extension in the notion of justification is insufficient is to show that induction, as it is actually used in ethics, is inseparably connected with a kind of reasoning that is neither deductive nor inductive. Such is the thesis of this chapter. In order that this central thesis may not be misunderstood, it is necessary to explain briefly how I am using the word "induction."

By "induction" I mean that sort of reasoning by which a hypothesis is confirmed or disconfirmed by establishing the truth or falsity of its implications. To show that the consequences of some hypothesis are true is to provide evidence for its acceptance; to show that one or more of its consequences are false is to refute it. It is this sort of reasoning, so important to science, to which I refer by the word "induction." The word is often used in a much narrower sense than this. By "induction" philosophers often mean extrapolation, reasoning from some members of a class to some generalizations about the entire class. At other times, the word is used in a much wider sense than mine. In this sense, any argument in which the truth of the premises would make the conclusion probable is inductive. I have no intention of legislating against either the narrow or the wide senses of the word. My purpose is simply to explain that, as I use the term, it refers to the confirmation or disconfirmation of hypotheses.

Thought experiments

The fact that something like scientific induction has an important place in ethics is brought out most strikingly by the frequent use of thought experiments in settling, or at least debating, ethical issues. Just as scientific theories are accepted or rejected on the basis of the results of experiments conducted in the laboratory, so ethical theories are tested by their conformity to experiments carried out in the mind. This technique of testing an ethical hypothesis against thought experiments is not new; one finds Plato attempting to disprove the theory that the good consists in pleasure without knowledge by imagining the case of an oyster feeling pleasure but without intelligence or memory.[1] Still, it is in this century that the most widespread and systematic use has been made of the technique of thought experiment. The very term "thought experiment" suggests that thinking about imaginary cases is very like experimenting in the laboratory. Let us explore this analogy a bit.

The simplest sort of scientific experiment is that in which a single theory is tested in the laboratory or by observation in the field. One derives some verifiable prediction from the theory together with additional assumptions and then checks this prediction against the facts. For example, the hypothesis that the larvae commonly found in putrefying flesh come from the eggs of flies implies, among other things, that if one keeps all flies away from the flesh, no larvae will appear. The experiment might consist simply in surrounding the meat with a fine mosquito netting and watching for larvae. If no larvae appear, the hypothesis is confirmed; if the meat is soon crawling with larvae, the hypothesis is disconfirmed.

Suppose, now, that a teleological theory of obligation is proposed. The theory is that whether an action is right or wrong depend entirely upon the amount of good or bad it brings into existence. Let us test this hypothesis against James' lost-soul experiment.[2] Imagine that I could bring about a world in which millions would be kept permanently happy simply by consigning a certain lost soul on the far-off edge of things to a life of lonely torture. For the purposes of this experiment it must be assumed either that only happiness has intrinsic value or that in this case the intrinsic disvalue of the injustice involved is far outweighed by the value of the happiness gained. Would it be right or wrong for me to purchase this immense amount of happiness at this price of injustice? If this experiment in thought yields a positive result, the teleological theory of obligation is confirmed; if it turns out negative, the theory is disconfirmed.

These two experiments simply test a proposed theory, but frequently an experiment is designed to decide between competing theories. A crucial experiment is one that establishes one theory at the same time it refutes another. Its decisiveness depends upon the fact that the two theories imply different outcomes of the experiment at hand. Suppose the theory that the world is flat is faced with the daring hypothesis that the world is really round. A possible test case would be to watch a ship sail away into the sunset. The theory that the world is flat implies that the ship will gradually diminish in size as a whole, while the hypothesis that the earth is round implies that the ship will sink out of sight with the lower portion disappearing before the masts. When the experiment is actually tried, it turns out that the red sails can be seen after the hull has ceased to be visible. This result confirms the theory that the world is round and disconfirms the hypothesis that it is flat.

Moral philosophers have tried, with more or less success, to construct thought experiments on the same pattern. Two theories of value which were very popular in this country during the last few decades are hedonism and the interest theory of value. Hedonism maintains that pleasure is the good; the interest theory asserts that the good is the object of desire or liking. Savery devised several crucial experiments to determine which of these hypotheses is correct. One of the more interesting is that of the agonized oyster.[3] Imagine that an oyster is impaled upon an oyster fork in a most painful manner, but that he has no aversion to his present predicament and no desire to escape it. Is his condition a bad one or not? The interest theory of value implies that it is not at all bad; hedonism implies that it is very bad indeed. Whichever way one decides in this test case, one theory will be confirmed and the other disconfirmed.

The ideal of science is probably the controlled experiment. In such an experiment one factor is varied while all the others are held constant. By varying one factor at a time it is possible to discover which factors are causally related to the phenomenon under investigation. Thus when cattle are injected with a certain solution containing a specific germ, they become diseased in spite of the fact that food, housing, and all other factors are left unchanged. When cattle are injected with the same solution that has been sterilized, they do not become ill. My scientific friends tell me that this proves something about the truth of the germ theory of disease.

A perennial ethical problem is whether value is objective or subjective. The objectivist claims that value exists quite independently of the mind, outside of consciousness. According to this view an object can be good or bad even if there is no sentient being to be aware of it. The subjectivist holds, on the other hand, that value and disvalue depend upon the mind, and consequently can exist only within consciousness. To decide this issue James suggests a controlled thought experiment.[4] Imagine a world, not unlike ours, which contains no sentient beings at all. It might contain towering mountains, plunging waterfalls, moonlit pools, and sunsets; but it must contain no angels, people, or even animals. Now imagine that a single sentient mind enters this world to become aware of its rainbows and bubbling brooks. If changing this single variable introduces value and disvalue into this world, the subjective theory of value is confirmed. If not, it is disconfirmed and the objective theory is confirmed instead.

Thought experiments cannot always be stated as succinctly as the ones I have mentioned. Sometimes it may even require an entire book to bring to mind a single experiment.

Corneille's *Le Cid* may well be read as an extended thought experiment in which the code of honor is put to the test. Dostoyevski's *Crime and Punishment* describes an imaginary case history that serves as a crucial experiment to decide between the new utilitarian theory and the old-fashioned Christianity. The importance of plays and novels in confirming and disconfirming ethical theories should not be underestimated. If the moral philosopher wishes to be wise as well as scientific, he can learn a great deal from the literary artist.

Although the reader is probably familiar enough with the thought experiments I have mentioned, I want to remind him of their existence for two reasons. First, it is too easy to forget, especially if one is strongly tempted by the deductive model, how very common thought experiments are in our actual reasoning. A survey of the literature reveals that ethical theorists of almost every school have used thought experiments to establish or refute theories relating to most of the live issues in contemporary ethics. Clearly any discussion of justification in ethics must either explain how thought experiments can confirm or disconfirm ethical theories or explain away one of the ways in which we normally reason in ethics. Second, these examples make it clearer how appropriate the term "thought experiment" is, for all the main types of scientific experiment have their analogues in ethics. Because thought experiments include crucial experiments and controlled experiments as well as simply testing a proposed theory against its consequences, many of the features of the logic of science exist in ethical reasoning as well. To my mind this parallel between science and ethics is both striking and important. Yet very seldom have philosophers tried to explain in any detail precisely what a thought experiment is or why it should be taken to prove anything.

Science and ethics

It looks as though something very like the scientific method could be used in ethics because ethical theories, like scientific theories, are hypotheses to be confirmed or discon-

firmed by experiment. Ethics employs the same inductive reasoning so characteristic of the sciences. But just how far can
this analogy between science and ethics be pushed? The answer depends upon how genuine and far-reaching the analogy
between laboratory and thought experiments is found to be.
Well, what are some typical features of a scientific experiment? A scientific experiment is *1*) an operational procedure
2) by which the experimenter produces some result *3*)
which is known by observation and *4*) such that any other
competent experimenter could go through the same procedure
producing an observably similar result. It is this last feature
which explains the success of the scientific method in arriving
at agreed solutions to scientific problems, but it is itself explained by the first three features of an experiment.

How well does a thought experiment measure up to these
standards of an experiment? Only in a very loose sense can it
be said that there is any specified procedure to be followed in a
thought experiment. Thinking is, I suppose, doing something,
and occasionally the instructions for a thought experiment
may specify that the thinker is to do one thing before another.
For example, James suggests that the experimenter should
first imagine a world without any sentient beings and then
imagine the same world being perceived by an interested
mind. But usually the object, situation, or act to be contemplated in imagination is simply described with no instructions
at all as to how to go about imagining it. This is in sharp contrast to the typical scientific experiment where it is essential to
specify just what operations must be performed in what order
on what equipment in order to carry out the experiment.
Moreover, although there is a sense in which thinking is doing something, there is another sense in which it is not doing
anything at all. It is not acting on the outside world; it does
not produce any changes in the laboratory or in the field. In
this sense also it involves no operational procedure. Thinking
is doing, but it seems to be a very different kind of doing from
manipulating apparatus or taking samples systematically in
the field.

The most obvious difference between doing in the laboratory and doing in the mind is that the former is causally effi-

cacious in a way that the latter is not. This is not to say that thinking changes nothing. Even when it does not produce changes in the outside world through volition, it may still produce changes in the mind. Thinking may cause one to accept or reject a belief, become angry or forgive a friend, come to favor something or cease to desire it. And in a way the thought experimenter is trying to produce a change in his mind; he is trying to produce a state of mind such that he is thinking of the specified object, situation, or act. On the other hand, he is not trying to produce the object, situation, or act itself. Although his thinking must be actual, the case of which he is thinking may be merely possible. He must produce this test case in his mind, but this does not imply that he must make it actual. Therefore in the most basic sense he does not actually produce the test case at all; he merely thinks about what it would be like if he, or anyone else, were to produce it. In a laboratory experiment, however, the experimenter must actually bring about some result. The experimenter must produce his test case in the full sense of making it actual, bringing it about, causing it to exist. No merely possible instance will do in science. Unless an experiment produces actual results it is no experiment.

How does the experimenter find out what result he has produced? By observation. Essentially a scientific experiment is an appeal to experience. The scientist derives from his hypothesis some prediction about what would happen under certain conditions. The operational procedure is designed to bring about these conditions; the statement describing the actual results is known by observation. Since the only way of knowing what actually happens at any time and place is by experience, only observable results count in science. At the heart of a scientific experiment is this confrontation of the predicted result with the actual result, this checking of what the experimenter thought would happen against the facts of the case. But the thought experimenter does not measure his thinking against the actual case, for he usually has only a possible case in mind and it exists only in his mind. A thought experiment is not a way of checking our thinking against our experience of reality; it leads to nothing but more thinking.

Just as the procedure of a thought experiment can be carried out in the mind, so the result is only in the mind. At this point the contrast between thought experiments and scientific experiments is sharpest and most fundamental. Thought experiments allow no place for the observation, the appeal to experience, that is at the heart of science. It might be claimed that thought experiment does involve the observation of one's own mind, the introspective experience of oneself. But although one might thus observe what is going on in one's mind when one is performing the thought experiment, this seems to play no essential role in the experimenting. It would be essential if the experimenter were trying to find out whether some predicted state of mind became actual as a result of his thinking, but this is not what he is trying to establish. What the thought experimenter is trying to establish is that some possible object is good (or bad) or that some imaginary act is right (or wrong). To be sure, he may observe himself coming to the conclusion that the object is good or the act right. But the fact that he came to think this, which could be established by introspection, is not what he aims to discover by the experiment. What he aims to discover is some ethical statement about the test case, and this is not established by observing what he thinks about the test case. Instead it is established by thinking about the case. Thus a thought experiment is an appeal to thinking, not to experience. This is the crucial difference between experimenting in the mind and experimenting in the laboratory.

A more striking difference, although one that is less fundamental, is that there is much more disagreement in the case of thought experiments than in the case of experiments in the laboratory. A good scientific experiment is one that could be carried out by any competent scientist in such a way that all experimenters would agree on the observable results. The success of the scientific method in reaching agreement arises from this feature of experimentation. Just because this feature seems to be lacking in thought experiments, it would seem that the scientific method, even if it were applicable to ethics, could not hope for the same success in reaching agreement among moral philosophers. The difficulties are two. First, it is very difficult for the thinker to be sure that he is carrying out the thought experiment correctly. Savery asks one to imagine an oyster painfully impaled upon an oyster fork, but just how does one do that? James asks one to imagine a world unperceived by any sentient mind, but is one not introducing a sentient mind into that world by the very act of imagining it? Descriptions of thought experiments normally contain no step-by-step instructions for carrying out the thinking involved. But without any operationally defined procedure it is very hard to be at all sure that any two thinkers are actually performing the same thought experiment. They often seem to be, of course. They often describe what they are thinking in the same way; they often report that they are imagining the same sort of test case. But even then they disagree as often as they agree on the result of the experiment. Somehow observation seems able to lead to agreement on the results in a way that thinking does not. Two scientists will almost always agree on what the observed result of an experiment actually was; but two moral philosophers very often disagree about what conclusion to draw from experimenting in the mind. The fact of disagreement, whatever it may or may not imply, is as undeniable in thought experiments as it is rare in laboratory experiments.

On the whole it must be admitted that the term "thought experiment" is very misleading, for thought experiments are really not experiments at all. The point of an experiment is to *bring about* certain conditions and *observe* what will *actually happen*. Only by producing the conditions can one produce the result that is to test the hypothesis. The hypothesis is tested inductively because of the logical relation between the hypothesis and the predicted result on the one hand and between the predicted result and the observed result on the other. When one "experiments" in his mind, however, one need not actually produce the test case nor observe it to find out what it is like. In the strict sense, one does not experiment at all. There is some analogy between thinking up a test case in the mind and producing one in the laboratory, but this analogy breaks down at crucial points.

If these differences are not borne in mind, it is all too easy to confuse a thought experiment with thinking of an experiment. The latter is also of great importance for ethics. Dewey has shown us the importance of dramatic rehearsal in deliberation.[5] When trying rationally to decide what to do in a given situation, the agent or his adviser may try out each of the alternative courses of action in his mind. He will act out each of these courses of action in his imagination, and his imagination will call to mind the probable consequences of each. But all this is thinking of an experiment; it is imagining oneself actually doing something and predicting what will happen. This is not actually experimenting, for nowhere in dramatic rehearsal does one check the predicted result against the actual result. Still, it is thinking about an experiment, the experiment of performing the action in question. A thought experiment is not even an experiment in this attenuated sense of thinking about an experiment.

This is fortunate, for Wittgenstein has raised a basic objection to the procedure of thinking of an experiment. He gives the example of an engineer trying to justify his choice of dimensions for a bridge he is constructing in his imagination by conducting purely imaginary loading tests. Wittgenstein remarks that, although this may well be called imagining justifying his choice of dimensions, it is certainly not justifying an imaginary choice.[6] In other words, imagining an experiment does not actually prove anything at all because the whole point of an experiment is actually to try it and see what happens. Remove the actual doing and the observation of the actual result, and no experiment remains. Whether or not this objection is fatal to dramatic rehearsal, it does not apply to the sort of thing I have in mind at all. In fact, Wittgenstein implicitly concedes the validity of thought experiments, for his own remark is itself a thought experiment intended to justify his conclusion about thinking of an experiment.

If a thought experiment is not really an experiment or even thinking of an experiment, what on earth is it? To put the matter bluntly, a thought experiment is an argument. The description of the test case is the premise or set of premises of the argument; the statement that the imagined object is good or the possible act is right is the conclusion. Thus a thought experiment, at least in ethics, is a bit of reasoning that goes from factual premises to an ethical conclusion. The sort of reasoning involved is neither deductive nor inductive. The fact that it is a bit of reasoning explains why the thought experimenter need not produce any actual case. Reasoning need not begin with true premises; one can reason just as well from merely postulated premises. Therefore a possible case will do as well as an actual one. The fact that a thought experiment is an argument also explains why no appeal to experience is necessary. One does not discover the conclusion of an argument by observing what one thinks but by thinking through the argument; one does not discover the conclusion by noticing what one happens to think but by reaching the conclusion by thinking. In the end, to conduct a thought experiment is not to experiment but to reason; it is an appeal, not to experimentation, but to reasoning.

What kind of thinking is this reasoning? Thought experiments are sometimes called "experiments in imagination." They frequently call for the thinker to imagine an oyster impaled upon an oyster fork or a world with no sentient life in it. What is one supposed to do when he imagines the test case? We speak of the imagination in two very different ways. Imagining may be imagining *that* such and such is the case; in this sense imagining seems to be nothing more than conceiving possible facts or entertaining beliefs or postulating statements as true. But in another sense the imagination is contrasted with conception or belief or postulation. Imagining may be imagining *a case* of such and such; in this sense imagining means creating in the imagination an instance of some sort of thing. I do not know how this is done, but traditionally it has been thought of as calling to mind a little mental picture or image. Now in which of these two senses am I asked by Savery to imagine an oyster impaled upon an oyster fork? Am I asked to assume that an oyster is impaled upon a fork or am I asked to picture to myself a writhing bivalve upon a gleaming silver three-tined fork?

Essentially, I think, the former. I am required to assume the truth of the description of the test case and reason out the ethical conclusion that follows from it. The sort of thinking that is required for a thought experiment is that in which one accepts the statements that constitute the premises of the argument and then reach the valid conclusion from them. I would not deny that imagery may be present, but this does not seem to be essential. I say this because in the case of some thought experiments it seems impossible to have anything like concrete imagery. Suppose one is asked whether the pleasure a brutal torturer gets from inflicting pain on his victim is intrinsically good. One can probably picture a muscular, unshaven man pounding his huge fists into a screaming and writhing maiden whose pale white skin is in striking contrast to the red blood oozing from her wounds. But the size of the man's muscles or the presence of a beard is hardly relevant to the moral conclusion, while his brutality is not captured by this single instance created in imagination. No, the sort of thinking required is that in which one imagines that the description specifying the test case is true.

Although concrete imagery is not essential to a thought experiment, it may be helpful. What is essential is assuming that the description is true, but one cannot always make the truth of some description real to himself simply by reading or saying it to himself. But if one can create in his imagination an instance of the sort described, this somehow brings home the case to the thinker and gives a vitality to the assumption. It is still not actually believed, but it is accepted or taken for granted much more fully than before. One can, for the moment, think as though it were true, and this is the sort of thinking that is necessary to think through the argument. Moreover, the description of a test case is always abstract in that it leaves out many characteristics any actual case would have and general in that the predicates applied always fall short of the fully specific. But the value of anything, and therefore the obligation to do any action, in any actual case will depend upon the case as it is in all its concreteness and specificity. This does not imply that every feature will be relevant to the ethical conclusion, but an indefinite number will be, each in its infinite specificity. Now by imagining a case covered by a description one makes the case concrete and specific. In this way one may make it clearer what ethical conclusion really follows from the description. (One may also discover that something of importance has been left out of the description. In this way imagery may lead to redefining or refining the thought experiment with which one began.) Just how does concrete imagery make it clearer what really follows from a description? Probably in part by making it clearer just what the description means. Sometimes, however, I think that imagery operates in a more radical way than this. It substitutes one argument for another. For a bit of reasoning from certain descriptive statements to an ethical conclusion it substitutes a bit of reasoning from certain images to an ethical conclusion. Later I shall try to develop a theory of reasoning that is broad enough to allow images to function as premises. From the moment let me only remark that any empiricist who wishes to use experiences as the ultimate reasons for his factual beliefs cannot afford to restrict premises to beliefs, propositions, or statements.

Because a thought experiment establishes its result in a way so different from that in which a laboratory experiment establishes its result, it is misleading to classify them both together as experiments. At this point there is no analogy between science and ethics. It is in the way in which the respective results bear on the respective theories that the real analogy exists, and here the parallel is complete and precise. The inferred conclusion of a thought experiment functions just like the observed result of a laboratory experiment in confirming or disconfirming a hypothesis. Ethical theories, just like scientific ones, have specific consequences for particular cases. If these consequences are found to be true, this confirms the theories. If they are found to be false, the theories are disconfirmed. However differently the consequences may be found to be true or false, the truth or falsity that is found has the same logical relation to the hypothesis of which it is a consequence. Therefore, inductive reasoning has its place in ethics just as it has in science. The logic of science is also the logic of ethics; the confirmation and disconfirmation of hypotheses is common ground.

Nonempirical induction

Induction is so often associated with the empirical sciences that the two are often assumed to be essentially connected. It is then thought that induction is simply reasoning from experience. But from a logical point of view induction is not tied to experience. It is that kind of reasoning that justifies hypotheses in terms of their consequences. In the end it always involves an appeal to particular cases, but there is no need for these cases to be known by observation. In the natural sciences the truth or falsity of the consequences is established by experience, but in ethics it is established by thinking instead.

Thus ethical principles are established by nonempirical induction. The logic of this sort of reasoning is precisely the same in ethics as it is in the natural sciences. Some hypothesis is confirmed or disconfirmed by the truth or falsity of its consequences. But the premises of this ethical reasoning are entirely nonempirical. That a given or proposed hypothesis has a certain consequence is established by thinking out the implications of the hypothesis in question. That the consequence to be tested is true or false is established by thought experiment. At no point is any appeal to experience necessary or even relevant.

The existence of such nonempirical induction, interesting as it is for epistemology in general, is particularly important when it comes to the justification of ethical principles. None of the other possible interpretations of ethical principles is very promising. They can hardly be empirical generalizations because experience is incapable of establishing their truth. We do not find ethical characteristics given in sensation or introspection, nor has it been possible to give any satisfactory definition of ethical words in terms of empirical characteristics. But if ethical characteristics are not to be found in experience, clearly experience cannot show that they are always correlated with any other characteristics whatsoever. This seems to leave only the possibilities that ethical principles are self-evident or that they are arbitrary postulates. But to accept the dubious faculty of intuition and the realm of nonnatural characteristics in order to avoid ethical skepticism is a hard choice. Fortunately one who wishes to hold that ethical principles can be justified need not make that choice, for ethical theories can be justified by nonempirical induction. It will not, I suspect, be easy to discover principles that do not have false consequences; but where it can be done, one can give a rational justification for the ethical principle by induction.

To be sure, I am not the first to suggest that some form of nonempirical induction is possible in ethics. Where I may claim to have improved upon this suggestion slightly is in giving a somewhat more extended discussion of the thought experiments upon which this sort of reasoning rests. By doing this I have tried to show in what ways thought experiments are and are not like laboratory experiments and to make clearer how they can be nonempirical. In understanding the nature of this sort of nonempirical induction it is vital to distinguish it from two other sorts of "induction." First, there is mathematical induction. A typical case would be the reasoning by which it is shown that some general formula is true by showing that it holds for unity and that if it holds for n it holds for $n + 1$. I have no real objection to calling this mathematical induction, but it should be noted that it is not inductive reasoning as I have defined "induction." It is a very special form of deductive reasoning. It is not at all the sort of thing I have in mind here. Second, there is the traditional theory of intuitive induction. According to this theory, from a survey of a few instances of a kind, one is supposed to be able to see the truth of some generalization about all instances of this kind. Ross seems to have thought that at least some ethical principles could be known in this way.[7] Again, he may call this induction if he likes, but it is not induction in the sense that I have defined the term. It is not a *reasoning* from particular cases to the universal generalization at all. Instead, thinking about the particular cases is supposed to be a psychological preparation from intuiting the truth of a self-evident principle. The principle is to be justified, if a self-evident principle can be said to need justification, by the act of seeing that it is true, not by any reasoning from evidence. The sort of nonempirical induction I have in mind, however, is an alternative to intuition and self-evidence. Here the principle is inferred to be true on the evidence of the truth of some of its consequences.

If I am correct, ethical principles have an epistemological status that is often thought impossible. They are known entirely a priori. Yet they are not, at least in any useful sense, analytic. If "analytic" means nothing more than a priori, then I suppose that ethical principles are analytic. But to beg the question of the synthetic a priori in this way is neither fair to the opponent nor enlightening to the friend. One way of defining the analytic would be as that which can be established by an analysis of the words used, this analysis to be given by a definition. In this sense, at least, ethical principles are not analytic. One cannot justify the claim that they are true by giving a definition of the ethical terms used. I seem to be committed to a rather old-fashioned epistemology at this point, for synthetic a priori truths are usually thought disreputable these days. So be it. One of the tests of any epistemological theory is that its consequences for ethics should be true. If the hypothesis that all a priori principles are analytic is disconfirmed in ethics, then the only reasonable thing to do is to reject that epistemological dogma.

I am not quite going back to the Kantian synthetic a priori, however. Kant thought that ethical principles, if genuine, must be a priori, based upon reason rather than experience. And for him the two marks of the genuinely a priori are universality and necessity.[8] A priori truths apply to all possible, not just actual, instances; and they do not just happen to be true, they must be true. Ethical principles do seem to possess this universality that goes beyond actual instances. They are true for all possible cases; that is why they can be established by thought experiment. Perhaps in some sense they are necessary as well, but I doubt this. At least they lack the sort of necessity that is characteristic of self-evident truths or of the conclusions of deductive inferences. From a logical standpoint they are merely probable; they are hypotheses that go beyond the evidence and that are always corrigible in the light of further evidence. In spite of the fact that the evidence for them is a priori, they are just as tentative as any hypothesis in any natural science. The fact that ethical principles are established by nonempirical induction therefore, gives them a very interesting epistemological status as a priori hypotheses.

It does not follow from what I have said that all ethical generalizations are a priori. There is always an element of the a priori in ethics. But normally we classify as empirical any conclusion that is based in any way or in any part upon experience. Many ethical generalizations are probably of this sort. For example, that no human being is morally perfect is a hypothesis that could be justified only by observing actual human beings. Probably the rules of thumb that are so useful in deliberation are rough statistical generalizations that are based in part upon an experience of the sorts of situation that commonly arise and the normal effects of certain types of action. Still, I would contend that some ethical generalizations are entirely nonempirical. Utilitarianism, if true, would be an example.

Is this contention really tenable? Thought experiments may seem like pure thinking, but perhaps an empirical element is smuggled in somewhere. At least two serious doubts linger on. First, it sometimes seems that thought experiments are corrigible in the light of subsequent experience. If so, they can hardly claim to be entirely a priori. For example, one is asked to imagine the case of the pleasure a brutal man takes in torturing his victim. When I perform this experiment in my imagination, my conclusion is that his pleasure has intrinsic value, although it may also have bad consequences. But after experiencing a good thrashing at the hands of a chuckling bully, my conclusion may be that such pleasures are intrinsically evil. Does not this show that my first thoughts were simply thinking of an experiment? Not at all. It must not be taken for granted that my conclusion subsequent to the experience is a correction of the first; my experience may have caused me to reach a false conclusion. More important, even if my experience did correct my conclusion, just *how* did it do this? It did not, I think, show me that my original conclusion was unjustified by the premises as I originally interpreted them. Rather it showed me that I had not properly or fully understood the premises. My error did not lie in drawing the ethical conclusion but in imagining what the experience of torturing was like.

That is, my error lay in my understanding of the descriptive statements constituting the premises of the conductive reasoning, not in the inference from them to the conclusion. This relation between the nature of some experience and its value is entirely a priori and is never corrected by experience. It could not be corrected by experience, since one never finds the value in experience as he finds its descriptive characteristics. What is corrected by subsequent experience is either the description of it or the interpretation of that description.

Second, it sometimes seems that thought experiments presuppose some knowledge of causation. The hypothesis that one ought always to keep his promises might be tested by thinking of the case in which a person who has promised to meet a friend for golf at noon sharp happens upon a drowning man just before noon. If the conclusion is that the person ought to save the drowning man even if this makes him late, the hypothesis is disconfirmed. But any such conclusion clearly rests upon our knowledge of the consequences of leaving the drowning man in the water until after the golf game, the probability that the other golfer will become impatient and commit suicide, etc. Does not the presence of all this empirical information show that the thinking is far from pure reasoning? Not quite. What it does show, I think, is that the thought experiment has been incompletely described. As it stands it is a mixture of empirical prediction about what would happen in such a case together with an ethical judgment based in part upon that prediction. To have a genuine thought experiment one must make all this empirical prediction explicit in the premises. Then the thought experiment will consist in the entirely nonempirical reasoning from the premises to the ethical conclusion. But if the premises are empirical, then is not the conclusion based upon experience? Again, not quite. The conclusion of the thought experiment as such is something like this: In such and such a case it would be wrong to keep the promise. Or perhaps: If the act were of such and such a sort, it would be wrong to do it. Whether or not the empirical information packed into the antecedent is true, the conditional statement is true. It can be known just by thinking. The real moral of the tale is not that thought experiments are not really reasoning, but that what pass for thought experiments are often a mixture of conductive reasoning and empirical guesswork. These two must be carefully distinguished, for the way in which each is justified is quite different. What will happen in a given case can be known only empirically, but the ethical judgment of that case is entirely nonempirical.

My view is that thought experiments, when properly conducted, are pure reasoning. Upon the a priori conclusions of such thought experiments ethical principles are based. The reasoning from the possible cases to the universal principle is inductive. That such a purely nonempirical induction is possible is crucial when the question of justifying an ethical principle arises. That this sort of inductive reasoning plays an important role in ethics is shown by the frequent use of thought experiments in the recent literature.

CONCLUSION

The common assumption that all justification is deductive must be abandoned in the face of inductive arguments that canot be reduced to deductive form. The next move is to limit justification to reasoning, either deductive or inductive. Although induction has several important uses in ethics, the most interesting is that in which thought experiments are used to confirm or disconfirm an ethical theory. The logic by which the results of these experiments establish or refute ethical hypotheses is precisely the same as that by which the results of laboratory experiments or observations in the field establish or refute scientific hypotheses. These thought experiments themselves, however, are experiments only in name. Properly interpreted they are seen to be ethical arguments which infer some ethical conclusion from a set of factual premises that describe the test case. Since these ethical arguments are neither deductive nor inductive, we are once more forced to extend our conception of reasoning and with it our view of justification. To see just how we must extend our view of justification we must examine this third sort of reasoning at some length.

3. conduction

WHEN one has considered all the deductive and inductive arguments in ethics, there remain others to be taken into account. A few ethical arguments that fall into neither of the two traditional categories are the following: You ought to take your son to the circus because you promised. This is a good book because it is interesting and thought-provoking. Although he is tactless and nonconformist, he is still a morally good man because of his underlying kindness and real integrity.

In most cases this sort of reasoning derives its conclusion from a variety of premises each of which has some independent relevance. Typically, although by no means always, several reasons are given in such arguments; and in those cases where a single reason is advanced there are others which might have been given as well. Since what is characteristic of this sort of reasoning is the leading together of various considerations, it seems appropriate to label it "conduction."

The nature of conduction

How can one make clear the nature of this kind of reasoning? We have discovered its existence by noticing that certain arguments in ethics are left over when all deductive and inductive ethical arguments have been studied. It is tempting, therefore, to define a conductive argument as any argument that is neither deductive nor inductive. But such a negative definition gives no insight into the positive nature of conduction. More important, the sort of argument I have in mind is not the only sort of inference that refuses to fall into the two traditional categories of reasoning. At some point statistical or probability inference will require a kind of reasoning that is neither deductive nor inductive. I also believe that there is something that might be called explanatory reasoning: reasoning from a body of data to a hypothesis that will render them intelligible. And if the argument by analogy cannot be reduced to some sort of statistical inference, it must also be admitted as a distinct kind of reasoning. Obviously it is necessary to find some way to characterize the sort of arguments I have in mind to distinguish them from other sorts of arguments that are also nondeductive and noninductive as well.

Conduction can best be defined as that sort of reasoning in which 1) a conclusion about some individual case 2) is drawn nonconclusively 3) from one or more premises about the same case 4) without any appeal to other cases. Perhaps the most striking feature of all the examples of conduction I have given is that they all deal with particular cases; each derives a conclusion about an individual act or object from information about that same act or object. Thus, you ought not to have spoken so harshly because your words hurt her deeply, or Martin Luther King is a fine man because, in spite of occasional arrogance, he is an unselfish and courageous worker for his fellowman. Although the conclusion of a conductive argument is a particular judgment, conduction is not to be identified with that judgment alone; it is the reasoning leading to the judgment. If ethical judgment is rational, and I believe that at its best it is, then the ethical judgment of the particular case does not stand alone but is the conclusion of a rational argument.

This reasoning is not simply the application of deduction to the particular case, for it is inconclusive—that is, it is always possible for the conclusion to be false even though the premises are true and the inference valid. To be sure, we do sometimes reason deductively about particular cases. But when we do we connect the facts of the case to the ethical conclusion by means of a universal major premise. Granted that we sometimes argue in this way, I have argued in the first chapter that we do not always reason in this way. In conduction the truth of the premises does not necessitate the conclusion but only supports it to a greater or lesser degree. When deductive reasoning is applied to particular cases it has a very different sort of uncertainty. Although the premises, if true, necessarily imply that the conclusion is true, the premises may not be quite true of the particular case at hand. If they are close to the truth, then the conclusion may be an approximation to the truth. Still, the logical rigor of deductive reasoning is no guarantee of the complete accuracy of any applied deductive argument. This sort of uncertainty arises, not from the inconclusiveness of the implicative link between premises and conclusion but from the possibility that the premises made do not quite fit the case to which they are applied. In conductive arguments, on the other hand, even a perfect fit of premises to individual case is no guarantee of the truth of the conclusion because additional information may be uncovered to outweigh the given premises.

Another way of drawing a conclusion about a particular case from one or more premises about that same case is reasoning by analogy. If the book on my desk is like several others I have read in being long, published by an obscure publisher, and written by Tobias Dullasdust, then it is probably, like them, uninteresting. In such reasoning the conclusion is linked to the premises, not by a universal generalization, but by appeal to analogous instances. The point of this appeal to analogous cases is that in these cases experience has shown that certain characteristics (like length, being published by an obscure publisher, and being written by a certain author) have gone together with another characteristic (uninterestingness). But in conduction the link between premises and conclusion is not established on the basis of the experience of analogous cases; it is entirely a priori. Reflection upon the given information about the case at hand justifies one in reaching some further conclusion about that same case. Thus conduction is that sort of reasoning in which a conclusion about some individual case is drawn nonconclusively from one or more premises about the same case without any appeal to other cases.

The examples of conduction that I have given have all been ethical arguments, arguments which infer some ethical statement about some particular case from factual premises about that case. This is no accident because the great interest of conductive reasoning for the justification of ethical statements is that it shows how factual information can be relevant to ethics. One might wonder, however, whether all conductive arguments are ethical. Although it is sometimes suggested that ethics has a logic all its own, there is still something a bit suspicious about introducing a special sort of reasoning to justify ethical statements. This seems too much like an ad hoc hypothesis invented to save a theory in the face of all the appearances.

Fortunately for my argument, conductive arguments do occur outside of ethics. Wherever some descriptive predicate is ascribed on the basis of a family resemblance conductive reasoning takes place. In all such cases there are several criteria for the application of the term and each of these criteria may be satisfied to a greater or lesser degree and they may vary in importance as well. The fact that one or more of the criteria are satisfied in a particular instance is a reason for applying the term, but the inference is nonconclusive and does not appeal to the fact that the criteria have been found empirically associated with the term in other cases. For example one might give the following arguments: Bees have a language because they can communicate information about the location of flowers to one another. Hunting is a game because it is fun and involves a competition between the hunter and his prey. Although John can play only one instrument, and that not very well, he is still musical because he has a remarkable memory for music he has heard and composes upon occasion. In such examples factual conclusions about some individual case are drawn from information about that case.

One nondefinitive characteristic of conductive arguments is particularly worthy of notice. Conduction is always nonformal. Traditionally, logicians have distinguished between the form and the matter of an argument. The form is the logical structure of the argument; the matter is the subject matter or what the argument is about. The same syllogistic form, for example, may be used in arguing about men and mortality or dogs and animality or chemicals and atomicity. It is precisely because the subject matter does not affect the validity of most deductive inferences that a single deductive logic can apply to the deductive reasoning of philosophers, biologists, and chemists alike. The situation is very different in conductive reasoning. Consider "you ought to do it because you promised." Whether or not this is a valid argument depends upon the relevance of promising for obligation and not at all on the logical form of the argument. This nonformality of conductive arguments is awkward when it comes to assessing their validity, but awkward or not it is one of the basic characteristics of this sort of reasoning.

Patterns of conduction

For reasons that should be obvious, conductive arguments fall into three distinct patterns. These are formal patterns; they differ in logical structure alone. But since this is conduction, such formal patterns do not determine the validity of the arguments. Both valid and invalid arguments may be found in each of the three patterns. It is still useful to distinguish these formal differences, even though they do not provide a formal logic of conduction.

The first pattern is exhibited by any conductive argument in which a single reason is given for the conclusion. Examples might be "you ought to help him for he has been very kind to you" or "that was a good play because the characters were so well drawn." Although only one reason is advanced in this pattern, there are always (or at least almost always) other relevant considerations that might have been mentioned. The given reason is usually selected either because it is particularly obvious or because it seems to outweigh all the others. Although there is no leading together of considerations in the first pattern, this is still the basic unit of conduction because arguments of the other two patterns are simply combinations of these.

In deciding whether or not an argument of this pattern is valid it is necessary to determine whether or not the premise is relevant to the conclusion drawn from it. At this point it is tempting to construe conduction on the model of deduction and assume that there is a tacit premise which links the reason given with the conclusion drawn. For example "he has been very kind to you" is a reason for asserting "you ought to help him" only if one takes for granted "everyone ought always to help anyone who has been very kind to him." This deductive model is misleading for it obscures the fact that the argument is inconclusive; it is always possible for additional evidence to turn up that will show the conclusion to be false without in the least showing the given premise to be either irrelevant or false. On the other hand, the deductive model is not entirely out of place. It serves to remind us that conductive arguments are subject to logical criticism as valid or invalid, logically correct or incorrect, much as deductive arguments are.

In the second pattern of conduction several reasons are given for the conclusion. Examples are "you ought to take your son to the movie because you promised to do so, it is a good movie, and you have nothing better to do this afternoon" or "this is not a good book because it fails to hold one's interest, is full of vague description, and has a very implausible plot." Here, also there are likely to be relevant considerations, particularly on the other side, that are not mentioned. Nevertheless, enough reasons are given so that it is usually difficult to challenge the conclusion without questioning either the truth of the premises or the validity of the inference.

In this second pattern of reasoning several considerations, each of which may be independently relevant, are brought together into a unified argument from which a single conclusion is drawn. It is tempting to think of this bringing together on the model of calculation; one adds up the various considerations to get the total conclusion. This model is particularly appealing when one thinks of deliberation along utilitarian lines. When a contemplated action would have several good consequences, each of these is a reason for doing the action. One draws the conclusion that the action ought to be done by determining how much good each separate consequence would have and then adding up these amounts of value. But it is a mistake to think of this leading together of reasons on the model of calculation even here. This model is misleading, not only because it suggests that conduction is an almost automatic process that can be done according to mechanical rules, but also because one cannot assign amounts of value or obligation in the absence of any fixed unit of goodness or oughtness. Conductive reasoning adds up the independent reasons, not by a sort of calculation, but by thinking them together, by holding them together in the mind. This logical convergence of evidence is quite different from the mathematical addition of homogeneous units.

The third pattern of conduction is that form of argument in which some conclusion is drawn from both positive and negative considerations. In this pattern reasons against the conclusion are included as well as reasons for it. For example "in spite of a certain dissonance, that piece of music is beautiful because of its dynamic quality and its final resolution" or "although your lawn needs cutting, you ought to take your son to the movies because the picture is ideal for children and will be gone by tomorrow." In such arguments the arguer often attempts to state all the relevant considerations, or at least all the important ones. Still, even this pattern is inconclusive. By this I mean that, whether or not there are additional considerations in the actual case that would change the conclusion without showing the given premises either untrue or the original inference invalid, there always might be such. It always remains logically possible to find additional considerations to support or weaken the conclusion.

Since this pattern includes reasons against as well as for the conclusion, it raises the question of how one knows that the reasons for the conclusion are stronger than those against it. Perhaps the most popular model for this sort of conductive reasoning is weighing. One decides whether the argument is valid by weighing the pros against the cons. If properly understood, this model is a good one. The weighing should not be thought of as putting each reason on a scale, noting the amount of weight, and then calculating the difference between the weight of the reasons for and the reasons against. The degree of support is not measurable in this way because there is no unit of logical force in which to do the calculation. Nor should one think of the weighing as being done on a balance scale in which one pan is filled with the pros and the other with cons.

This suggests too mechanical a process as well as the possibility of everyone reading off the result in the same way. Rather one should think of the weighing in terms of the model of determining the weight of objects by hefting them in one's hands. This way of thinking about weighing brings out the comparative aspect and the conclusion that one is more than the other without suggesting any automatic procedure that would dispense with individual judgment or any introduction of units of weight. Probably one more refinement in the model is necessary if we are not be misled by it. To decide which of two small piles of pebbles is heavier, I can usually take one pile in one hand and the other pile in the other and heft both at the same time. But suppose that I must estimate the relative weight of two piles of stones. In this case I am only strong enough to take one or two stones in a hand at a time. Hence I must lift the stones in each pile one after the other in order to estimate their total weight. Similarly, there are limits to the number of considerations one can hold together in his mind at any single moment, even if this moment is a specious present. Consequently, it is usually necessary to turn over the pros and cons successively in one's mind in order to draw any conclusion from them. At this point the model suggests that it will be difficult, to say the least, to reach any reliable conclusions about the validity of conductive arguments in the third pattern. This suggestion is not, I fear, inappropriate.

On the whole it is helpful to think of conductive reasoning in terms of the model of weighing construed in this way. Still, one must remember two things: it is only a model and it is not always helpful. Like any model, it may be used to suggest features of conduction that we might otherwise overlook. But to discover what, if anything, there is in conductive reasoning to correspond with some features of the model, we must, in the end, think in terms of conduction itself. Moreover, this model does not *define* conduction, for weighing of the evidence does not occur only in conductive reasoning. One also weighs positive and negative instances in many statistical inferences, but this is a different sort of weighing involving numerical ratios. Still another sort of weighing takes place in some explanatory reasoning. A proposed hypothesis may explain certain facts very well but leave other facts unexplained or even render them incongruous. To decide whether the data support the hypothesis on the whole may require the balancing of intelligibility against unintelligibility. Thus, although the weighing of pros and cons is typical of conduction, it is certainly not restricted to this form of reasoning.

Even in conduction, the model of weighing is not always helpful. It fits best the third pattern of conduction where the logical problem is to estimate the relative logical force of the pros and cons, the reasons for and the reasons against the conclusion. It fits the first and second patterns less well. Although we can think of one or several reasons as giving weight to or weighing for a conclusion, to do so seems to clarify very little. Since the best model can mislead if pushed too far, we should not insist upon the model of weighing except where it is obviously appropriate.

The logic of ethics

Expressions like "the logic of ethics" and "the logic of moral language" are quite common these days, but can there really be any logic of ethical reasoning? The answer depends upon just what logic is supposed to be. In the very wide sense in which logic is simply the analysis of reasoning from an epistemological standpoint, I can hardly deny, right in the middle of an epistemological analysis of ethical reasoning, that a logic of ethics is possible. But taken in a narrower and more interesting sense, logic is that discipline which distinguishes between valid and invalid arguments. A glance at a few standard treatises on logic suggests that logic performs its function in at least four ways. It provides lists of fallacies against which any given argument may be checked. It develops certain test procedures, such as Venn diagrams or truth tables, by which it is possible to separate valid from invalid arguments. It specifies the criteria of validity, the marks by which a valid argument can be recognized. And it formulates rules of inference which, if followed, guarantee that the reasoning will be valid. To what extent, then, can there be a discipline which supplies lists of fallacies, test procedures, criteria of validity, and rules of inference for ethical arguments?

Many ethical arguments are deductive in form, and to most of these ordinary deductive logic is readily applicable. Since the validity of most deductive arguments depends upon their form alone, the ethical subject matter can be disregarded by the logician. Therefore the traditional lists of fallacies, test procedures, criteria of validity, and rules of inference contained in the standard works on deductive logic apply to ethics just as they do to any other field. Moreover, deductive logic is being extended in various ways these days. Various logicians are working out deontic, axiological, and normative logics along several different lines. Just how far the boundaries of deductive logic can be pushed, just how many of these special deductive logics can be firmly established, I do not know. There is nothing wrong with the attempt, however; in principle such logics are quite possible. How useful they will be depends upon the power of the principles discovered. I doubt whether such logics will take us very far, but any progress at all in this area is welcome. Finally, it appears that certain deductive ethical arguments, such as some forms of the practical syllogism, are valid because of their content rather than their logical form. If so, ordinary deductive logic, which is purely formal, can be no measure of their validity or invalidity. In general, it seems safe to say that deductive logic, ordinary or special, can apply to most deductive ethical arguments.

The status of inductive logic is a subject of more controversy. There are those who deny that there is any such thing on the grounds that induction is not a separate and valid form of reasoning. Since I have already rejected this view, I believe that inductive logic is possible in principle. In fact, various studies in the logic of confirmation and the rather elaborate principles of statistical inference seem to provide the basis for inductive logic. Unfortunately, certain logical and epistemological problems remain to be solved before inductive logic can claim the same systematic coherence and rational support as deductive logic. In any event, to the extent that there can be a logic of confirmation and disconfirmation it would seem to be as readily applicable to inductive ethical arguments as to inductive arguments of any other kind.

When one turns to conductive ethical arguments the situation is much less promising. Clearly there now exists nothing like a fully developed and firmly established logic of conduction. Worse yet, there is reason to doubt that the attempts to found such a logic will ever lead to anything. These doubts hinge upon the fact that the validity of a conductive argument always depends upon the content of the argument rather than its logical form. This nonformality of conductive argument implies that, whatever the logic of conductive ethical arguments might be, it could not be a discipline separate from ethics that would pass judgment upon the inferences used in ethics. There is no way to judge the validity of such ethical arguments while ignoring their ethical content.

Although I cannot go very far toward clarifying the distinction between logical form and subject matter, it may be helpful to notice how it is related to the equally unclear classification of symbols. It appears that the symbols making up any statement can be grouped into three classes—logical terms, predicate constants, and individual constants. Examples of logical terms are "all," "some," "or," "if   then," "not," "may," and "must." Predicate constants include "red," "soluble," "intelligent," "tree," "good," and "wrong." Individual constants might be "this," "here," "now," "London," "he," and "John." Formal logic is made possible by the fact that the validity of many arguments depends exclusively upon the logical terms they use. Conductive arguments are nonformal in the sense that their validity depends upon the predicate constants they contain as well as the logical terms they use. In no case, however, do the individual constants affect the validity of an argument. In this sense, validity remains universal even when it is not formal.

What does this nonformality of conductive reasoning imply about the possibility of a logic of conductive ethical arguments? As far as fallacies are concerned, it obviously implies that there can be no list of formal fallacies in this area. However, there presumably could be informal ethical fallacies corresponding to the traditional fallacies such as the fallacies of composition or *argumentum ad baculum*. If I were to construct such a list, I would begin with the egoistic fallacy and the moralistic fallacy. The egoistic fallacy is the logical error of ruling out any consideration that does not have a bearing upon the agent's own welfare as irrelevant to a conclusion about what that agent ought to do. The moralistic fallacy is drawing some conclusion about the rightness or wrongness of an action from evidence that is relevant to its moral goodness or badness instead. I see no reason why such a list of specifically ethical fallacies could not be constructed. But if such a list were to be useful in distinguishing between valid and invalid ethical arguments, two conditions would have to be fulfilled. The logical errors would have to be tempting enough so that people would be commonly misled into using and accepting such arguments; yet the type of argument must be clearly enough mistaken so that it could be seen that it was invalid upon reflection. There is some doubt whether both of these conditions could be satisfied to any great extent at the same time. Still, it might be that a few fallacies of ethical reasoning could be identified, established to be such, and described sufficiently to serve as checks against plausible errors.

Could there be any test procedures for conductive ethical arguments? I am not sure, but I doubt it. All of the text procedures with which I am familiar seem to depend upon the formal nature of most deduction. For example, Venn diagrams can be used to test syllogistic inferences only because the logical relationships between the logical words such as "all," "some," "is," and "not" can be treated in terms of the inclusion and exclusion of classes *without* any consideration of the defining characteristics of these classes. Again, it is possible to use truth tables to test the validity of certain inferences only because logical words can be defined in terms of the truth or falsity of the propositions upon which they operate *without* any consideration of the content of these propositions. But the validity of conductive arguments cannot be determined without considering their subject matter, for their validity is nonformal. I suppose someone might invent some test procedure that would depend upon the predicate constants in an argument instead of ignoring these, but I find myself unable to imagine what such a procedure would be like. Certainly the success of all the existing test procedures seem to arise from their ability to ignore the predicate constants in the arguments to which they apply. Therefore, until someone comes up with a radically different sort of test procedure, I shall assume that there can be no tests for the validity of conductive ethical arguments.

Another form a conductive logic might take would be a specification of the criteria of validity in conductive arguments. This would be like what the traditional rules of the syllogism do for one sort of deductive argument. One way of testing the validity of a syllogistic inference is to see whether the middle term is distributed at least once, whether there are two negative premises, etc. These are the features by which invalid syllogisms can be detected and valid ones identified. Again, there are certain rules of thumb that serve as criteria for the strength of an argument from analogy. The greater the number of instances, the greater the variety within the known instances, etc. the more logical force the argument from analogy has. Are there any characteristics of conductive arguments whose presence can be readily detected and which are marks of validity or invalidity?

One way of reading Toulmin's *Reason in Ethics* is as proposing two criteria for one species of conductive ethical argument.[1] The two criteria of validity for any inference from the facts of the case to a conclusion as to the agent's duty in that case are that the argument either appeals to the moral code of the community to which the agent belongs or to the suffering or inconvenience to the members of the community that his act would cause or prevent. Now it does not seem to me that these criteria are either necessary or sufficient to guarantee the validity of an inference to an agent's duty in a given situation. Other sorts of consideration seem perfectly relevant to what one ought to do. For example, that the act will cause many people to be happy is a reason why one ought to do it. Again, the moral reformer is not necessarily arguing invalidly even when he ignores the accepted code of his community and appeals to something other than suffering or inconvenience, such as justice. Toulmin might reply that in such cases one is not inferring any duty, that the notion of the specifically moral ought presupposes the moral code of a community. But I see no reason to accept this narrow definition or conception of duty. Nor are Toulmin's criteria sufficient. To appeal to the moral code of one's community may be a very bad reason if that moral code is perverted. Would a Nazi really be giving a good reason for spitting on a Jew if he pointed out that such action was required by the code of his group? In the end Toulmin's attempt to provide criteria of conductive arguments for judgments of duty will not do.

Is it simply that Toulmin has not managed to discover the right criteria or is there something mistaken in principle about trying to find criteria of conductive ethical reasoning? Perhaps we could answer this question if we could see just why Toulmin failed in his attempt. For one thing, his criteria are too narrow. There are many sorts of reason that are relevant to conclusions about what one ought morally to do besides the two Toulmin mentioned. To be sure, he managed to encompass a wide variety of considerations under his single criterion of appealing to the moral code, for any developed moral code includes many principles. But once it is realized that the appeal to a moral code is not always valid, Toulmin's single reason falls apart into as many reasons as there are tenable principles in the moral code. Therefore, any attempt to find criteria of conductive reasoning along Toulmin's lines would seem to lead to a very wide range of criteria, particularly if it is to extend beyond inferences to duty to include inferences to other sorts of ethical conclusions. Another difficulty with Toulmin's program is that he reduces all such arguments to the first pattern, arguments in which an ethical conclusion follows from a single factual reason. Obviously criteria of validity for first-pattern arguments will not enable one to judge the validity of third-pattern arguments; that is, criteria of relevance are not enough to serve as criteria of logical force. It is the latter that are necessary if we are to determine the validity of arguments in which the pros are weighed against the cons. Toulmin tries to avoid all third-pattern arguments by building a hierarchy into his logical system. Thus the appeal to the moral code is supposed to be valid only where the moral code applies unambiguously to the act in question. Where there is any conflict in principles, instead of weighing the conflicting duties one simply forgets the moral code and appeals to avoidable suffering or inconvenience instead. In this way third-pattern arguments never can arise for Toulmin. But it seems to me that they do arise and that any logical system that tries to do away with the need for weighing pros and cons is false to the facts of ethical reasoning. If I am right that many ethical arguments do involve both positive and negative considerations, then it will take a very different sort of criterion to determine the validity or invalidity of such arguments. Thirdly, in what sense will the criteria discovered in this way be criteria? Any useful criterion should be an easily detectable mark that can be shown to be a mark of validity independently of the argument to which it is to be applied. But as the number of kinds of consideration that are relevant multiplies and as provision is made for degrees of logical force, it looks less and less as though one could find any criteria that are independent of the specific content of the argument to be judged. This is just what one would expect in the case of a nonformal form of inference like conduction. But then the nonformality of conduction would seem to doom the attempt to discover any useful criteria of conductive ethical reasoning.

This leaves that part of logic which formulates and applies rules of valid inference. Could there be principles of conductive reasoning? Since the validity of a conductive argument in no way depends upon the individual constants it contains, it should be possible in principle to formulate rules for conduction. Every valid argument belongs to a class of arguments which differ from it only in the individual constants used, and every member of this class is valid. Similarly, every invalid conductive argument is a member of a class of logically similar arguments all of which are invalid. Therefore, it should be possible to formulate a rule for each such class of conductive arguments declaring that all arguments of the specified kind are valid (or invalid).

In principle this is quite possible, but in practice it is

not so easy. To judge the validity of conductive arguments in the first and second patterns one must know whether or not the premises advanced are relevant to the conclusion drawn; in the third pattern one must also know how much logical force the pros have against the cons. Now it might not be too hard to formulate rules of relevance for conduction. Examples might be "the fact that an experience is pleasant is a reason for concluding that it is good" or "the fact that an act would produce disvalue is a reason against doing that act." Such principles might be established in the same way that the principles of deductive logic are, by induction from clear cases of valid argument. Once established by appeal to clear cases, these rules of relevance might then be applied to arguments whose validity is in doubt. Thus one might realize that his own pleasure is a reason for judging his own experience good but not recognize the connection in the experience of someone else, or one might grant that he ought not to do what would produce bad results for his friend but not make the same inference in the case of a stranger.

Let us suppose that some logician, such as Toulmin, has proposed a set of rules of conductive ethical inference. Would we have anything comparable to our existing deductive logic? There would be some analogy, but three differences are painfully apparent. 1) The rules of conduction would be much less firmly established. The principles of deductive logic are usually sufficient to justify the claim that some particular argument is valid because these principles are themselves usually accepted. But it would be much harder to establish any rules of conduction so firmly that they would be generally accepted. It is always possible to appeal to intuition, but there is every reason to believe that logicians' intuitions about the principles of ethical inferences will be no more unanimous than moralists' intuitions about ethical first principles. If the inductive appeal to clear cases is to be effective, all the clear cases must be valid. If some arguments of a specified class seem clearly valid while others seem clearly invalid, no universal rule can be formulated with any great confidence. This sometimes seems to be the situation with ethical arguments. For example, children may feel that "it hurts me" is clearly relevant to "it ought not to be done" but may emphatically deny that "it hurts you" is relevant at all. That this logical conflict is not limited to children is shown by the fact that the issue between ethical egoism and ethical universalism can be a serious problem among intelligent and responsible philosophers. Another situation which occurs much more frequently and which equally undercuts the possibility of establishing rules of relevance is that in which no member of the specified class is clearly valid or invalid. If one is in serious doubt about the validity of the argument "John is Mary's father so Mary ought to help John even though he deserted the family just before Mary was born," one will probably be just as uncertain about the validity of every argument just like this one except for containing the names of different individuals. In such a situation there are no clear cases from which one can induce any rule of conductive inference. 2) Even supposing the rules of conduction could be firmly established, they would be much less powerful than the rules of deductive logic. The power of deductive logic lies in the fact that a single set of a relatively few principles can be applied to a very large number of arguments in a wide variety of fields. This is possible because the validity of most deductive inferences depends upon their logical form only. Therefore, differences of subject matter can be ignored by the deductive logician. This is not so in conduction. Since conductive reasoning is nonformal, the rules of conduction must specify the subject matter of the argument, for example that pleasantness is relevant to goodness. Every change in the content of a conductive argument may affect the validity of that argument. Therefore, it would be necessary to have a new rule of conduction for every new predicate in the argument. This logical fact throws serious doubt upon our ability to formulate anything like a complete conductive logic or to apply any fragment we might possess. At best, any rule we could discover would be very weak in the sense that it would apply to only a very restricted range of ethical arguments. 3) Even where these rules of relevance were applicable, they would often be insufficient to establish the validity or invalidity of a given argument. In any argument of the third pattern, it is not enough to know whether the premises are or are not relevant to the conclusion; one must also know how much logical force the reasons for the conclusion have in comparison to the reasons against the conclusion. To determine the validity or invalidity of any reasoning from both pros and cons, rules of relevance must be supplemented with rules of force. There is serious doubt that this can be done.

It has sometimes been suggested that one could formulate rules of logical force by specifying which kinds of reasons take precedence over which other kinds. Examples might be "that some act causes harm takes precedence over the fact that it causes good" or "moral reasons always take precedence over prudential reasons." Any such program is faced with two grave difficulties. *a*) Any specified factor can be present in a situation in various degrees. There can be more or less harm or many different degrees of good. Now it is probably true that we condemn causing harm to others more than we would failing to produce an equal amount of good, but these amounts are not always equal. It is false to say that potential harm always outweighs potential good, for a very large good will outweigh some slight harm. Nor is it easy to specify in any set of logical principles just what amount of good is required to outweigh each possible amount of harm. The same sort of difficulty clearly arises for every other pair of factors that can occur in ethical reasoning. To be of any real help the rules of logical force would have to specify the priority for every degree of each factor for each possible pair of factors. Such a set of rules would be very complicated indeed. *b*) But the complications are not over, for the relevant factors do not always occur neatly in pairs, one pro balanced against one con. There may be all sorts of combinations of factors with several pros and several cons. Any rules of logical force that will enable us to judge the validity of conductive arguments which incorporate all the relevant information must tell us which combinations, where the nature of the combination is a function of the degree of each factor as well as which factors are combined, take precedence over which other combinations. Each such combination has its own logical force and would require a separate rule of force. In the end very little generalization is possible here.

The upshot of all this is that to determine the validity of conductive arguments one would need a rule of inference for each set of predicates, where asserting a different amount of the same factor constitutes applying a different predicate. I willingly grant that in principle such a set of rules of ethical reasoning could exist, although such a logic of ethics would be so complicated that it is hard to imagine it actually being brought into existence. At the very least, it is clear that we do not now judge the validity of ethical arguments by any such logic, for nothing like such a set of rules of inference has been proposed, much less firmly established, by anyone. Moreover there seems little point in trying to bring such a logic into existence. Just because conductive reasoning is nonformal, the content of any rule of inference must be identical with the subject matter of the argument as far as all the predicates go; only individual constants may vary. In any case in which the validity of the argument is in serious doubt there would seem to be as much doubt about the correctness of the corresponding rule. Whether one is pondering the rule of inference or the inference itself, there seems to be no alternative to weighing the pros and cons, to reflecting on all the considerations advanced and drawing the valid conclusion. The appeal to logical rules seems pointless here, for one can just as well weigh the reasons in the original argument.

My conclusion, then, is that there can be no logic of ethics in any very interesting sense. The ordinary logic of deduction and induction can apply to those ethical arguments that are deductive or inductive, but ordinary logic is no more a logic of ethics than it is a logic of biology or of geometry. When one turns to conductive reasoning, however, any helpful logic would have to be specifically ethical because the validity of conduction depends upon its subject matter. Just for this reason, there can be nothing like deductive logic to enable us to judge the validity of conductive ethical arguments. It might be possible to draw up a short list of tempting fallacies, but this would not take us very far. It does not seem possible in practice, whatever the possibilities in principle may be, to establish test procedures, criteria of validity, or rules of inference in conductive ethical reasoning.

Nonformal reasoning

There are those who feel that this conclusion requires the further conclusion that conduction is not really reasoning. If there can be no logic of ethics, particularly if there can be no logical form, rules of or criteria for conduction, then conduction is not really valid reasoning at all. Obviously, it is up to me to defend my claim that conduction is a genuine kind of reasoning.

The reason that there cannot be any logic of conduction is that the validity of any conductive argument depends upon the content of the argument. By contrast, whether or not a deductive argument is valid normally depends on the logical form alone. It is only a step to the view that validity is tied to logical form in such a way that there could be no such thing as nonformal reasoning. Hence, conduction cannot be a genuine kind of reasoning.

Now is it true that validity is a purely formal matter? Since I insist that conductive arguments can be valid while admitting that their validity does not hinge on their logical form, I will obviously deny this premise of the argument. But since my critic denies that conductive arguments ever are valid, I cannot simply assert their validity without begging the question. One thing I can do is to give examples of conductive arguments, like "you ought not to do that because it causes avoidable pain" or "you ought not to do that because it would make him unhappy and he has been kind to you," which are so obviously valid that even my critic can recognize their cogency as reasoning. In this way I can support my general thesis by nonempirical induction.

Another thing I can do is to take the fight into the enemy's camp by arguing that even deductive arguments are not always formally valid. It does seem as though the validity of most deductive arguments hinges on their form alone, and deductive logic does manage to ignore the subject matter of reasoning. Still, there are a few arguments that seem to be deductively valid even though they are not covered by formal logic. The argument "since this is green, it is extended" is one example; Black's version of a practical syllogism is another.[2] My conclusion is that the validity of an argument is not always a purely formal matter.

It is hard to be sure, of course. One difficulty is that it is always possible to save the comprehensiveness of formal logic by interpreting these arguments as enthymematic. If we add the premise "everything that is colored is extended" and assume that "anything green is colored," we can easily transform "since this is green, it is extended" into a formally valid inference. The difficulty is that adding such premises often makes the arguments useless for the purposes of justification. In the case at hand, to assume that everything colored is extended seems to beg the question. In other cases, like those in which we use conductive ethical arguments, the arguer may not be in a position to justify accepting that additional premise. If he does not want to base his argument on any such unjustifiable premise, it seems unfair to require him to do so. Therefore, I would prefer not to treat these arguments as enthymematic in spite of the logical convenience of doing so.

Another difficulty is that the notion of logical form is far from clear. As long as one sticks to arguments like the traditional syllogisms or the inferences that can be validated by truth-functional logic, the claim that validity is a purely formal matter seems to raise no problems. But when one turns to borderline cases like the ones to which I appeal, it is far from clear how much depends on logical form. There seem to be at least three different ways of defining logical form. *a*) The logical form of an argument may be everything determined by the purely logical words it contains. The problem then is to distinguish between logical and nonlogical words. Perhaps a logical word is any word upon which the validity of the argument depends. It is then analytically true that the validity of any argument is a purely formal matter. But it might then follow that "ought," "happy," and "kind" are logical words because the validity of "you ought to do that because it would make him happy and he has been kind to you" depends in part upon these words. And in any event, it settles a controversial matter simply by definition. One might avoid this by defining a logical word by listing all such words. But then one can always argue that "ought" and "happy" should be added to the list or, if not, that the validity of some arguments is determined by words not on the list. Finally, it is doubtful that one can sort out the logically relevant and irrelevant features of an argument simply by sorting out the words it contains into two groups. Consider our old friend "all men are mortal, Socrates is a man, therefore Socrates is mortal." Now "mortal" and "man" are usually classified as nonlogical words on the grounds that they can be replaced by any other predicates without affecting the validity of the argument. But notice that they must be replaced by predicates; one cannot introduce adverbs or quantifiers and still have a valid argument. And they must be replaced uniformly; one could not substitute one predicate for the first occurrence of "mortal" and another for the second. Since some words are logically relevant in some respects but not in others, one cannot sort out the factors that affect validity by sorting out the words into two neat piles.

Another way to define logical form is to start at the other end of the dichotomy between logical structure and subject matter. *b*) The logical form of an argument is everything but its subject matter. When thought of this way, it seems fairly clear that the syllogism does not depend upon its subject matter because the argument "all animals are irrational, Fido is an animal, therefore Fido is irrational" has a very different subject matter from our old Socratic friend yet preserves everything upon which the validity of either hinges. But it is less clear whether an argument about all men has a different subject matter from one about some men, or whether arguments that one ought to do something because he promised have a different subject matter from arguments that one ought not to do something because it would be unjust. And it certainly seems that "since it is green it is extended" is valid only because of its subject matter. Therefore, if logical form is defined as the opposite of subject matter, the appropriate conclusion would seem to be that logical validity is not a purely formal matter.

With the development of uninterpreted systems for the manipulation of marks on paper, there has arisen a third notion of logical form. *c*) The logical form of an argument is its symbolic structure quite apart from the meaning that is given to any of its symbols. In this view the ideal of reasoning is the manipulation of uninterpreted symbols according to explicit transformation rules. I would not wish to deny the value of this sort of manipulation; but as Whitehead observed its value lies precisely in avoiding all reasoning. Since no thinking is involved, this is not reasoning so much as a logical test procedure to be classified with the use of Venn diagrams and truth tables. And these manipulations are logic, rather than some other sort of game, only because the rules for manipulation are deliberately devised to accord with a reasoning that is independently valid. Now it might be that it is possible to devise a system of symbolic manipulation such that every valid inference could be validated by using it, but this is far from obvious. There certainly seem to be valid arguments that escape any of the systems devised so far. Therefore, in many of the arguments we now use the validity does not hinge on purely symbolic manipulations. Not all reasoning is as yet formal in this sense. My conclusion is that conductive ethical arguments cannot be denied validity-value on the grounds that they are nonformal. If logical form is defined so widely that every feature of an argument upon which its validity hinges is included, then all reasoning is indeed formal; but in this sense conduction is formal too. It is more natural to give some more restricted meaning to "logical form." But on none of the other usual interpretations can it be asserted with any confidence that all reasoning is purely formal.

Reasoning without rules

Another challenge to the validity of conductive arguments arises from the fact that there is not, and probably cannot be, any logic of conduction. Genuine reasoning can exist only where there are rules to distinguish valid from invalid reasoning. But there are no rules of reasoning that govern conductive ethical arguments. Therefore these are not really reasoning. The crux of this challenge is the assertion that there can be valid reasoning only where there are rules of reasoning. Although this is a very popular slogan, perhaps just because it is so popular, it is seldom explained or criticized. To my mind, however, two questions badly need asking: What kind of rules are presupposed by reasoning? And why are such rules required?

First questions first. The rules required are, I suppose, logical rules. But what kind of rules are logical? *1*) The goal of the modern logician seems to be derivation rules. These are rules governing the derivation of one formula from other formulas in an uninterpreted calculus. Derivation rules are necessary in such a purely formal system just because it is impossible to reason in any literal sense with completely meaningless symbols. Such rules are advantageous because they reduce to the minimum any need for fallible judgment and because they assure that everything about the manipulation of symbols shall be explicit. As far as I know, no logician has invented any such calculus to correspond to any part of the area of conductive ethical arguments. For any given set of conductive arguments such a system could be invented, but the resulting calculus would have no more general application because the validity of any conductive argument depends upon its subject matter. Hence the construction of logical calculi in this area is a rather trivial activity. But surely the existence of valid reasoning does not presuppose the existence of any such calculus of derivation rules, for the inferences formalized by Hilbert and Ackerman, say, were valid before they invented their logical system just as the syllogism was valid long before Aristotle. As a rule the logician tries to construct his calculus so that it will reflect some sort of reasoning that is recognized to be valid independently of his system. To be sure, the inventive logician can think up queer logics which suggest new, and sometimes strange, ways of reasoning. But if these queer logics become too queer, they are no longer considered logics but only symbolic games of some similar sort. This indicates that even here our standards of validity are outside of and independent of the derivation rules in any uninterpreted calculus.

Sometimes the logician is thought of, not as inventing rules, but as discovering and formulating rules of inference existing prior to any systems of logic. But what could these rules be before they are discovered? 2) Often they are thought of as syntactical rules. Syntactical rules are one sort of linguistic rules, those governing the relations of one word to other words. Since language is essentially a rule-governed activity, the meaning of any word consists in certain rules for its use. According to the view being examined here, these rules are basically of two kinds—semantical rules and syntactical rules. Semantical rules connect the word with the world; they govern its application to certain sorts of objects or its use in certain sorts of situations. Syntactical rules, on the other hand, connect the word with other words; they govern what is implied by the word and what in turn implies it. Thus syntactical rules are rules of reasoning at the same time as they are rules of meaning. Now what is really wrong with this view is the over-simple conception of meaning as reference that lies behind it. But even without examining that conception, it is clear that this view will not serve as a basis for challenging the validity of conduction. For in some broad sense of "semantical rules," all the expressions used in conductive ethical arguments are governed by semantical rules. If rules of reasoning are meaning rules, then these words, since they are perfectly meaningful, are governed by such rules. Moreover, I doubt whether the meaning of a word requires syntactical rules *in addition to* semantical rules. I grant that the logical relations in which a word stands are determined in some way by its meaning; what I deny is that these logical relations are governed by a separate set of rules. I do not think it would be possible for one to give semantical rules for the use of a word and then find oneself confronted with the task of deciding what syntactical rules should be added. But if the semantical rules already determine the syntax of the expression, there is no need to recognize any distinct class of syntactical rules at all. Therefore, although the validity of reasoning is in some way determined by the meaning of the words used, the rules which give the word meaning are not in themselves rules of reasoning. And insofar as they are rules of meaning, such rules exist for the words used in conductive ethical arguments as much as for any others; in fact, the very same words that are used in such arguments can equally well be used in deductive or inductive reasoning.

3) Finally, rules of reasoning may be thought of as regularities implicit in valid reasoning. Precisely because it claims validity, all genuine reasoning must be implicitly universal. No reasoner can claim that some consideration is a good reason today but deny that it is a good reason tomorrow, unless he admits that he was mistaken in his earlier reasoning; no reasoner can claim that some consideration is a good reason when he advances it but a bad reason when someone else gives it. Implicit in the claim to validity is the principle that a given consideration is either always or never a good reason for the conclusion drawn from it. Therefore, genuine reasoning is always rulelike and presupposes that there are general rules to which it conforms. I will admit that all reasoning does presuppose rules in this sense. But this sort of rule exists for conductive arguments as well as any others. If any conductive argument is valid, then every other argument from the same sort of premise to the same sort of conclusion is equally valid. Unfortunately, we are usually unable to formulate these rules of reasoning in other than trivial form because the validity of such arguments depends upon their subject matter. But these rules are still implicit in our reasoning in spite of our inability to discover and express them in any helpful way. Since there are rules implicit in conductive reasoning, it cannot be denied to be valid reasoning on the grounds that it is not implicitly regular.

The other question that needs to be asked is this: Why are rules required for genuine reasoning? Once more a number of different answers are given. a) Reasoning requires rules because it claims objective validity. If the claim to validity is to be really objective, it must hold good for all reasoners. But this rules out claiming that a consideration is a good reason

when I give it but not when you give it or that it is a good
reason when my Monday self gives it but a bad one when my
Tuesday self gives it. Therefore, the universality of reasoners
implicit in the claim to objectivity requires a universality in
the reasoning all these reasoners accept as valid. It follows
that there must be general rules implicit in any valid reasoning As far as I can see, this is a sound argument. The claim to
validity does seem to be essential to any reasoning and it does
seem to imply that reasoning be regular in this sense. But in
this sense, as I have already remarked, conductive ethical arguments are as regular as any others.

  b) Sometimes it is claimed that reasoning requires rules
because the conception of validity is a normative concept.
Valid arguments are arguments that ought to be accepted, and
invalid arguments should not be used or assented to. The
whole point of distinguishing between valid and invalid reasoning is to prescribe what we may or must not do as reasoners. Since the notion of validity is prescriptive and since it is
rules which prescribe, there must be rules of reasoning. Even
if "valid" were a prescriptive term, I doubt that it would follow
that there must be rules of reasoning. True enough, rules do
prescribe; but so do other things like singular imperatives.
"Hey you, open that window here and now" prescribes, but it
is surely no rule of action. Besides, I do not think that "valid"
has prescriptive meaning. It is hard to tell, of course, because
the notion of a prescription is so very vague. But I interpret
logical words like "valid" and "invalid" to have critical meaning.[3] They are used to make claims within the process of reasoning and have no meaning when taken out of that process.
If I am correct, so far from reasoning presupposing any rules
of validity, the very notion of validity presupposes the process
of reasoning.

  c) At other times it is said that reasoning requires rules
because reasoning claims correctness and the claim to correctness is possible only where there are criteria of correctness.
Unless there are rules of reasoning to serve as criteria of validity, there can be no question of even claiming validity. But
why must these criteria of validity be rules? We use color
samples as our criteria for identifying colors and thermometers

as our criteria for temperature, but these do not seem to be rules or very much like rules. It should at least be explained why the only thing that could serve as a criterion of validity is a rule. And why must we have criteria anyway? This in itself is a large question requiring a separate section.

But the conclusion of this section should be clear by now. It is not enough to argue that conductive ethical arguments cannot be valid because there are no rules of conduction. Although logicians have not formulated any set of rules governing conductive inferences, these inferences are implicitly regular and the words used in them are governed by meaning rules. And if other sorts of rules are absent in conduction, there seems no reason to think that any other sort of rule is required to ensure the validity of conductive inferences.

Validity without criteria

The third, and most basic, challenge to the validity of conductive arguments rests on my admission that there can be no useful criteria of their validity. Clearly the claim to validity is essential to reasoning. But this claim to validity loses its significance where there is no way to distinguish between correct and incorrect claims. Thus the claim to validity is out of place where there are no criteria by which valid arguments can be told from invalid ones. Since there are no criteria of validity in the case of conductive ethical arguments, conduction cannot be genuine reasoning.

What can be said in reply to this challenge? Before trying to answer it, it will be well to try to understand it. Just what is a criterion supposed to be? Let us begin with a few examples. One can estimate the weight of medium-sized objects by hefting them in his hands, but a more accurate way of weighing objects is by using a set of scales. One can feel the heat of a room as soon as he walks into it, but a more reliable measure of heat is a thermometer. One can appeal to a sample in a color chart to tell whether he has correctly identified the color of an object by just looking at it. And although an argument may seem invalid when one tries to think it through, one will decide that it really is valid if it turns out to have all T's on the last line of its truth table. Criteria are things like scales, thermometers, color samples, and truth tables. Now let us try to generalize a bit. *a*) A criterion is something to which one can appeal to check on the correctness of some judgment. If one is not sure whether he has estimated the weight of a stone correctly, one can put it on the scales; no matter how confident one is that the wall is mauve, one may change his mind if it fails to match a color sample entitled "mauve." The point of having criteria is to have some test of the correctness of one's judgments. *b*) A criterion must be other than that of which it is a test. Every judgment claims correctness for itself, and usually a judger is fairly confident that he is right. Anything that could serve to correct or substantiate this claim to correctness must be in some sense external to and independent of that on whose behalf the claim is made. *c*) A criterion is more reliable than some alternative basis for judgment. One can judge the color of a wall by just looking at it, at least if he has learned the meaning of the color words in our language. But we discover that just looking is not a very reliable way of judging color because we find that different lookers disagree about the color of a wall or a rug and that even a single person may change his mind or remain undecided after careful looking. One can, of course, look again, but even this does not resolve all disagreement or doubt. On the other hand, we find that most of this uncertainty is resolved by appealing to color samples. Similarly, disagreements about weight or heat are usually resolved by appealing to scales or thermometers. We conclude, therefore, that color samples, scales, and thermometers are reliable enough to serve as criteria.

Now if this is what criteria are, can there be any criteria for the validity of conductive ethical arguments? Unfortunately not. I do not insist that there can never be a criterion for any conductive argument; possibly we can find criteria in the case of a few sorts of inference. But by and large there is no way to judge the validity of these basic ethical arguments but by thinking them through and feeling their logical force. This is a pity because thinking through an ethical argument is a very unreliable way of judging its validity, as we discover every day when even careful thinkers can disagree about the validity of even a fairly simple ethical argument. Does it follow from this absence of criteria that conductive ethical arguments lack validity-value? Fortunately not. To be sure, it almost follows, and this is why this challenge is so very plausible. It is true that the claim to validity is essential to reasoning and that where there is no way of establishing the correctness or incorrectness of such a claim there can be no genuine reasoning. Hence, *if* the only way of distinguishing between valid and invalid arguments were to appeal to criteria of validity, then it would follow that conductive arguments are not really reasoning. But there is a way of distinguishing between valid and invalid conductive arguments—thinking through the arguments. Admittedly, this is a very unreliable way of judging validity, but it is always possible to check up on any verdict arrived at in this way simply by thinking through the argument again. And if this does not resolve all doubt, one can always think the argument through once more. This may not be as satisfactory as having criteria of validity, but at least it is enough to give meaning and substance to the claim to validity.

Not at all, some readers will insist. Well, precisely what is missing here that would be supplied by criteria of validity? *a*) A criterion of validity is something to which one can appeal to check the correctness of any verdict of valid or invalid reached by thinking the argument through. Reflection upon my own procedure and observation of my fellows convinces me that we often do decide whether or not a conductive argument is valid by thinking it through, and that we may correct our first impression by thinking it through again more carefully or in a cooler hour. This might be admitted, but my reader may insist that thinking through is a test of validity only because it is itself subject to some other test. *b*) A criterion must be other than that of which it is a test. I will admit that this otherness is essential, not just to criteria, but to any genuine test. Anything that could possibly serve as a check on the correctness of a given judgment must be something other than that judgment itself. But thinking through an argument is other than judging its validity. Although the thinking through may result in a verdict of valid or invalid, it is not the same thing as that verdict. In the same way looking at a wall is not the same thing as judging it mauve. Therefore, looking at an object can serve as a check on the correctness of a color judgment; sometimes we do correct our color judgments by looking again. The kind of otherness required in any genuine test exists in the case of thinking through an argument. What is lacking is a very different and unnecessary otherness, another test by which to check the reliability of the first test. Consider the scales. One can check one's estimate of the weight of an object by hefting it in his hands. Since the hefting is other than the judging, the hefting serves as a check on the judging. But the procedure of weighing on a set of scales is not only other than the judging, it is also other than the hefting. Now it is sometimes claimed that the hefting is a test of the correctness of the judging only because one can appeal from it to the scales. I certainly do not see why this should be so, and I think that I see why it could not be so. One test cannot corroborate another unless each is some test independently. The weighing and the hefting can serve as checks on each other only because each is an independent check on the judgment of weight. Now there can be no ultimate test of reasoning except reasoning itself; any attempt to check up on the validity of reasoning by appealing to some independent criterion would itself be reasoning. One might be able to test one kind of reasoning by another sort of reasoning just as one can check the verdict of just looking at the color of the wall by looking at a color sample held against the wall. Sometimes this second-order reasoning is possible, but in the case of conduction even this is often impossible. What one can do is check the validity judgment based on one thinking through of the argument by another thinking through. The basic test of the validity of any bit of conductive reasoning is another bit of conductive reasoning of the same kind; if one is not sure whether one has thought through the argument correctly there is nothing to do but think it through again. This thinking through is other than the judgment of validity it is supposed to test and even other than the original thinking through from which that judgment arose. This is all the otherness that is required in any genuine test of correctness. But it may seem as though something is still lacking. *c*) A criterion is more reliable than the usual basis of judgment. What is lacking is any reliable test of correctness or validity. We usually speak of criteria only where one basis of judgment is more reliable than another. For example, the color sample is a criterion of color as opposed to just looking, and the scales are a criterion of weight as opposed to just hefting. It seems inappropriate to speak of thinking an argument through as a criterion of validity because it is not opposed to any other less reliable way of estimating validity. But one can hardly claim that *every* genuine test of correctness has to be *more* reliable, for there can be more reliable tests only if there are also less reliable tests. I suppose that what is thought to be lacking in the case of thinking through an argument is not more reliability but just reliability at all. If we all came to the same conclusion about the validity of arguments we thought through, then the absence of any other text would not bother us very much. But the fact that every careful and repeated thinking through leaves us disagreeing about the validity of conductive ethical arguments assures us that thinking is a most unreliable method of judging validity. This I concede. But an unreliable test of validity is still a test of validity. Thinking through an argument is a way of determining the correctness of its claim to validity even though it is a notoriously unreliable way. Because it is so unreliable, we badly need criteria of validity. But the claim to validity is still genuine as long as there is some way, no matter how unreliable, to check its correctness.

CONCLUSION

My thesis in this chapter has been that, in addition to deductive and inductive arguments, ethical reasoning includes conductive arguments. We all use this sort of argument in reaching conclusions about what ought to be done in particular situations and what individual things are good or bad. It would be inconsistent for the philosopher, who recognizes the validity of many of these arguments as a practical man, to deny that they are a genuine kind of reasoning. His philosophical preconceptions might, of course, tempt him to try to reduce them to deductive form; but I have argued in chapter 1 that this cannot be done. Here I have tried to show that any such reduction is unnecessary because the usual reasons advanced to deny validity to conduction are insufficient. Conduction is as much a sort of reasoning as induction or even deduction.

These three kinds of reasoning are separate but equal; none can be reduced to the other and all are necessary in the justification of ethical statements. It follows that the conception of justification must be extended once more. Not all justification is deduction; it is not even enough to admit that induction can justify as well. If conductive arguments really are valid reasoning, then they, too, serve to rationally justify their conclusions. And if there are other kinds of reasoning as well, as I suspect that there are, then they can also be used in justification. The conclusion seems to be that to justify a statement is to derive it from one or more acceptable premises by valid reasoning of any sort. Have we at least arrived at an adequate view of justification?

Before confronting this question directly, it will be helpful to try to clarify the nature of reasoning itself. If to justify is always to reason, just what is it to reason? As long as reasoning is limited to deducing, this question does not seem terribly urgent. Our familiarity with deductive arguments and our ability to handle them with the powerful techniques of logic lull us into imagining that we understand the nature of deduction. But once induction, conduction, and goodness knows how many other forms of reasoning are admitted, our conception of reasoning seems to be losing its clarity and solidity. What is reasoning, anyway?

4. reasoning

I have argued that the justification of ethical statements requires at least three distinct kinds of reasoning: deduction, induction, and conduction. But induction is quite different from deduction, and conduction is very different from both. In what sense can they all be said to be reasoning? In this chapter I hope to answer this question by explaining my view of the nature of reasoning.

A clear conception of the nature of reasoning is also vital if we are to answer several other questions that arise in reflecting upon our topic, justification in ethics. Can justification be identified with reasoning from acceptable premises? If not, is justifying analogous to reasoning? What is it that makes a consideration a good reason for some ethical conclusion? Why is it that good reasons justify a conclusion? Are some ethical arguments merely persuasive or unpersuasive rather than valid or invalid? The way in which any philosopher answers these questions depends upon his conception of reasoning.

Reasoning and persuading

Where are we to look for an adequate theory of reasoning? I suggest that we start with the activity of reasoning and ask ourselves what we are doing when we reason. One might start elsewhere. Some choose to begin with psychology and investigate the nature of human reason, the faculty of intuition, or our capacity to understand. Others prefer to begin with the objects of reasoning, propositions subsisting in a

Platonic realm or concepts existing in the human mind. Presumably one is to explain the activity of reasoning in terms of our cognitive faculties or the objects of cognition. But since the existence of such faculties or objects might well be doubted and their explanatory value is problematic until it becomes clearer just what they are to explain, it is better to ignore them at first and investigate the activity of reasoning directly. The existence of reasoning can hardly be denied. Our task is to explain its nature.

From the first we are embarrassed by the fact that reasoning seems to be not one activity but many. For one thing, reasoning has both public and private forms. We reason with one another when we discuss the truth of some statement, propose arguments for and against it, and debate the final import of the evidence. But the individual is also reasoning when he silently resolves his doubts by considering the evidence or thinks out the implications of his beliefs. For another thing, reasoning, whether public or private, proceeds in different directions. Sometimes it begins with premises that are accepted and moves to some conclusion; then it is discovering a truth or drawing an inference. At other times it begins with some conclusion and either presents the evidence to support it or searches for the considerations to test it; then it is justifying or testing a claim to truth.

One way, and probably the obvious way, to deal with this variety in the forms of reasoning is to abstract what is common to all these processes and investigate this essence of reasoning. Unfortunately, it is not easy to do this as a preliminary step in reaching a theory of reasoning because it is hard to distinguish between essential and nonessential aspects of each form of reasoning until one has carried out his investigation to the point of understanding the nature of reasoning itself. If one simply ignores every apparent difference and concentrates on what is left, he is in danger of finding that what little is left falls far short of any genuine reasoning. Therefore, I suggest that we begin with one form of reasoning, develop a theory to explain that form, and then test our theory by applying it to the other forms of reasoning.

Which form shall we pick as a starting place? Preferably

some public form of reasoning, some sort of discussion. The advantage of such a form is that the reasoning gets itself expressed in language; we have the reasoning laid out, as it were, in the publicly observable utterances of the speakers. At least the existence of these utterances cannot be denied and we can know what it is we must explain. To begin with private reasoning would immediately plunge us into the problematic. It is not that the process of thinking can be seriously doubted, but that it seems impossible to give any characterization of this process that does not beg serious epistemological issues. No doubt we will have to leave the public realm before long, for the sounds or marks must be meaningful and the speakers thoughtful for genuine reasoning to be taking place. Still, let us postpone this attempt to probe the human mind as long as possible and begin our search in the relatively clear light of public discussion.

Among discussions let us take as our model the attempt to support some statement already made. It cannot be taken for granted, of course, that what is true of conversations in which one speaker defends his statement against the attacks of others is also typical of conversations in which the speaker explains to others what follows from some mutually accepted premises or in which undecided speakers are united in trying to determine what they should assert. Still, it is the process of establishing a statement with arguments that is most obviously relevant to my present enterprise of understanding justification in ethics. If we can find a theory that seems to explain this form of reasoning, it will be time enough to worry about its applicability to other forms of reasoning.

If we take as our model those conversations in which one person is trying to defend some statement against the attacks of other people, what is reasoning? The obvious answer is that reasoning is persuading. That the purpose of reasoning is to persuade is indicated by the occasions when we engage in reasoning. We never bother to give arguments for our statements when our audience already accepts them; we begin reasoning only when some hearer expresses doubt or disagreement or when we suspect some unexpressed doubt or disagreement on his part. Moreover, we stop presenting arguments as soon as, but only when, the hearer is persuaded; or if we do break off reasoning sooner, it is with the sense of frustration. The fact that reasoning ends happily only with persuasion suggests that its end is to persuade.

Nor is this tie between reasoning and persuading limited to the standpoint of some speaker seeking to defend his statement. The reasonable audience is determined to accept only valid arguments. Now when does one judge that an argument presented to him is valid? Usually when one is persuaded by it. As a rule one does not recognize the validity of an argument as long as he remains unpersuaded by it nor is one persuaded by an argument he takes to be invalid. This coincidence between being persuaded and judging valid is striking and calls for some explanation. In my own case, of course, the explanation is not hard to find. Naturally I am persuaded by valid arguments only, this is precisely what one would expect of a perfectly rational man. But the fact that other, less rational, men usually judge an argument valid when and only when they are persuaded by it cannot be explained in this way. Perhaps in the end this coincidence can be explained only by saying that reasoning is persuading.

In spite of such persuasive arguments, the reasonable man may be reluctant to identify reasoning with persuading. To begin with, there are many ways of persuading without using valid arguments. Quite apart from giving invalid arguments, instruction by rote often persuades the pupil without giving any reasons at all. Indoctrination and brainwashing are extensions of such nonrational persuasion. And if it is not a mere figure of speech to speak of the hidden persuaders, subliminal advertising can persuade without reasoning. Not all ways of producing conviction are persuading, but even within the limits of persuading one finds more than reasoning.

Even when persuading does take the form of advancing considerations, it cannot be identified with reasoning *tout court*, for one may reason without persuading. We sometimes want to say that a speaker has actually proved his case—has really given true, valid, and sufficient reasons in support of his conclusion—even though his audience remains unpersuaded. For example, a mathematician or scientist may present a genuine proof of some theorem or theory that is not generally accepted until years later.

Such a man may well feel disappointed and frustrated; he has not entirely achieved his aim as long as his audience remains unpersuaded. Still, it is not enough to admit that reasoning is not persuading but insist that at least it is trying to or intending to persuade. For one thing, we do not say that a speaker who fails to persuade by presenting sound arguments has failed *in* his reasoning or *as* a reasoner. For another, a rational and responsible speaker will refrain from using invalid arguments even though he may believe that they would persuade his audience. Under normal circumstances, he believes that he ought not to use certain forms of persuasion. But he need not condemn such reasoning on purely moral grounds as he might condemn "persuasion" with a rubber hose; he is condemning such arguments on logical grounds. He believes that he ought not to use such arguments *because* they are invalid. Therefore, reasoning cannot be identified with persuading even in its aim.

Just as the failure of an argument to persuade does not establish its invalidity, so its success in persuading does not prove its validity. The traditional fallacies, in fact, are those forms of argument that tend to persuade in spite of their invalidity; one would not bother to catalog completely implausible types of argument. Since a speaker often persuades his audience by deliberately using invalid arguments, we cannot identify reasoning with persuading or even trying to persuade.

Another way of putting this point is in terms of relevance. Not every consideration that can be advanced is a reason; only relevant considerations are really reasons. But what is the difference between relevant and irrelevant considerations? It will not do to say that relevant considerations are those that persuade, for we want to say that a hearer can fail to see the relevance of some consideration presented to him or that he can be taken in by irrelevant considerations. The line we draw between relevant and irrelevant premises does not always coincide with the line between those premises that do and those that do not persuade.

This is primarily because a consideration that persuades

one man may not persuade another. The psychological effectiveness of an argument varies from hearer to hearer and from time to time with a single hearer. Yet central to reasoning is the claim to validity, the claim that the argument is in some sense correct and that anyone who rejects it is mistaken. This claim is not restricted to any single speaker or his present audience but is intended to be impersonal or objective in some way. Such a claim may turn out to be untenable in the end, but it is at the core of reasoning and must be taken into account by any thory that would explain what reasoning is.

Well, where are we? We cannot identify reasoning with persuading because a speaker can reason without persuading and persuade without reasoning. Yet there seems to be some essential connection between these two activities. Consider those fortunate occasions when a speaker manages to do both, to persuade by reasoning. Has he managed to do two things at once as I do when I type and chew gum at the same time? No, there are not two separate activities going on side by side, one reasoning and the other persuading. Rather there is one activity of giving arguments that can be characterized in two ways, as reasoning and as persuading. The arguing can be criticized logically as valid or invalid, or it can be described psychologically as persuasively effective or ineffective.

Now what is the relation between these two ways of characterizing this single process? If it were possible to analyze our critical vocabulary in terms of persuasion without making "valid" synonymous with "persuades," then there would be a way to eat our cake and have it too. We could explain both those features of arguing that tempt us to identify reasoning with persuading and those features that prevent such an identification. Such an analysis promises to be difficult at best and may prove impossible, but it seems well worth attempting.

The claim to validity

The model of reasoning I have chosen to use is that of a speaker trying to defend his statement against the challenges of his audience. The reasoning speaker is trying to persuade the hearers by arguing. The unit of reasoning is an argument, a bit of language consisting of one or more premises, a conclusion, and an implicit claim to validity. A premise is any consideration (that is, anything that can be considered or attended to) which counts or is thought to count for or against the conclusion. The conclusion is something that ostensibly is to be accepted on the basis of the premises. Premises and conclusion are held together or unified in the argument by the claim that the conclusion follows validly from the premises or that the premises are valid reasons for the conclusion. Although the arguer does not say in so many words that he is claiming validity for his argument, he is reasoning only if he is prepared to make such a claim. The claim to validity is what distinguishes reasoning from persuading.

This claim to validity that is implicit in every argument becomes explicit in critical judgments directed at arguments. One may pass logical judgment upon an argument and say "my argument is valid" or "all of your arguments are invalid." To become clear about what one is claiming in arguing we must become clear about what one is saying of an argument when one calls it valid or invalid. What do these critical terms mean? To say that an argument is valid is to claim that when subjected to an indefinite amount of criticism it is persuasive for everyone who thinks in the normal way; to say that an argument is invalid is to claim that when subjected to indefinite criticism it is unpersuasive for everyone who thinks in the normal way. This analysis of validity contains at least four notions that require some explanation.

1

First and foremost, I am asserting that reasoning is necessarily tied to persuading because to claim that an argument is valid is to claim that it is persuasive. Being persuasive is a dispositional property, but it is more like being fragile than like being soluble. To say that something is soluble is to say that it is capable of dissolving; therefore, one occurrence of dissolving is sufficient to establish solubility. But the fact that something breaks does not necessarily prove that it is fragile, for even the toughest and most resilient things break under sufficient stress and strain. To say that something is fragile is to say that it tends to break, that it breaks readily or easily. This is not to say that it is always breaking or fragile things like glasses and china would be relatively useless. Fragile things are expected to break only when the conditions of breaking are present, when they are dropped or struck or otherwise subjected to disruptive forces. Nor is it always required that they break when acted on by such forces, for the force may be slight or counteracted by some other force. Still, to say that something is fragile is to say that it usually breaks when breaking conditions are present.

Similarly to say that an argument is persuasive is to say that it usually persuades when the conditions of persuading are present. Thus it is not enough that the argument persuade on one or a very few occasions, nor is it required that it invariably persuade even when the conditions of persuading are present. What is required is that it usually persuade under these conditions. What are the conditions of persuading? That the person to be persuaded accepts or has the premises of the argument, that he rejects or doubts its conclusion, and that he pays attention to or thinks through the argument. One need not be persuaded by an argument whose premises he rejects or even seriously doubts; I add the words "or has" to allow experiences to function as premises in arguments. Again, one cannot really be said to be persuaded by an argument if he was already completely persuaded of its conclusion before the argument was brought to his attention. However, if his acceptance was tinged with some real doubt which vanished after the argument, then he can be said to have been persuaded by the argument. Finally, no argument can be expected to persuade anyone who is unaware of it. The person must pay attention to the argument or think it through in order for it to be psychologically effective. Therefore, to say that an argument is persuasive is to say that it usually persuades one who accepts or has its premises, who rejected or doubted its conclusion just before being subjected to the argument, and who thinks through the argument.

To say that an argument persuades, even under the most favorable conditions, is, I suppose, to use a figure of speech.

Strictly speaking it is always some speaker who persuades some hearer by means of the argument. But it seems a happy figure of speech to say that the argument does the persuading because the same argument can be presented by any number of different speakers and can even produce conviction in someone who thinks it through for himself without having it presented to him by any speaker. The cash value of this metaphor is that reflecting on the premises of a valid argument whose premises one accepts creates or reenforces acceptance of its conclusion. Just as a speaker persuades when his words cause his hearer to accept something, so an argument persuades when its premises cause some thinker to accept its conclusion. This analogy is built right into our ordinary language, for we do not hesitate to speak of arguments as persuasive or unpersuasive. It is through this notion of persuasiveness that reasoning is tied to persuading.

2

Although it is natural to suppose that every argument is either valid or invalid, it does not appear that arguments can be sorted neatly into two groups, the persuasive ones and the unpersuasive ones. Still, the claim to validity is not the claim that an argument is persuasive under any conditions but that it is persuasive *when subjected to an indefinite amount of criticism*. By criticism I mean a process of thinking about and discussion of the argument. This process is criticism of the argument because it serves to test its claim to validity. It is not easy to say just how much is included in thinking and discussing. Certainly thinking through the argument is included as well as reasoning about the argument. One reasons about an argument when one produces second-order arguments intended to prove that the original argument is or is not valid. But thinking includes much more than reasoning. It includes the attempt to understand the meaning of any expressions used and the thinking that is understanding their relations. Thinking would also include experiencing to the extent that any of the premises are experiences, and having emotions, attitudes, and deciding to the extent that these are the conclusions of reasoning. "Thinking" is used in a very wide sense when it defines the process of criticism. Some such notion is important, however, because the unthinking use of language is not really criticism at all.

Still, discussion normally plays a large part in criticism, even though it must be thinking discussion. Discussion includes stating the argument, reformulating the argument, explaining it more clearly, arguing about its validity, explaining any of the key expressions used in the argument. Presumably it does not include arm-twisting, the administration of drugs, threatening with arm-twisting, or hypnosis, although it is not clear just how the line between discussion and other forms of language aimed at changing the subject's mind is to be drawn. In any event, it is clear that the process of criticism is a process of thinking and discussing in very wide senses of those terms.

It is crucial for my purposes that this process be defined descriptively and not critically.[1] I must not say that one is criticizing an argument when he is reasoning validly about it but not really criticizing it when he is advancing irrelevant considerations. This is because I am trying to explain critical terms like "valid" and "relevant" in terms of this process of criticism. Then to define the critical process by means of such terms would be to use obviously circular definitions. Such definitions might be correct enough, but they could not hope to clarify anything but the syntactical or logical relations between a closed set of terms. Again, I must not say that criticism takes place only when the participants are rational or exercising their rationality to the fullest, for these are also obviously critical terms. Even more dangerous is the temptation to use covertly critical terms. For example, one might say that criticism requires that one be thinking "clearly" or that one "fully" understand the meaning of the expressions used. Clarity of thought is not an introspectable property to be defined by empirical properties; fullness of understanding is also not a descriptive concept. Both make critical claims that arise from the process of criticism and cannot be used to define that process. It follows that the process of criticism will include all sorts of confused thinking, half-understood language, invalid argument, and irrelevant considerations. The process of criticism is a very imperfect one indeed.

But if actual criticism is such an imperfect process, how can it give rise to and be any test of ideal claims to validity, relevance, and truth? Part of the answer lies in the fact that the process of criticism is indefinite in extent. Although criticism to date is always imperfect, it is also incomplete. Thus the critical claim always goes beyond the actual to a something more that is potentially infinite; no matter how far the process of criticism has been carried or how confident its verdict, the validity challenge can always be made anew and tested by carrying the process further. The process of criticism is indefinite in at least two directions, in time and in the number of participants. Just as no amount of criticism is too small to give some support to a claim to validity, so no amount is sufficient to establish such a claim beyond challenge. Potentially the process can go on forever in time; it is temporally indefinite. Criticism is also indefinite in extent. What I mean is that no matter how many people may agree that an argument is valid or invalid, the possibility always remains for someone else to come along and disagree. Discussion is a social process, and the community of discussers is potentially infinite. The process of criticism is indefinite in that it is always open to extension in time or open to new participants. The ideality of the claim to validity does not arise from the fact that later discussions are likely to be more correct than earlier ones or the fact that new discussers are apt to be more rational than those who have already had their say. Rather the claim is ideal in that it always goes beyond the verdict of any actual thinking discussion and is subject to correction in the light of more of the same. It is because the activity of reasoning is, at least potentially, set in the context of an indefinite process of criticism that it can claim anything like logical validity.

The process of criticism is generated by doubt and disagreement. Psychologically it is doubt and disagreement that motivate us to engage in this process; epistemologically it is only doubt and disagreement that require any such process. Each of these is more basic in its own way. A single individual can criticize his own reasoning without discussing the matter with anyone else; and since all thinking is essentially private, ultimately all reasoning and criticizing must be egocentric. Therefore in the end it is doubt, rather than disagreement, that matters. But doubt is often a product of disagreement, for I will usually doubt my own opinion when I find that others disagree. And doubt itself can be thought of as a sort of disagreement within the self, a conflict between tendencies to accept and reject. Therefore, disagreement can well be taken as a model of all doubt. It is, I think, a valuable model, but let us not forget that it is a model and not the thing itself. It can serve as a model because disagreement and doubt share something, a conflict between acceptance and rejection, but there are important differences between this conflict when it lies within the individual self and when it exists between distinct selves. Out of such conflict arises the process of criticism. The end of criticism is the resolution of this conflict, whether within the self or between selves. Psychologically criticism ceases when unanimous acceptance or rejection is reached; epistemologically criticism projects an ideal agreement of all the participants.

This ideal of universal agreement in critical judgments is possible only if the process of criticism separates arguments into two distinct groups, the persuasive and the unpersuasive. This separation should not be thought of as like the sorting of white sheep and black sheep into two pens, but as like the dyeing of toy sheep, some white and some black. That is, the process of criticism does not so much discover which arguments are antecedently persuasive or unpersuasive as make them persuasive or unpersuasive. Criticism sustains the persuasiveness of some arguments or even makes originally unpersuasive arguments persuasive; in the case of other arguments it destroys or diminishes what persuasiveness they had. In this way a sort of unanimity of persuasiveness emerges from the process of criticism. At any stage of actual criticism this unanimity is incomplete and imperfect, but an ideal of perfect unanimity is projected from this very imperfect process of producing partial and imperfect agreement. The claim to validity is the claim that the argument is persuasive when subjected to an indefinite amount of criticism.

3

The claim to validity projects an ideal of universal agreement; it claims that the process of criticism will separate arguments into the universally persuasive and the universally unpersuasive. Is it realistic to project such a universal agreement? Is it permissible to claim such a universal persuasiveness for any argument? Only, I think, if one restriction is built into the claim. All one can reasonably claim is that a valid argument will, through the process of criticism, remain or become persuasive *for everyone who thinks in the normal way.* Hard experience indicates that no amount of critical discussion will make any very complicated argument persuasive for a feeble-minded person. It is unrealistic to expect that an insane person will be usually persuaded by some valid arguments, those concerning his fixed ideas or compulsions. Quite apart from the facts of psychological differences, it seems logically possible that different men might think in basically different ways so that what persuaded one man would not persuade another no matter how long critical discussion were carried on. It is only for men who think in the same way that the process of thinking and discussing will lead to unanimity. Therefore, the claim to validity must be restricted to those who think in the normal way.

What is it to think in the normal way? It is not just to agree with the majority on the validity of this or that argument. By a *way* of thinking I mean something more basic than present judgments on one or several issues. Nor does thinking in the normal way mean being persuaded by the same arguments that in fact persuade the majority. Again, it is not just what happens to persuade a person now that counts. By a *way* of thinking I mean something more like a *tendency* to be persuaded by some *sorts* of arguments and not by other sorts. The notion here is that what persuades one depends upon the nature of his mind and that underlying the many variations in one's mental state or condition is a relatively stable individual mentality. Now the claim to objective validity presupposes that there is something like a *normal* way for the human mind to work. This normality is not identical with the consensus of present agreement or the present persuasive force of various arguments but by a uniformity of persuasiveness that is *usually* there in the thinking of *most* men on any given *sort* of argument. Normality does not require complete uniformity of all men but only of most men, and it must be determined separately for each kind of argument. It is not necessary that all men think alike in all reasoning, but only that most men are similarly persuaded or unpersuaded by any given sort of argument. If there were not in fact such a psychological uniformity in the human mind, it would be pointless to claim anything like objective validity.

Thus the claim to validity is grounded in human psychology. This is not to say that a valid argument is valid because (in any logical sense) all or most men think in the same way; the facts of psychology are not grounds for the claim to validity in the sense of being reasons for it. Much less is it to say that claiming validity is asserting that all men think alike; "valid" makes a critical claim rather than describing any psychological fact. Still, the word "valid" can mean what it does in our language only because in fact there is a normal way for the human mind to work. A critical term claiming that some given argument is, when subjected to an indefinite amount of criticism, persuasive for everyone who thinks in the normal way has a use in our language only because there is a normal way of thinking.

It follows that, although the claim to validity is objective, its objectivity is restricted to a community of like minds. Its claim is universal in that it applies to everyone, but it has a limited universality in that the community is limited to those who think in the normal way. It is not at all clear just how limited or widespread this community of like minds is. Perhaps some human beings, such as the very feeble-minded, are forever excluded from it. Others, like the temporarily deranged or the drunk, may be excluded from it from time to time but not permanently. Probably most of us are excluded from it in this or that respect. We may think in the normal way in most respects, but there may be certain classes of arguments in which our minds just work differently. Still, the claim to validity presupposes a normal way of thinking which is sufficiently widespread to allow the process of criticism to function as a test of that claim. This claim can hope to be established only because it is limited to those who think in this normal way.

4

To say that an argument is valid is to make a *claim*. I emphasize this point because I believe it is essential to notice that words like "valid" and "true" have a very special sort of meaning, what I call critical meaning. They are used within the process of criticism and become meaningless when separated from that process of thinking and discussing. Just what the word "valid" means depends upon where it is used in the critical process. Saying that an argument is valid may be a way of announcing that one is prepared to defend it, or challenging all hearers to refute it if they can, or reaffirming one's acceptance of the argument after criticism, or conceding that one has at last accepted the argument under critical pressure, or proclaiming that one has defended it successfully.

If one thinks of the critical process as generated by disagreement, then an appropriate analogy is with the language of trial by combat. The challenge is a form of language that invites someone to engage in mortal combat and usually initiates the trial process. This combat is usually terminated by an admission of defeat or a proclamation of victory or both. The challenge, the admission of defeat, and the proclamation of victory are not to be looked at as comments upon the combat made from outside; their meaning lies in the way in which they operate within that trial itself. Similarly, the words "valid" and "invalid" function to initiate the process of criticism and to render its verdict.

If one thinks of the critical process as generated by doubt, then a more appropriate analogy is with the language of trial by temptation. I am tempted to avoid an awkward situation by telling a lie but I feel guilty at the thought of lying and must somehow overcome or give in to this temptation to lie. Since this is a trial within the individual soul, there is no formal language like that of the duel, but some of the struggling may be verbalized as expressions of inclination or self-condemnation and, eventually, as an expression of some fixed decision. What is important for understanding critical language is seeing how such language might play a role in the trial by temptation itself. Perhaps just because the process is mostly unverbalized there is a tendency to dramatize it as a form of combat between a higher and lower self or between oneself and Satan.

What these two forms of trial, trial by combat and trial by temptation, have in common is the element of struggle. And some of the language connected with these outer and inner struggles gains its meaning from the role it plays in the struggle itself. Now critical language is also essentially tied to inner and outer struggle, but this time an intellectual struggle carried on by discussion and thinking. Winning or losing consists in making an argument persuasive or unpersuasive. The words "valid" and "invalid" do not so much describe the results of this struggle as challenge someone to participate in it, proclaim victory after some period of struggling, or concede defeat in the struggle. It is this sort of meaning to which I refer as critical meaning or claiming.

In my view, to argue is to make a claim to validity on behalf of the argument one is using. Although this claim is not expressed in so many words, it is implicit in the argument form itself. This claim becomes explicit in critical judgments that apply the words "valid" or "invalid" to the argument. These words derive their meaning from the role they play in the process of criticism, a process of thinking and discussion which sustains or destroys the persuasiveness of argument. To say that an argument is valid is to claim that when subjected to an indefinite amount of criticism it is persuasive for everyone who thinks in the normal way; to say that an argument is invalid is to claim that when subjected to an indefinite amount of criticism it is unpersuasive for everyone who thinks in the normal way.

In many ways my analysis is very Peircean.[2] Peirce suggests that "true" means something like "will be believed by all scientists at the limit of the process of investigation"; I hold that "true" means roughly "will be believed by everyone who thinks in the normal way after an indefinite amount of criticism." Our analyses are similar in that both emphasize the process within which belief arises and is fixed and both define truth in terms of the psychological notion of belief or acceptance. We differ primarily on two points. While Peirce thinks primarily of the process of investigation, the process of arriving at belief, I think primarily in terms of the process of criticism, the process of attacking and defending and explaining beliefs. And while he thinks of the word "true" as *describing* the *outcome* of such a process carried to the limit, I think of "true" as making a *claim* to be tested *within* a process that has no limit.

This second difference is the more important, for it protects my conception of truth from some of the standard objections to Peirce's definition. *1)* According to his view one must wait until the end of the process of investigation to know which beliefs are true. On my view one is justified in making a judgment of truth or falsity at any moment within the process of criticism. *2)* On Peirce's definition it appears that one discovers which belief is true by counting noses, by waiting to see whether all scientists agree in the end. My view is that one discovers which belief is true only by participating in the process of criticism and that no mere enumeration of the results will do. *3)* It seems logically possible that at any given moment of time, including the last, all scientists might happen to come to a false conclusion. Since this would not be possible if Peirce's definition were correct, his definition must be mistaken. Since my conception does not define truth in terms of any single moment of time, this logical possibility does not touch me. Moreover, my theory even explains the fact that at any moment of time it is an open question whether or not the agreed opinion is true because it defines truth in terms of an open-ended process of criticism.

While my conception of truth avoids the obvious objections to Peirce's, it retains the important advantage at which he aimed: it defines truth in terms of empirical concepts. Although our understanding of the nature of truth is adequate for everyday purposes, it gets us into trouble when we begin philosophical reflection. Since we cannot observe any empirical property of trueness, we are tempted to postulate some non-natural property to explain how we can recognize the truth. To explain the distinction between true and false statements we are led to postulate a realm of facts to which our utterances may correspond or fail to corespond. Yet it is not clear just what sort of relation correspondence is or how we ascertain its existence in any given case. It seems to me that, if at all possible, some analysis of the notion of truth is very desirable. But to define "true" in terms of other epistemic notions such as "correct" or "reasonable" is not much help, for the *definiens* is as obscure as the *definiendem*. Hence the great advantage of defining the truth in terms of a process of criticism that can be empirically described. In this section I have given an analysis of "valid" parallel to my definition of truth. My hope is that it is Peircean enough to be helpful without repeating the mistakes of traditional pragmatism.

A definition of reasoning

Now let us return to the activity of reasoning. My model is a speaker presenting considerations to defend one of his statements against the challenges of his audience. The advantages of this model are that the reasoning gets itself expressed in language where it can be observed and that such defensive reasoning seems most directly relevant to justification. What is it that makes this activity reasoning? Not that the speaker is persuading his audience, for he may be reasoning even when he fails to get his audience to agree with him. Not that he is trying to persuade, for one can try to persuade by nonrational means. What makes his activity reasoning is the way he is trying to persuade; the speaker is trying to persuade his audience by arguing, by presenting arguments for his statement. Implicit in any argument is the claim to validity, the claim that when subjected to an indefinite amount of criticism the considerations offered are persuasive for everyone who thinks in the normal way. It is this claim to validity which makes his activity reasoning subject to logical criticism instead of mere persuasion to be judged as psychologically effective or ineffective only.

It is interesting to see how far beyond my original model this claim to validity has taken me. My model is a one-sided conversation in which a speaker tries to persuade his hearers;

his audience is either passive, or at most, resistant. But the claim to validity is the claim that the argument is persuasive for everyone who thinks in the normal way when subjected to an indefinite amount of criticism. Therefore, in arguing the speaker is making a claim that can be sustained only if he opens himself to the criticism of his audience. In this way what began as a one-sided conversation can always become transformed into the give-and-take of discussion, what began as the attempt of one speaker to persuade his audience can become a contest of mutual persuasion.

So far reasoning remains public in two distinct ways. It is a process of conversation involving two or more people, and it consists of linguistic utterances that are observable by all those people who happen to be about at the time. But the claim to validity soon takes us out of this public realm into the individual mind. The speaker is claiming that his argument is persuasive, and persuasiveness is a psychological matter to be established by changes in this or that individual mind. Moreover, the claim to validity is limited to those who think in the normal way, another psychological factor. Finally, the ultimate test of validity is whether or not the individual thinker finds himself persuaded by the argument after engaging in the process of criticism. Thus, not only must one go beyond the public arguing into the private thinking of the arguers, but in the end private thinking takes epistemological priority over public talking. What this all means is that the one-sided activity I have taken as my model is reasoning only because it makes a claim that goes far beyond that activity to the potentially infinite process of criticism which is two-sided and at least as much private as public.

Now that it is clear that my model of reasoning can be understood only in the context of a process of criticism, it is time to try to formulate a definition of reasoning that will be applicable to other forms as well. Provisionally, I suggest this definition: Reasoning is using one or more arguments. The notion of an argument is an ambiguous one. By an argument we often mean a bit of language consisting in one or more premises, a conclusion, and an implicit claim to validity. The conclusion is some statement that is supposed to be accepted because of the premises. The premises are considerations presented in support of the conclusion. These are unified into a single argument by the implicit claim to validity. But at other times we mean by an argument, not the bit of language, but that which is formulated in the language. We say, for example, that in the case of an enthymeme the argument is partly unexpressed. And surely a person can think out arguments to himself without making any public utterance. To what extent such thinking must be verbalized is unclear, but at least arguments need not be utterances. Instead of removing this ambiguity, I shall preserve it; for it will enable me to formulate a definition of reasoning that applies to both public and private forms, both conversations in which some speaker presents an argument and thinking in which he does not make any utterance.

The notion of using an argument also belongs in the first instance to the linguistic realm where it is contrasted with that of mentioning an argument. I use an argument when I try to establish some conclusion with it. One mentions an argument when he says " 'you ought to do that because you promised' is valid." One may also mention an argument when one describes its logical form or when one explains its meaning. A similar distinction applies, I believe, to the level of unexpressed thinking. One thinks with an argument when one reaches some new conclusion by means of the argument; one thinks about an argument when one ponders its meaning or judges its cogency. By using an argument, then, I mean thinking with it or arguing with it as expressed in language.

There are many forms of reasoning because there are many ways of using arguments. First, there are public and private uses. That is, one can use arguments in his speaking or writing as well as in his unexpressed thinking. Second, there are the uses in reaching, testing, and justifying some conclusion. In some uses of argument, one begins with the premises and infers the conclusion from them; this is an activity of coming to a conclusion by reasoning. At other times the conclusion is given and one tries to defend or attack its claim to truth by means of argument. On still other occasions one uses arguments to test a conclusion which has not been firmly accepted or rejected as yet. In this way my definition seems to cover a wide variety of forms of reasoning.

However, it is probably not wide enough yet. The speaker who tries to persuade some hearer by arguing is using arguments, but the hearer who may be attending to these arguments and even opening himself to their logical force is not himself using the arguments presented to him, at least not in any ordinary sense of using arguments. Again, someone who is thinking through some argument to judge its validity before deciding whether to accept and use the argument is not using it. Yet in both cases I would be inclined to say that these people are reasoning. Let us, therefore, say that one is also reasoning when he follows an argument that is being used by another or that might be used by another. Reasoning, then, is using or following one or more arguments. The core of this activity of reasoning is the claim to validity implicit within it; where this claim is present one is reasoning.

In another sense, of course, one is not always reasoning when he merely claims that his arguments are valid. We sometimes use the term "reasoning" in a narrow sense such that a person is not really reasoning when he advances invalid arguments; only when he argues validly is he really reasoning. This ambiguity need cause no serious confusion provided it is kept in mind. In this narrow sense, to reason is to use or follow valid arguments. Analogously, we sometimes say that only good reasons are really reasons; irrelevant considerations only seem to be reasons. But in the wider sense, a person is giving reasons whenever he advances any considerations as long as he is claiming validity for them. To say that a person is reasoning in this narrow sense is to say that he is reasoning in the wider sense of using or following arguments and to say that these arguments are valid. Since this narrow sense can be defined by the broader one, let us ignore it from now on.

Therefore, I propose this definition: *Reasoning is using or following one or more arguments*. I do not claim any finality for this definition. Not only should it be possible to express the definition more happily, it may well turn out that it does not draw the boundaries between reasoning and the process of criticism at quite the right place. What I do contend, however, is that it is the right kind of definition. The most enlightening way to think of reasoning is as a family of processes defined by an implicit claim to validity. Thus essential to reasoning is its relation to a larger process of criticism in terms of which the notion of validity has its meaning. Whatever activities one may wish to include in the family, the immediate members of the family must include inferring, testing, and justifying as well as both public discussion and private thinking. I can only hope that the family portrait I have drawn conveys what it is to belong to the reasoning family, for then it can claim to be an adequate conception of the nature of reasoning.

Anticipating my critics

I cannot, of course, hope to answer every objection that any critic might make to my position. But there are certain criticisms that are so obvious that even I can anticipate them and so fundamental that I cannot afford to ignore them. To these I shall try to reply here. First, it may be objected that it is a mistake to analyze validity in terms of persuasiveness because this commits something like a category mistake. The persuasiveness of an argument is a psychological matter depending upon the rhetorical skill of the arguer and the predispositions and intellectual capacities of the audience; the validity of an argument is a purely logical matter that in no way depends upon the verbal skill of the arguer or the prejudices and limitations of his audience. Since logic cannot be reduced to psychology, it is a mistake to define validity in terms of persuasiveness.

I agree that logic cannot be reduced to psychology, but I do not admit that I have done this. Although I have used the notion of persuasiveness in my analysis of validity, I have not equated the two. This is because my analysis includes more than persuasiveness, primarily a reference to the process of criticism. Now granted that a logical term like "valid" is not to be equated with any psychological term like "persuasive" or even "persuasive after thoughtful discussion," it does not at all follow that psychological terms can play no part in an explanation of our notion of validity. Logic may be distinct from psychology even though it is essentially connected with it. In fact I have tried to make clear just how different the two are by insisting that "valid" has critical meaning. To *claim* that an argument is valid under indefinite criticism is very different from *describing* an argument as persuasive after criticism; it is to challenge one who disagrees to critical combat or to render the verdict of the critical struggle rather than to state any psychological property of the argument. Far from reducing validity to persuasiveness, I have insisted on their fundamental difference as critical and descriptive terms respectively.

Another criticism of my analysis is that I make the content of the critical claim so vague that no verdict could ever arise from the process of criticism. The claim is that a valid argument is, when subjected to an indefinite amount of criticism, persuasive for everyone who thinks in the normal way. How is anyone to determine in the case of any given argument whether or not this claim is correct? Presumably he is to think about the argument and discuss it with other thoughtful men. But consensus seldom arises from this process, and when it does it usually dissolves as the participants change their minds in the light of further criticism or as new participants enter the discussion. Since unanimity is seldom achieved and the process of criticism is open-ended both in time and those participating, how can this process actually reach any verdict on the claim to validity?

Well, it never can reach any final verdict. At no point can one be sure that a given argument is valid; any critical judgment is always subject to revision in the light of further criticism. But the fact that no actual amount of criticism is sufficient to place a critical judgment beyond further challenge does not imply that limited amounts of criticism are insufficient to justify a tentative judgment of validity. To justify any given judgment of validity all that is necessary is to meet whatever challenges are actually made to it. These challenges will be made by those who reject or doubt the critical judgment and are participating in the discussion with the judger. It is often possible to continue the critical discussion to the point where those participating come to agree on the validity or invalidity of the given argument; and where agreement does not arise, the judger may at least completely resolve all of his own doubts. To this extent, then, he has succeeded in justifying his judgment of validity. To put the point another way, the process of criticism may succeed in making some argument persuasive or unpersuasive for some limited group. To this extent it reaches and justifies a verdict of valid or invalid by that group. Recognizing the tentativeness of the judgment and the fact that at any time further justification may be required does not preclude recognizing that for the moment the justification may be sufficient.

But perhaps I have not been quite fair with my critic. It is not just that any finite success in the process of criticism is always subject to revision in the light of further criticism; it is that we so seldom achieve even finite success. Sometimes we manage to reach agreement on the validity of an argument within a limited group after limited discussion, but very often one must decide whether an argument is valid even though agreement has not emerged from the discussion. This is particularly true of some ethical arguments like those that infer ethical conclusions from factual premises or appeal to other-regarding consequences. After extensive discussion among thoughtful men, there may still be disagreement over the validity of such arguments; some may be persuaded by them and others unpersuaded. Yet one may make a critical judgment under such circumstances, and such a judgment is not improper or arbitrary. My view is that each individual should accept or reject an argument on the basis of whether he finds it persuasive when he thinks it through. But what right has the individual to judge on the basis of his own thinking when he cannot achieve agreement by discussion with other thinkers? Basically, I suppose, it is that one has no choice but to trust his own thinking. He can appeal to the verdict of others only insofar as he is aware of it, and to do so is to engage in reasoning. The reasoning of others is relevant to my conclusions only as it becomes a premise in my own reasoning. And if the reasoning of each individual is not to be granted some credibility, then agreement does not increase credibility. One should be troubled by any disagreement and should reconsider his own judgment and try to resolve any differences, but meanwhile one should, because one must, accept his own judgment as correct. Therefore, incomplete and imperfect as the process of criticism is, it does justify drawing conclusions as to the validity of this or that argument.

A third criticism of my analysis of validity is that it undermines the objectivity of the claim by being relative. The claim is that a valid argument will when subjected to indefinite criticism be persuasive for everyone who thinks in the normal way. I interpret this claim as having significance only within a critical community of like minds. But to make it thus depend upon the psychology of a given group, no matter how large, is to make it subjective. To be really objective the validity of an argument should be independent of how we think, it should be a fact built into the universe to be recognized by our thinking not created by it.

I do not believe that the objectivity of reasoning can be saved by making validity something completely outside of and independent of the human mind. Suppose that there were something outside the human mind to serve as the basis of valid reasoning. How could one ever appeal to this something to justify his claim that a given argument is valid? To do so would itself be reasoning. Is this to be justified by another appeal to something external? In the end reasoning must stand on its own feet and not require any external support.

What is required for the claim to validity to be objective is that the correctness of the claim should not be decided by the present opinion of the claimer. There must be something outside the judgment of validity to serve as a test of its correctness. But on my analysis there is, for any given judgment of validity is potentially subject to an open-ended process of criticism in terms of which it may be revised. Not only does this process go beyond the present state of mind of the judger; it is social in that it involves the discussion of thinking men. To be sure, it is limited to those who think in the normal way, but this limitation does not destroy the distinction between seeming valid and being valid. It is this that is at the heart of objectivity. To be objective is to be subject to criticism, to be such that the distinction correct-incorrect applies. The fact that this distinction arises out of a critical process of a limited community does not make the process unreal or its verdict a purely personal matter. It is a public matter even if the public is restricted; it is objective in the only sense that is relevant to epistemology.

A final criticism of my position is that it unduly restricts our ability to recognize the validity of an argument. Admitting that we sometimes come to the conclusion that a given argument is valid by reasoning about it, in the end we recognize the validity of many arguments by thinking them through and finding ourselves persuaded by them. We judge them persuasive because we find ourselves persuaded by them. But a person can be persuaded by an argument only when he accepts or has its premises and does not accept its conclusion. This seems to imply that one cannot recognize an argument to be valid by thinking it through either when he does not accept its premises or when he already accepts its conclusion. Yet surely we can do just this; we can recognize an argument as valid even under these circumstances.

The reply to this criticism involves several factors. For one thing, very often we may be recognizing the validity of such arguments by reasoning about them rather than by thinking them through. For example, I realize that "Wellman is prejudiced because Wellman is a philosopher and all philosophers are prejudiced" is valid by noticing that it falls under a principle of logic rather than by feeling its logical force directly. For another thing, acceptance and rejection are matters of degree. Hence some doubt about the premises and a moderate acceptance of the conclusion still leave room for the thinker to be persuaded. Finally, in some cases we judge the validity of an argument by imagining ourselves in the other fellow's shoes. Thus a person who does not accept the premises of a given argument can still imagine what it would be like to accept them and make a good guess as to whether they would then persuade one of the conclusion; again, one who already accepts the conclusion completely can imagine what it would be like to doubt it and judge whether the premises would remove this doubt. Our ability to project ourselves into the position of a reasoner with different convictions depends in part upon our ability to entertain beliefs we do not have and in part upon the fact that our minds are presupposed to work alike, that is in the normal way. It seems to me that together these three factors explain how it is possible to recognize the validity of arguments whose premises we do not accept or have or whose conclusions we already accept.

CONCLUSION

In this chapter I have outlined my conception of reasoning. Reasoning is using or following arguments. An argument consists of a conclusion, one or more premises, and an implicit claim to validity. It is this claim to validity that is central to and characteristic of reasoning. To say that an argument is valid is to claim that, when subjected to an indefinite amount of criticism, it is persuasive for everyone who thinks in the normal way. Thus reasoning is an activity which derives its epistemic dimension from the fact that it is at least potentially embedded in a much larger process of thinking and discussion which sustains the persuasiveness of some arguments and destroys the persuasiveness of others.

This theory can easily be extended to provide an interpretation of many other logical expressions. For example, a "reason" is any consideration that is claimed to be valid; to say that a reason is valid is to claim that when subjected to an indefinite amount of criticism it is persuasive for everyone who thinks in the normal way. A "good reason" is a consideration that is claimed to be and actually is valid. The distinction between "relevant" and "irrelevant" considerations is the distinction between those considerations which continue to make a difference to our acceptance or rejection after criticism and those which do not affect our critical conviction.

Now if my definition of reasoning is accepted, it can very plausibly be held that conductive arguments are reasoning in the same sense that the most respectable proofs in Euclid are reasoning. Moreover, this view has a great advantage for one concerned with ethics in that it is applicable to emotions, attitudes, and decisions as well as statements and beliefs. Emotions, attitudes, and decisions can be the conclusions of genuine reasoning because all can be modified by advancing or reflecting on considerations, and the arguments used or followed in changing them can be judged persuasive or unpersuasive after indefinite criticism. Since attitudes and decisions are central to ethics, one must either have a theory of reasoning that applies to them or abandon all attempts at rational justification in ethics.

5. justification

WHEN philosophers argue about how, or even whether, ethical statements can be justified, their conclusions are usually determined in large measure by their presuppositions about the nature of justification itself. It is often taken for granted that to justify a statement is simply to deduce it from acceptable premises. I have tried to show that this conception of justification is much too narrow by arguing that inductive and conductive arguments can justify their conclusions even though they cannot be reduced to deductive form. The recognition of the fact that there are several kinds of valid reasoning suggests that to justify a statement is to derive it from acceptable premises by valid reasoning of any sort. Alas, even this wider view of justification is not broad enough.

Justifying as reasoning

Clearly, justifying and reasoning are not identical, for not all valid reasoning is justifying. *a*) When a mathematician deduces "two plus two equal four" from the axioms of his system, he is certainly reasoning. Yet it is very doubtful that he is justifying his conclusion, for he is far more confident of the truth of "two plus two equal four" than of most of his axioms. The point of his reasoning is not to justify his arithmetical conclusion but to systematize his knowledge of mathematics. *b*) The scientist may tentatively accept some working hypothesis and then proceed to draw out its various implications. In thinking through the implications of the hypothesis he is reasoning, but he is hardly justifying any conclusions about the truth of the hypothesis itself or the statements that follow from it. Of course, he may go on to confirm or disconfirm the hypothesis by establishing the truth or falsity of its consequences, but until he does take this further step, he is reasoning without justifying. *c*) It is possible to construct, follow, and even use valid arguments that do not at all justify their conclusions. This happens when one knows the premises to be false or when one has no reason to believe them true. One can infer any conclusion he pleases by arbitrarily postulating the required premises, but such reasoning hardly justifies the claim that the conclusion is true. To put the point paradoxically, some perfectly logical proofs do not prove anything. Hence, reasoning is not always justifying.

It is less clear that not all justifying is reasoning. Often it is. If some statement is challenged, the obvious way to defend it is to give evidence of its truth. Good reasons, if they really are good reasons, serve to justify the conclusion they support. In all such cases one is justifying by reasoning and justifying is nothing but reasoning.

It is easy to think of other cases, however, in which justifying is not reasoning in this sense at all. *1*) Suppose that I say to my neighbor, whose reckless son has just broken my picture window with his baseball, "that was a wicked thing for John to do." My neighbor might challenge my ethical statement by point out that John is only a child. I then reply "he is still old enough to know better." In saying this I am not giving a reason for my ethical statement in the ordinary sense of a consideration to establish its truth. The fact that John is old enough to know better is hardly evidence for my statement that his action was evil, for to point out that John has acquired some knowledge of good and evil would be just as relevant (and in the same way) to the statement that he had done some morally good act. Nevertheless, my reply does help to justify my ethical statement. If John is not old enough to know better, if he has not acquired the status of a moral agent, then he is not the sort of entity to which one can appropriately apply the terms "morally good" and "wicked." If my neighbor can show that John is too much of a child to be a moral agent, then I must admit that my condemnation was unjustified, not because my statement was false but because it was out of place. One justifies a statement by showing that it is not inappropriate or out of place as well as when one gives reasons to prove that it is not false. 2) Suppose that I do give reasons to support some ethical statement I have made. Someone may then challenge the validity of my reasoning. One way to meet this challenge is to reformulate my argument to make it clearer. If my reformulation enables the challenger to recognize the validity of my argument, I have justified my implicit claim to be reasoning validly. But I have not justified this claim by further reasoning. I have not proved my argument valid; I have not used any second-order argument to support my ethical argument. Instead I have revealed the validity of my argument; I have simply made clear what my argument was. When one explains an argument, one may justify its claim to validity without giving reasons for the conclusion "it is valid." 3) If someone were to deny an ethical statement I had just made, I might ask "what evidence do you have that my statement is false?" or more simply "why?" Although I am hereby asking my opponent to give reasons for his denial, I am hardly supporting my own statement with reasons. Questions, and the doubt they may express, are hardly evidence to establish the truth of a conclusion; these are not reasons in any ordinary sense. Yet one can defend an ethical statement by asking questions or expressing doubt. One way to meet an attack on an ethical statement is by forcing the attacker to assume his share of the burden of proof. If he cannot justify his denial, then he cannot claim to have shown my statement to be unjustified. To this extent, then, I can defend my claim to have made a justified statement simply by asking questions. Examples like the three just given show that justifying is not always reasoning.

But long-lived presuppositions die hard, especially when they are unexpressed and therefore unexamined. Let us reexamine these examples to see whether they could be interpreted in such a way as to save the identification of justifying with reasoning. 1) Although "he is old enough to know better" may not be a reason for "that was a wicked thing for John to do," it is a reason for " 'that was a wicked thing for John to do' has truth-value." This suggests that when justifying does not seem to be reasoning, it may be transposed into reasoning on some higher level. Thus justifying might turn out to be reasoning in some indirect way after all. I would not deny that the discussion with my neighbor might be put into this new key. He might charge that my ethical statement is without truth-value because it is out of place and I might reply by giving reasons for " 'that was a wicked thing for John to do' has truth-value." I would then be justifying the conclusion " 'that was a wicked thing for John to do' has truth-value" by reasoning. But how would *this* reasoning serve to justify the statement "that was a wicked thing for John to do"? The whole point of the discussion is that I am trying to justify my original statement in the face of my neighbor's challenge. In our transposed discussion his charge "your statement is without truth-value" is not a reason against my statement, and my conclusion that my original statement has truth-value, although it is supported by reasoning, does not itself support my ethical statement by reasoning. Therefore, to transpose this sort of justification into reasoning is to leave unexplained the way in which this reasoning bears on the statement to be justified. Even when justifying can be transposed into reasoning on another level, it will not do to identify the justifying with this reasoning in a new key. Moreover, such transposition is not always possible. One would not really want to say that "how do you know that?" is a reason for "you do not know what you are saying," although it has something to do with the justification of the claim to know.

2) How might one reinterpret the case of justifying the claim to validity of an argument by reformulating the argument in such a way that its meaning, and thus its logical force, becomes clear? One would have to show either that reformulating an argument is giving a reaon for it or that this sort of explanation does not really justify its claim to validity. The first alternative will not do for reasons already given. Suppose one construes the justification to amount to something like this: This reformulation is clearly valid, any argument and its reformulation have the same validity-value; therefore, the original argument is valid. What does the conclusion of the reasoning, "the original argument is valid," have to do with the origi-

nal argument? Well, it obviously justifies the claim to validity of the argument. But one cannot infer the argument from the statement that it is valid, for an argument is not the sort of thing that can be a conclusion of reasoning. Thus the way in which the conclusion of the reasoning justifies the argument cannot itself be by reasoning. Once more reasoning in a new key, while possible, turns out to leave a gap between the reasoning and that which is to be justified. The other alternative does not seem much more attractive. Can one say that reformulating an argument never justifies its claim to validity? Well, is one justified in brushing aside the charge that an argument is invalid? I think not. When the validity of an argument is challenged, the argument needs to be justified. One way to meet this challenge would be to prove that the argument in question is valid. Since this is reasoning, presumably it would be accepted as genuine justification. But one can also meet the same challenge by reformulating the argument or explaining its meaning so that the challenger sees its validity for himself and withdraws his challenge. Now, is this justifying the argument? If the argument needed justification before the explanation was given but no longer needs justification afterwards, it is hard to see why one would deny that reformulating is justifying. To insist that it cannot be justifying because it is not reasoning would be to beg the question whether all justification is reasoning. It seems more reasonable to admit that explaining an argument is justifying its claim to validity even though it is not a form of reasoning.

   3) The role of questions and doubt in justification remains to be explained. It will not do, I think, to exclude them entirely. At the very least they call for or necessitate justifying. The person who makes an ethical statement cannot justifiably brush aside the questions "what reason do you have to assert that?" or "how do you know?" as beside the point; nor can one justify his deepest convictions by what Peirce [1] called the method of tenacity, one part of which is ignoring or suppressing whatever doubts one may have. Questions, and the doubt they express, do challenge ethical statements, and the convictions they express. Whatever justification may be it must include meeting questions and doubts. On the other

hand, one cannot explain the relevance of questions and doubts by interpreting them as reasons for our ethical conclusions. To hold that "what reason is there to think philosophy worthless?" is a valid reason for the statement "philosophy is worthwhile" is surely to stretch the meaning of the word "reason" considerably. One can always redefine a word, but would one want to say that the more doubts there are on some ethical issue the more reasons one has to draw an ethical conclusion? The only remaining alternative seems to be to maintain that questions and doubts necessitate justifying but cannot be used to justify; they pose a real challenge to an ethical statement but cannot support any such statement. This is an untenable position because justification is called for only where there is a choice between contrary statements. To justify "pleasure is good" is to establish it as opposed to "pleasure is not good." But if "what reason is there to think pleasure is not good?" really challenges the statement "pleasure is not good," then it might, if unmet, show that acceptance of that statement is unjustified. To do this would necessarily go some way toward showing that its contradictory, "pleasure is good," is relatively more justified. Therefore, one can justify a statement in some cases by posing questions of anyone who would deny its truth. Again, not all justifying is reasoning.

I have belabored this point because it is crucial. The most basic question in the whole area under investigation, "what is justification?," is usually ignored as requiring no special consideration. Everyone knows, or thinks he knows, that justifying an ethical statement is nothing but giving good reasons for it. Unfortunately, this is not so. Far more than this is required to justify the claim to have made a true statement. This is partly because there are relevant challenges besides the truth challenge and partly because there are justifying responses which are not reasons. Far from being solved by my discussion of ethical reasoning the problem of the nature of justification is only posed more urgently by everything I have said so far.

Challenges

Although justifying is sometimes nothing but reasoning, at other times it is something other than reasoning. This is because some challenges that are pertinent to an ethical statement cannot be met with reasons and those challenges that can be met with reasons can also be met in other ways. Since the challenges to an ethical statement extend beyond any possible reasoning, justification must be similarly extended. The key notion, therefore, is that of a challenge rather than that of a reason. If one wishes to become clear about the nature of justification, one must begin with the challenges that make it necessary.

What is a challenge? The paradigm cases seem to be the gentleman issuing a challenge to a duel and the knight issuing a challenge to a trial by battle. In these cases a challenge demands some response; it calls for someone to engage in a specified process. Why should the challenged party bother to put himself to this test? Because his honor is at stake; his claim to be a gentleman will be overturned if he fails. Thus in the paradigm case a challenge calls for some response because it threatens some claim. When I speak of a challenge in the context of justification, I am using the word in an analogous sense. Here, too, a challenge calls for some response because it threatens some claim, in this case the claim to rationality.

The claim to rationality takes many forms depending on that for which it is made. Statements and beliefs make a claim to truth; they claim that the reasons for them outweigh the reasons against them. Although one would not speak of an attitude as true, it seems natural to speak of appropriate and inappropriate attitudes. Actions and decisions are neither true nor valid, but we do not hesitate to claim rightness for them; without this claim to rationality there would be no ethical problems at all. On behalf of emotions the proper claim seems to be the claim to be suitable or reasonable. These are all forms of the claim to rationality because they are all claims about the weight of the reasons. In every case the claim is that the belief, attitude, or decision on whose behalf the claim is made will withstand and be supported by the process of reasoning.

Because challenges may threaten this claim in various ways, there are several distinct dimensions of justification. In making an ethical statement one is implicitly claiming that the statement is true, that reasoning would lead one to accept rather than reject the statement. Truth challenges question or deny this claim directly. Truth-value challenges might be said to undermine or cut the ground out from under this claim rather than to oppose it; if an utterance can be shown to be neither true nor false, then it is quite beside the point, rather than mistaken, to continue to claim that it is true. Similarly, the meaningfulness challenge undermines the claim to truth in an even more radical fashion; obviously no meaningless utterance can legitimately claim to be true. Validity challenges threaten the claim to truth in quite another way, by criticizing the reasoning by which that claim must ultimately be defended. And so it goes. The different kinds of challenges threaten the claim to rationality in different ways.

What is it that all these challenges have in common that makes them challenges? They all claim to be upsetting. I deliberately choose the ambiguous term "upsetting" because it reminds one of two features which seem to me essentially connected in the nature of a challenge. To upset may be to disturb psychologically as when an insulting remark upsets a young lady; to upset may be to disturb or overturn physically as when a strong wind upsets an old sailboat. Analogously, a challenge usually disturbs the person at whom it is directed because it threatens to overturn some claim to rationality he is making. It is the claim to be upsetting that is definitive of a challenge. Like the claims to truth and validity, this is a critical claim, a claim to be judged by the outcome of the process of criticism.

Exactly what is the content of this claim? To say that something is upsetting is to claim that it tends to upset every normal person when subjected to an indefinite amount of criticism. In this context "tends to upset" means "unless counteracted, causes one to reduce or withdraw or withhold the claim to rationality when it is directed to a person who accepts, has, or understands it." Statements, beliefs, and attitudes upset one only when one accepts them himself. Experiences and doubts upset only the person who has them. Explanations upset only when they are understood. I do not claim that in this paragraph I am explaining what we ordinarily mean by the word "upsetting"; I am trying to define the word in a way that will make it useful in the analysis of justification. I am using the word "upsetting" to label a critical claim implicit in our everyday practice of justification but not explicitly and precisely spelled out in our ordinary language. The core of this critical claim is that a challenge causes one to reduce or withdraw or withhold a claim to rationality; this can be seen in the way in which challenges actually operate in the give-and-take of discussion. But to claim that something is upsetting differs from describing it as causing someone to withdraw or withhold a claim to rationality in two ways. First, it attributes only a disposition to the challenge. It is not required that a challenge cause this result on every occasion but only that unless counteracted it cause this result when the conditions of upsetting (when accepted, had, or understood) are fulfilled. Second, it has critical rather than descriptive meaning. It does not describe the challenge as having this tendency to upset; it claims that when subjected to an indefinite amount of criticism it will have this tendency for everyone who thinks in the normal way. Anything that implicitly makes this claim to be upsetting is a challenge.

Growing out of this central and defining characteristic of a challenge are several features that bear materially on the nature of justification. Every challenge is a challenge of something; by its very nature it is aimed at some object, something making a claim to rationality. Thus a challenge is always relative to that whose rationality is being threatened. If I say "Sally is a wicked woman," someone may object either "what evidence do you have of her indiscretion?" or "it is very rude to say that in public." The former remark challenges the truth of my statement; the latter challenges the rightness of my act of uttering the statement. It is important to be clear about this relational feature of challenges because justification requires only that pertinent challenges be met. In this respect, being a challenge is like being a reason. Statements are not reasons in and of themselves; they are reasons for or against something. The same statement may be a reason relative to one conclusion and not a reason (quite irrelevant) to another conclusion. Similarly, a remark may be a challenge to one statement but not at all a challenge to another statement.

In another way a challenge is more like a premise than it is like a reason. A statement P may be a reason for another statement Q even though no one who makes or hears the statement realizes this logical fact; but a statement is a premise only when it is used as a premise by some speaker or thinker. A statement is made into a premise by being used in an argument. Similarly something is made into a challenge by being used or taken as such; only when the speaker or thinker claims that it is upsetting is anything a challenge. "He is selfish" can be used as a challenge to the statement "he is morally good"; but it may also be admitted as a nonchallenging truth by the person who knows that it is more than offset by other good-making characteristics.

This fact, that something is a challenge only when it is used or taken as such, suggests that I have been using the term too broadly in my previous discussion. I think that this is not so, provided it is understood that I am using the word "challenge" in a technical sense that goes beyond ordinary usage. In the paradigm case a person issues a challenge to someone else. The words he utters are used as a challenge in that they are a formula being used in the act of challenging. Strictly speaking, it is the person who is challenging with the words; the utterance in itself does no challenging. But just as it is convenient to think of a statement as making a claim to truth, so it is convenient to think of a statement as issuing a challenge. The convenience of this extension lies in the fact that the same sort of challenge might be issued by any of a number of speakers and who is uttering the challenge makes no difference to its logical properties. Accordingly, I shall continue to speak of statements and questions as making implicit claims to be upsetting and as being challenges. This is a harmless shorthand as long as it is realized that these are challenges only as they are used by speakers to issue challenges. However, I wish to extend the notion of a challenge even further than this. I wish to speak of unexpressed beliefs, doubts, experiences, and attitudes as challenging some thinker at times. Although it is stretching our language to say that these issue challenges, it seems less farfetched to say that they pose challenges. But in saying this it is important to remember that they pose challenges only when and insofar as they are recognized by the thinker as threatening some claim to rationality. In this very wide sense, it is only when taken as challenges by the thinker that his beliefs, doubts, experiences, and attitudes are challenges for him. In this way the similarity between being a challenge and being a premise is preserved. Relevant considerations are premises in an individual's thinking only insofar as he recognizes their relevance; similarly something is a challenge for a thinker only insofar as he recognizes that it threatens to upset some claim to rationality. Something becomes a challenge only when it is being used to issue a challenge to another person or by being taken to pose a challenge to oneself.

This leads naturally into another feature of every challenge. A challenge is necessarily directed at someone on some occasion. Every challenge is relative to the person for whom it is a challenge and the occasion on which it is a challenge. The doubt of another person is no challenge to my conviction, and the doubt I will feel tomorrow is no challenge to my conviction today. Of course, the doubt of another may challenge my belief if he expresses it in a demand for reasons addressed to me; but if he does not express his doubts in my presence, then his doubts are not any challenge for me. Again, the challenges Thrasymachus and Socrates issued to each other become challenges for me now only when I become a participant in the discussion recorded in book one of the *Republic* by reading or reflecting upon it.

It is important to distinguish between genuine and feigned challenges because only the former need to be met. An utterance that appears to challenge some claim to rationality may turn out to be a counterfeit in either of two ways: either the speaker is not seriously claiming that it is upsetting, or he does not himself accept or understand it. Suppose that I assert vehemently that Hitler was a thoroughly wicked and inhuman man. Someone might reply "but his eyes were true blue." It is barely possible, I suppose, that the speaker takes his reply to be evidence against my assertion; blue eyes indicate Aryan stock and no Aryan could be really wicked. But if he recognizes the irrelevancy of his remark, then he is not seriously claiming that it is upsetting, that it would tend to upset every normal person after an indefinite amount of criticism. And if he is not making any claim to upsettingness, then he is only feigning a challenge. Someone else might respond to my assertion that Hitler is thoroughly wicked and inhuman by saying "but he personally distributed food and clothing to needy families without any publicity." If true, this reply does show that Hitler was not as completely wicked as I had assumed, but is it true? If the speaker does not himself believe it true, if he has just pulled a statement out of the air and uttered it without any conviction at all, then he, too, is just pretending to challenge me. Every genuine challenge must 1) make a serious claim to be upsetting and 2) be accepted, had, or understood by the person who uses or takes it as a challenge. If either condition remains unfulfilled, then what may seem to be a challenge is only a feigned challenge.

Before turning to responses, let us sum up our conclusions about challenges. A challenge is anything that claims to be upsetting. To be genuine it must also be accepted, had, or understood by the person who uses or takes it as a challenge. Every challenge is relative in several ways. It must be a challenge *of* something making a claim to rationality. It must be made *by* someone prepared to claim that it is upsetting. And it must be a challenge *for* someone *on* some occasion; every challenge is directed at someone at some particular time. These relational features of any challenge go a long way toward defining the nature of justification.

Responses

Every challenge calls for some response. In paradigm cases, a response is a linguistic utterance by a different speaker and later in time than the challenge to which it is a reply, but for my purposes the notion of a response needs to be extended in three ways beyond such clear cases. First, one speaker can anticipate the challenge of another. One sometimes replies to a challenge before it is made because one expects that it will be made in any event. Second, a speaker can respond to his own challenge. Although typically justification involves conversations in which the give-and-take is between different persons, reasonable men often participate in the criticism as well as the defense of this own statements. Third, a response need not be a linguistic utterance. If I take my new tie outside and examine it closely by daylight because I have begun to wonder about its true color, my visual sensations may properly be considered a response to my doubts. When one justifies some statement or conviction or action to oneself, one need not say anything aloud and not everything one does will be saying things even to oneself. It is in this somewhat extended sense of the term that justification consists of responses.

A response, in this sense, can be analyzed in a manner that is now familiar to the reader. The defining characteristic of a response is its implicit claim to be reassuring; anything that makes such a critical claim is a response. To say that something is reassuring is to claim that it tends to reassure anyone who thinks in the normal way when subjected to an indefinite amount of criticism. "Tends to reassure" means unless counteracted does reassure anyone who accepts, has, or understands it. I am not using "to reassure" in its ordinary sense but to mean to cause one to reduce or withdraw or withhold a challenge. Although this does not have anything to do with emotional reassurance, it does have something to do with the assurance with which one accepts and maintains that which has been challenged.

It is important to remember here that what makes anything a challenge is that it is used as one; it is only when issued as or taken to pose a challenge that anything actually challenges. This has a direct bearing on what it is to reduce, withdraw, or withold a challenge. Consider this short conversation:

> "Sally is wicked."
> "But she is very kind."
> "Yes, she is far too kind to strange men."

This dialogue consists of an ethical statement, a challenge to its truth, and a response to that truth challenge. If we suppose that the response is sufficient to justify the original statement and that the challenger is reasonable, then it follows that the second speaker will withdraw his challenge. This does not imply, however, that he will withdraw his statement that Sally is very kind. He will probably continue to assert this statement whenever it is relevant, for its truth has not been put in question at all. What he will do is to cease issuing it as a challenge to "Sally is wicked." The response need not cause him to back down on his implicit claim to truth on behalf of the statement but only on his claim that it is upsetting. Similarly, he will withhold this challenge on future occasions in that he will not issue this statement as a challenge, but he may well continue to make and defend the statement in spite of the response. To withdraw a challenge is to withdraw its claim to be upsetting; to withhold a challenge is to refrain from using it *as* a challenge.

Like a challenge, a response is relative in several ways. First, a response is relative to the challenge to which it is responding. It claims to be reassuring, but only with respect to some specific challenge. By its very nature a response is a response *to* something; if it happens to bear on anything else, that is by accident. This indicates that primarily a response rebuts some challenge rather than supports a claim. Supporting a claim that has been challenged is one way, but only one way, of responding to a challenge. Seeking to attack or undermine the challenge is another; such responses defend the claims challenged only indirectly by removing the challenge to them. Thus every response faces some challenge, even though it may glance back over its shoulder at the claim being challenged. Second, a response is relative to the person responding. It is only when issued as or taken to be a response that anything is a response. Every response must be used *by* someone as a response, for only then is any claim to be reassuring made on its behalf. While the claim to truth is intrinsic to any genuine statement, the claim to be reassuring is adventitious to any statement and accrues to it by the way in which it is used by some particular speaker or thinker. Third, a response is relative to the person and occasion *at* which it is directed. The supporting evidence my friends possess constitutes a response to my challenge only insofar as it is brought to bear on my challenge at some stage of our conversation. Only when it is used as a response to me does it claim to be reassuring with respect to my challenge. These three sorts of relativity are built into the nature of every response.

Just as it was necessary to distinguish between genuine and feigned challenges, so one must distinguish between genuine and feigned responses. To be genuine a response must not only make a serious claim to be reassuring but also be accepted, had, or understood by the person using or taking it as a response. Any speaker who either interjects a remark that he realizes does nothing to meet a given challenge or that he himself is not prepared to assert or able to understand only pretends to respond to that challenge. His utterance is an empty gesture without any justificatory significance.

It is also convenient to distinguish between adequate and inadequate responses. The adequacy of a response is, of course, relative to the challenge it is intended to meet. To say that a response is adequate to a given challenge is to claim that after indefinite criticism anyone who thinks in the normal way and who accepted, had, or understood both the challenge and the response would withdraw or withhold the challenge. To say that a response is inadequate is simply to deny that it is adequate.

To judge whether or not a response is adequate to a given challenge requires weighing the response against the challenge. This is closely analogous to weighing the reasons for some conclusion against the reasons against that conclusion. In one respect, it is somewhat simpler, for one never has to weigh many responses against many challenges as one must sometimes weigh several pros against several cons. This is because every challenge is a challenge to some claim to rationality and every response is a response to some challenge. One might weigh one response against several challenges in the case where someone tries to meet several challenges to a given statement with one reply, and one might weigh several responses against one challenge in the case where the speaker makes more than one reply to a single challenge to his statement. Typically, however, one is called on to weigh only a single challenge. In the course of any considerable discussion of some ethical issue many challenges will be issued and many responses will be made. But it would be ridiculous to try to weigh all the challenges against all the replies, for not all the challenges are aimed at the same claims and not all the responses are replies to the same challenge. To overlook this relativity of challenges and responses would be as silly as to weigh all the reasons for one statement against the reasons against another statement or to try to sum up the conclusion of many arguments by weighing all the pros against all the cons even though the arguments had quite different conclusions. Thus the notion of the adequacy of a response is much like that of the weight of the evidence. Both involve some sort of weighing of opposed factors, and in both cases one must be careful to ensure that the factors being weighed are commensurate.

One last point needs to be made. Although responses are essentially different from challenges, one and the same thing can be both a response and a challenge. For example:

> "Killing is always wrong."
> "Not when one is fighting a just war."
> "There is no such thing as a just war."
> "How do you know?"

I am assuming that the ethical statement "killing is always wrong" initiates the conversation; if so, it neither challenges nor responds to anything that went before. "Not when one is fighting a just war" challenges the truth of the ethical statement that precedes it; but since that statement is not a challenge, it is not a response in the technical sense in which I am using that term. "There is no such thing as a just war," however, is both a response to and a challenge of the statement immediately before it. Likewise, the last sentence in this truncated dialogue is both a challenge and a response to the statement which precedes it. In fact, it is typical of the give-and-take of ethical debate that a speaker will respond to some statement by challenging it. This does not imply that being a response is the same as being a challenge, but only that these two characteristics are compatible and often conjoined. Nevertheless, for the purpose of analyzing justification it is essential not to confuse them.

The nature of justification

Exactly what is justification? The various words that express our conception of justification seem to fall into three classes—verbs, adjectives, and nouns. We say that someone will justify, is justifying, or has justified his statement, belief, or action. We speak of a statement or act as justified, unjustified, or unjustifiable. And we talk about the justification of something. My strategy is to take the verb forms as basic and then define the adjectives and nouns in terms of these; my hope is that the verb forms can themselves be analyzed in terms of the notions of a challenge and a response.

What do we mean by "justifying"? Justifying a statement, belief, attitude, emotion, or action is meeting challenges to it. To meet a challenge is to give an adequate response which is accepted, had, or understood by the challenger. An adequate response is one that after indefinite criticism would cause *anyone* who thinks in the normal way and accepts, has, or understands both challenge and response to withdraw or withhold the challenge; the adequacy of a response is an impersonal status to be determined by the ideal outcome of criticism. But whether the response is actually accepted, had, or understood by the challenger depends upon the accidents of his personal biography and psychological makeup. Therefore, whether a given response meets a given challenge is relative to the challenger and even the occasion on which the challenge is made. A reason advanced may be accepted by one member of the audience and not another; an explanation offered may be understood by someone today but no longer understood tomorrow when his mind is less clear or he has come to recognize some ambiguity. Hence a response may meet the challenge of one person on one occasion and not meet a precisely similar challenge of another person on this occasion or the same person on another occasion.

Although relativizing the notion of meeting a challenge in this way may seem objectionable at first, I believe that it is necessary and desirable. *1*) It does not rule out making responses that are not in fact accepted, had, or understood by the challenger. For one thing, the way to discover whether or not some response really meets a challenge is normally to make the response and see whether or not it is then challenged in its turn. Moreover, one may make a response *and then* go on to get it accepted, had, or understood by further discussion or thinking. Although the response does not meet the challenge until one manages to get it accepted, had, or understood, it can come to meet the challenge during the course of the process of justification. *2*) Unless some such restriction is placed upon those responses that actually meet a challenge, it will be possible to meet any challenge in an easy and trivial way. One can always pull some statement, question, or explanation out of thin air and claim to have met the challenge. If someone should challenge my statement that I am now typing on the back of a turtle instead of a table, I can airily respond that the hard shell and long claws of the object prove it to be a turtle. If someone points to the slim legs of tubular steel, I can ask "how do you know this turtle does not have four artificial limbs?" Surely such responses do nothing to meet the challenge at hand. *3*) The restriction I have imposed on responses that meet a challenge is the right sort of restriction for my sort of theory. I am trying to interpret justification as a psychological process of causing challengers to withdraw their challenges. Observation indicates that only responses that are accepted, had, or understood by the challenger will be psychologically effective. Hence, insofar as it is a psychological process, justifying must be anchored in the actual beliefs, doubts, and comprehensions of the participants. 4) Nevertheless, such anchoring in psychology does not reduce justifying to a purely psychological process because it also involves critical claims at other points. For example, the claim that the given response is adequate goes beyond its efficacy in convincing the challenger on this occasion. Thus one may actually meet a challenge even though the challenger does not admit that one has done so. Moreover, although some statement with which one responds may or may not be actually accepted by the challenger, this does not settle its claim to truth; the statement may meet one challenge because, in part, it is accepted yet itself be open to further challenge and require further justification. 5) Finally, this requirement helps to explain why reiteration and circular arguments do not constitute justification. Why cannot I meet a truth challenge to my ethical statement simply by repeating my statement in a loud and emphatic tone of voice? What is wrong with giving P as evidence for Q, Q as evidence for R, and then giving R as evidence for P? On my view such procedures fail to meet the challenge because anyone who would challenge the conclusion would necessarily not accept the reason given to justify it. For various reasons, then, it seems quite proper to say that only accepted, had, or understood responses meet the challenges to which they are addressed.

If to justify is to meet challenges, how long must one go on meeting challenges before he has finished the job? One "has justified" something to someone when one has met every challenge (in the wise sense) that has actually been made to it on that occasion, by that challenger. One can meet a challenge either by showing that it is not really upsetting or, in the case of statements or questions, by refuting the assertion or resolving the doubt. Moreover, each and every actual challenge must be met before one can claim to have finished the task of justifying. Occasionally, one response will serve to meet several challenges, and several responses each of which is inadequate may together meet some challenge. But one cannot leave any challenge unanswered or offset the inadequacy of one response by more than meeting some other challenge.

Every challenge must be met. Not every possible challenge, however, but only those challenges that are actually made on this occasion. Thus one may have finished the job on this occasion but find that on another occasion there are additional challenges to be met. Finally, one may have justified something to one challenger but not to another. A speaker may manage to meet every challenge made by one person but not every challenge made by another either because the latter made more challenges than the former or because he did not accept, have, or understand some response that the former did. Thus whenever it can be properly said that someone has justified something, implicit in this statement is a reference to the person to whom and the occasion on which the justifying was completed.

Now let us turn to an example of the adjectival form. To say that a statement, belief, attitude, emotion, or action "is justified" means that the possible responses meet every possible challenge to it. The sort of possibility involved here is not that of logical possibility. A possible response is one that is available, one that it would be humanly possible to think up, that might be accepted, had, or understood by a normal human being, and would constitute genuine response if made. A possible challenge is one that, given human nature and the human condition, might be made and, if made, would be a genuine challenge. Thus to say that something is justified goes beyond saying that it has been justified. It has been justified if the actual responses meet every challenge actually made on this occasion, but it is justified only if every possible challenge could be met by an indefinite continuation of the process of justifying. While "has been justified" makes a critical claim about the actual outcome of some actual process of justification on some particular occasion, "is justified" makes a critical claim about the ideal outcome of an indefinite process of justification that could not actually take place in time. Just because this latter claim is not limited to any actual occasion of justifying, it is impersonal in a way in which the former is not. One can be said to have justified something only to someone on some occasion; but a statement or action is not justified to me or to you, it simply is or is not justified. This is because to say that it is justified is to claim that all possible challenges, all the challenges anyone at all could make, are met by the possible responses. Although the claim that something *is* justified goes beyond the claim that it *has been* justified, the latter is the basis for the former. The only test of whether or not something is justified is whether or not it can be justified by someone on some occasion. In one sense the process of showing that something is justified can be completed and in another it cannot. Any given test can be completed; whenever one tries to justify something one either has or has not done so when he rests his case. On the other hand, new tests are always possible simply because new challenges are always possible. One cannot finish the job of showing that all possible challenges can be met because one cannot actually make all possible responses on any actual occasion of justifying. This does not mean that the claim that something is justified is arbitrary and unjustifiable; what it means is that, although it can be established tentatively by the outcome of actual processes of justifying, it is always possible to demand additional tests. Until such additional challenges are actually made, however, it remains true that the claim has been justified.

The noun "justification" is ambiguous. The word "building" may refer to the process of building or the product built; one could say "building a tall building is dangerous." In somewhat the same way, "justification" may refer to the process of justifying or to that which does the justifying. One might say either "justification is more difficult in ethics than in science" or "the justification for his perceptual beliefs is in part his sensations." In the former sense, justification is the name of the process of meeting challenges; in the latter sense, it is a collective name for the responses that meet some set of challenges.

There are many other words that I might try to define, but I believe that I have said enough to indicate how I would continue my analysis. In my view justification is to be understood essentially as a process of responding to challenges made. It may be observed and described as a psychological struggle in which one person tries to force another to back down or one person struggles to come to terms with his own doubts and conflicting convictions. But it is more than a psychological struggle because at its core are certain critical claims like the claims to truth, validity, to be upsetting, to be reassuring, and to be adequate. Therefore the actual outcome of any particular psychological struggle never settles once and for all the issues being fought over in the process of justification. It is this peculiar ambivalence of justification that enables what we actually do in discussion and thinking to serve as a test of critical ideals like truth, validity, and being justified.

The need to justify

Not everything stands in need of justification. I may well be asked to justify my statement that my height is five feet ten inches, but I would hardly know how to respond if asked to justify my height. It is not so much that I search for a justification I cannot find as that justification seems quite beside the point. What sorts of things, then, do call for justification? Beliefs, for one. But why? What is it about a belief, for example, that makes it the sort of thing that requires justifying? In the first instance it is the fact that it can be challenged. Only where a challenge can be made is it necessary, or even possible, to meet that challenge. It is because my height cannot be challenged that it needs no justification.

This just pushes the question further back. What is it about beliefs that makes them open to challenge? It is that they make an implicit claim to rationality, a claim to correctness in the light of all relevant considerations. The believer need not explicitly make any such claim; he may say simply "snow is white" instead of " 'snow is white' is true." Still, the claim is there implicitly in the indicative grammatical form and the serious tone of voice. These make a claim to rationality even when it is not explicit because the claim is explicit on other occasions, it could be explicit when it is not, and whether explicit or not the reasonable man will recognize the relevance of reasons to his belief. The relevance of reasons remains even when no explicit claim to rationality is made.

Here we take one step further back. What is it about beliefs that gives them this implicit claim to rationality? It is the fact that there are reasons for and against them. It makes sense to claim rationality only where there are reasons by which this claim could be tested, and wherever there are such reasons this claim is implicit if not explicitly made.

But what is it about beliefs that allows reasons to be given for and against them? A reason is some consideration that after an indefinite amount of criticism is persuasive for everyone who thinks in the normal way. It follows that reasons can exist only where persuasion is possible. Here we are down to bedrock, the stable foundation of human psychology underlying the epistemological structure of reasoning. Beliefs require justification because they are persuadable, because they are modifiable by discussion and reflection. Persuadability may not be a sufficient condition of the claim to rationality, for there might be persuasion without any fixed pattern of persuasion shared by all normal human beings; but persuadability is at least a necessary condition of reasoning. No amount of talking or taking thought can add one cubit to my height. It follows that to claim rationality for my height would be quite beside the point, and where no claim can be made it cannot be challenged and need not be justified.

Beliefs require justification because they are persuadable. Attitudes, emotions, and actions are also modifiable by discussion and thinking. Since they, too, are persuadable, the claim to rationality can be made on their behalf and they need justification as well. And statements require justification because they put into words beliefs or attitudes that themselves stand in need of justification. Should doubts be added to this list? Since doubts seem to be modifiable by reasoning, I am inclined to think that they should be included, but as a special case. I do not think that doubt can make the kind of claim to rationality that belief or attitude can, the claim that in the end the reasons for it outweigh the reasons against it. The only appropriate final conclusion of the process of reasoning is some conclusion; doubt, whether it be the suspension of judgment or the inclination to both accept and reject some judgment, seems appropriate only during the preliminary stages of reasoning. Still, it remains true that one can give reasons for and against doubt. Therefore, one can make some sort of a claim to rationality on its behalf; one can claim that, in the light of the available evidence, doubt is the reasonable, if tentative, conclusion. That is, doubts can be reasonable or unreasonable even if they cannot be correct or incorrect. To this extent they implicitly claim rationality and do stand in need of justification.

What of experiences? Empiricism has traditionally held that the experiences arising from sensation and introspection are the ultimate data of knowledge because they need no justification, but the reasons given for the ultimacy of experiences have varied. Among these reasons have been the alleged facts that the mind is passive in sensation, that experiences are vivid and clear, that they are self-contained and do not refer beyond themselves, that by definition the given is incorrigible, and that experiences make no claim to correctness. This last is the real explanation as far as it goes. Experiences need no justification because they make no implicit claim to rationality that could possibly be challenged. But why is the claim to rationality quite out of place here? Because there can be no reasons for or against experiences since experiences are unpersuadable Since no amount of discussion or thinking can cause one to reject an experience, all claims about which experiences are supported by the process of reasoning are beside the point.

Experience is not the only ultimate in knowledge; thinking is equally essential and equally ultimate. The claims to truth, validity, and adequacy are all relative to the normal way of thinking; these claims are universal only within the community of like minds. Now does the normal way of thinking need any justification? I think not. Although the choice of how to think in the future requires justification, one has no choice as to how to think in the present. All critical claims are defined in terms of the normal way of thinking, but this way of thinking makes no claim on its own behalf. Why would any such claim be out of place here? Because someone's way of thinking is unpersuadable. Discussion and reflection can change *what* one thinks, the conclusions he draws and the arguments he uses, but they cannot modify *how* one thinks, the basic pattern of psychological connections now in his mind. Which considerations persuade one and which responses cause one to withdraw challenges are as much givens for one as are experiences. Since one's way of thinking is unpersuadable, no claim to rationality can be made or challenged where it is concerned.

My conclusion is that experiences and ways of thinking are ultimates in justification but do not themselves require any justification. Beliefs, attitudes, emotions, actions, statements, and in a limited way doubts are the sorts of things that do need justifying. These things need to be justified because they make a claim to rationality which can be challenged. Everything else, including natural objects and their states, needs no justification and plays no part in justifying either.

Having decided what needs justification, I must consider when it needs justifying. Ethical statements, for example, need justification, but one need not always be engaged in justifying one's statements. My view is that a statement, or anything else, needs to be justified when and only when it is actually challenged. Why does a statement need to be justified when it is challenged? Or, since statements have no needs, why does a speaker need to justify his statement when it is challenged? The beginning of the answer is obvious. The speaker needs to justify his statement simply because it has been challenged and a challenge may cause him to withdraw the claim to rationality on behalf of his statement. So what? Why not withdraw that claim? Why bother to make any such claim in the first place? These questions really boil down to the problem of why one ought to engage in the process of criticism. One ought to make and defend claims to rationality because doing so increases the likelihood that one's beliefs, attitudes, emotions, and actions will be correct and on their correctness depends much of the value they contribute to human life. There is a very strong pragmatic reason for using one's reason and participating in the process of criticism.

This sort of justification cuts off two tempting escapes from the burdens of justification. First, why does one need to meet the challenges of another when one does not himself share these challenges? For example, someone may ask me "but how do you know that?" when he has real doubt and my conviction is undoubting, or someone may challenge my statement with some assertion that he believes to be true and I know to be false. In a very real sense these are challenges for him but not for me; since I do not have the doubt or accept the statement, these will not upset me. Nevertheless, I should try to meet his challenges because by so doing I will put my claim to rationality to a more severe test. It is all too easy to rest complacent with one's convictions and to brush aside with little or no consideration the evidence against them. Taking seriously any challenge that anyone issues is one way of increasing the probability that one will not be fooled by the mere appearance of correctness. Second, why not go on claiming rationality but let others do the justifying? We all do this at times. When my statement is challenged, I sometimes say "well, there are reasons but I do not know just what they are." I say this, but only reluctantly and as a temporary expedient. One wants to engage in the process of criticism oneself because only as one hazards one's own convictions by subjecting them to that process does criticism serve to ensure their correctness. One may sit back and allow others to dig up the reasons and formulate the arguments, but only as one sooner or later rethinks one's own convictions in the light of such criticism is one likely to achieve the correctness one wants. In the end it amounts to this: one needs to justify one's statements, beliefs, attitudes, emotions, and actions because only by participating in the process of criticism can one reach the justified statements, beliefs, attitudes, emotions, and actions one needs to live the good life. Therefore, one needs to justify something when it is challenged.

Moreover, one needs to justify it only when it is actually challenged. Why only then? One might try to go on to bigger and better things; one might want to continue the process of justifying until every possible challenge has been actually met. It is possible, I think, to anticipate a challenge, to actually meet it before it is actually made. This may even be worth doing if it causes someone to withhold a challenge he was about to make. But it is a waste of time to meet challenges that no one is tempted to make simply because they are possible challenges. The whole point of justifying is to subject the claim to rationality to the test of criticism. But this claim is tested by the psychological struggle between one who is trying to defend it and one who is trying to force its withdrawal. The claim goes beyond any given psychological struggle of course, but it is actually tested only by some actual struggle between minds or within one divided mind. If it takes two to make a fight, it also takes two to constitute genuine criticism—not necessarily two people but at least a challenge as well as a response. One *can* actually respond to a merely possible challenge. But unless confronted with an actual challenger, one has no test of whether the response actually meets the challenge and, therefore, no way of determining whether the claim to rationality has or has not been successfully justified. There is simply no point in trying to continue the process of justification when there are no longer actual challenges to be met. My conclusion is that only those things that make an implicit claim to rationality stand in need of justification and that one needs to justify them when and only when this claim is actually challenged.

When justification is needed, how much is needed? When can one stop and say that one's statement, for example, has been justified? My theory clearly implies that it is enough to meet all the relevant challenges that have actually been made. Meeting a challenge is responding to it in a way that would, after indefinite criticism, cause any normal person to withdraw or withhold that challenge. When one has thus responded to all the relevant challenges that have actually been made, one has given sufficient justification.

By what test is it determined that one has really met a given challenge? I may sincerely believe that I have met some challenge when I have not, and my opponent may stoutly deny that I have met his challenge when in fact I have. Since the claim to have met a challenge is a claim that the response would cause any normal person to withdraw the challenge, the test is whether or not some particular challenger in fact withdraws his challenge. This test is not as decisive as one might wish. Only if his withdrawal would not be retracted in the light of further discussion and reflection and if all normal persons would do likewise, does it fully establish that the challenge has been met; and the failure to withdraw a challenge does not count if it arises from incompetence. In spite of these provisos, the only test of whether or not some response really does meet some challenge lies in the outcome of a psychological struggle in which the challenger is trying to cause the speaker to withdraw the claim to rationality on behalf of his statement and the speaker is trying to cause the challenger to withdraw his challenge. In this contest victory goes to the man who forces the other to withdraw in the face of the psychological pressure exerted by challenges and responses. If the challenger in fact withdraws his challenge, the speaker has really won a victory and has done all he needs to do to justify his statement.

When the challenge is withdrawn, his victory is complete. This does not imply that his victory is final. The challenge which has been withdrawn on this occasion can always be made again, either by another challenger or by the same person after he reconsiders the matter. But the fact that the claim to have met a challenge is always subject to further testing does nothing to show that it is not really tested by a single round in the contest. In fact, if no single round in the contest were really a test, then the endless series of rounds would be no test either. When a given challenger withdraws his challenge, the speaker has won this round of the struggle. If additional rounds can always subject the claim to further testing, it is for the same reason that completed rounds were genuine tests. Each round can be complete, and in that sense justification can be sufficient, even though the series of rounds is potentially infinite, and for that reason justification can never be final. Not only can the same challenge be re-issued at any time, but other challenges can always be made. There is no limit to the new challenges that can be made to any statement. In this respect, too, victory is never final. Like the claim to have reasoned validly, the claim to have met a challenge is grounded in but always goes beyond the critical contest by which it is tested.

Rules for the direction of the mind

From time to time philosophers have laid down rules intended to guide the inquirer toward justified acceptance or rejection. Probably most famous of all is the Cartesian dictum that one should doubt every proposition until it is clearly and distinctly known to be true. More recently Clifford [2] has maintained that one ought to doubt every statement until it is established as probable by scientific investigation; this is simply the old Cartesian distrust of the unproved stated in terms of a newer conception of the scientific method. On the other hand, there have been those who have proposed what might be called anti-Cartesian rules. Peirce has contended that one ought to continue believing whatever one finds oneself believing until doubt actually arises.[3] Austin has even suggested that one ought to accept any statement anyone makes unless there is some special reason to doubt it.[4] Each of these rules has been argued for in many ingenious ways, but I do not wish to examine these arguments here.

Instead, I wish to ask what these rules are designed to accomplish. They are not, I take it, primarily intended to determine our acceptance or rejection after investigation is completed; it is the business of investigation itself to discover what one is justified in accepting. One purpose of these rules is to enable one to decide what to accept or reject prior to investigation, for it seems clear that one needs something to work with if one is to discover any new truths or justify anything whatsoever. A second purpose of these rules is to fix the burden of proof within the process of investigation. The Cartesian rules imply that, while acceptance or rejection require justification, doubt requires none. The anti-Cartesian rules imply that it is doubt that stands in need of special justification.

It seems to me that the rules to which I have referred

are all inadequate on both counts. It is a mistake to place the burden of proof on acceptance, *or* rejection, *or* doubt to the exclusion of the others; none of these is more inherently justified than the other two. All three can be challenged; therefore, all stand equally in need of justification. Neither acceptance nor rejection nor doubt can be exempted from its burden of proof because all three make some claim to rationality. The truth seems to be that some burden of proof lies with anyone who makes a claim to rationality, for any such claim is open to challenge. If one party asserts something and another denies it, each is called upon to justify his own statement; it is up to the asserter to make good his assertion and up to the denier to defend his denial. And if some third party cares to challenge both statements and claim that doubt is more rational than either, then he must accept his burden of showing that his doubt is reasonable. Anyone who enters into the contest that is justifying takes upon himself a burden of proof determined by the claim he makes. The only way to escape this burden is to make no claim and to withdraw from the entire process. There is no safety in denying rather than asserting or in doubting rather than either.

Because neither acceptance nor rejection nor doubt is exempt from its burden of proof, there is no way of determining which is justified prior to the process of investigation. If the question of whether to accept or reject or doubt comes up, there is no way of settling it other than to go through the process of responding to whatever challenges raise that question. At the same time it can be added that there is no need to justify acceptance or rejection or doubt until the question does arise, until some challenge is actually made. Until challenged one may accept or reject or doubt as the spirit moves one. What one cannot do is to justify oneself by citing some general rule claiming an inherent justifiability prior to all justification. There is no justification prior to the process of justification. Fortunately, none is needed. In part, the rules I have mentioned are solutions to an unreal problem.

My theory of justification commits me to certain rules for the direction of the mind that are somewhat different from the more traditional ones. I will state them briefly with little explanation and no justification simply to illustrate my viewpoint. *1*) Accept or reject or doubt as you are inclined until you are actually challenged, but seek out challenges and challenge those with whom you disagree. In one way this rule is like the usual anti-Cartesian rules; it is conservative. It does not call for any wholesale rejection or doubting as a preliminary to serious investigation, but allows one to go on accepting what one has been accepting until challenged. However, it does not claim that acceptance is any more reasonable in itself than rejection or doubt. It does not always permit one to hold fast until there is some reason to doubt, for not all challenges are reasons. Finally, it adds a provision that was only implicit in the usual rules, that one should seek out challenges and challenge others. Although there is no need to justify until one is challenged, it is also true that the reasonable man will not evade and will even welcome challenges. *2*) Defend your claims and challenges as long as you can. Once justification is called for, one should enter into the process as fully as possible. Whether one is fighting for acceptance or rejection or doubt, one should shoulder one's burden of proof and attempt to cause one's opponents to back down by every valid argument or adequate response at one's command. No doubt one is often required to break off the contest for practical reasons, such as the lack of time or more pressing obligations, but the ideal is to carry the struggle through to a decisive conclusion. *3*) Conform your acceptance or rejection or doubt to the outcome of the process of justifying to date, but be prepared to carry the process further at any time. The process of challenge and response really settles the question of what is justified, but it settles this question only as long as no new challenges are issued.

Although these rules differ somewhat from others which have been proposed, I do not present them as exciting news. They are, I believe, the rules we all accept before, during, and after engaging in the give-and-take of justification. Still, they are worth mentioning because they make it clearer exactly what is involved in justifying and, in particular, the importance of its temporal nature as a process with a beginning, a middle, and an end. These rules may also serve as useful reminders of the mutual obligations the participants in this process have to each other arising from the claims they wish to make and defend. The only way to avoid such burdens is to withdraw from all justifying and give up the claim to rationality. That is a price too high for any reasonable man to pay.

6. infinite regresses

I have given my answer to the question "what is justification?" in terms of a challenge-response model. The philosophical importance of this model is that it implies that we should think of justifying, not so much as giving reasons, but more fundamentally as meeting challenges. This way of thinking about justification suggests, alas, that genuine justification can never take place. Since new challenges can always be made, the job of meeting challenges can never be completed. The problem posed by the challenge-response model of justification is that of halting infinite regresses in justification. Let us see how such infinite regresses arise and whether they make it impossible fully to justify any ethical statement.

It is always possible to challenge the truth of an ethical statement. Although this challenge might be met by any of several responses, the central and only fully satisfactory response is to support the original statement by giving reasons for it. This reasoning, whether it be deductive, inductive, or conductive, necessarily rests on one or more premises. As a rule, any of these premises can in turn be questioned; at this point the truth challenge is simply repeated on a new level. This new challenge requires a new response which is usually another bit of reasoning which itself rests on one or more additional premises. But this move simply provides an opportunity for continuing the game; each new premise assumed is open to question in its turn. In this way there is generated a series of reasons for reasons for reasons stretching on and on.

How far does this series of reasons extend? If every reason requires support by some prior reason, it looks as though justification could never get finished, or, to vary the metaphor, that there is no firm foundation upon which to build any ethical conclusion. There would seem to be no way to avoid this infinite regress unless sooner or later one could come to a reason that did not itself require the support of any further reason. This would be what I shall call an ultimate reason. It would be a premise to which one could appeal to justify the claim that some conclusion is true but which would not itself stand in need of any such justification. Traditionally, the rationalists have found such ultimate reasons in self-evident propositions and the empiricists in experiences.

Although rationalists and empiricists disagree about the nature and source of ultimate reasons, they agree that there are such. In fact, most philosophers have thought that there must be ultimate reasons if skepticism is to be avoided. On the other hand, the idealists and the pragmatists have argued that justification can get along without any ultimate reasons and that, in fact, there are none. Clearly we must ask whether the attempt to justify becomes an empty pretense when it does not rest on ultimate reasons.

The demand for indubitables

An ultimate reason would provide a premise from which to argue for the conclusion in question but which could not itself be questioned because it is beyond any possible truth challenge. Why is it so commonly thought that justification is genuine only if it can appeal to such ultimate reasons? Since the quest for certainty is so closely associated with the name of Descartes, let us begin by examining his arguments. *1*) Knowledge is distinguished from mere belief by its certainty. Any conclusion based upon premises that could possibly be doubted is itself subject to doubt.[1] Therefore, one can claim to know that a conclusion is true only if it is derived from indubitable premises.

This Cartesian argument appears to be impeccable provided one accepts his definition of knowledge. Knowledge, in this sense of the term, does require ultimate reasons. Unfortunately, knowledge, in this sense, is unattainable; we never can be certain. Yet it is misleading to conclude that all we can achieve is mere belief, for there still remains the distinction between rationally justified belief and unjustified credulity. If one defines knowledge in terms of rationally justified belief, then one need not embark upon the quest for certainty. One can accept the possibility of error as long as there is the probability of truth. Better a genuine probability than a precarious certainty.

However, Descartes has another argument which is not so lightly brushed aside. 2) Only indubitable premises can guarantee true conclusions. No matter how probable one's premises may be, the possibility of error remains. And false premises often lead to false conclusions. Therefore, one who reasons from probable premises is bound to reach false conclusions occasionally. Moreover, in the case of any given conclusion there is no way of knowing that this is not one of those unfortunate, if rare, occasions. Therefore, there is always reason to doubt any conclusion based upon premises that are less than indubitable.[2] And if one has reason to doubt a conclusion, one is rationally unjustified in accepting it.

I would agree with Descartes that one always has reason to doubt any conclusion derived from dubitable premises. That is, one should always accept such a conclusion tentatively and be prepared to reject it upon further investigation. Where I would not agree is in drawing the further conclusion that one is rationally unjustified in accepting any conclusion which there is reason to doubt. This step in the Cartesian argument overlooks two things. First, the mere possibility of error does not count against accepting any particular conclusion because it applies equally to every possible conclusion. Accepting any particular conclusion always involves a choice between it and a set of alternative conclusions. Therefore, any reason to accept or not to accept a given conclusion must be a reason to accept or not accept this conclusion *as opposed to* those other conclusions. Since the possibility of error constitutes a reason to doubt every alternative conclusion, it can never be a reason to reject any conclusion in particular. Although it is a genuine reason to doubt, it cancels out when the question of acceptance or rejection arises. Second, if the possibility of falsehood is a reason to doubt a conclusion, the possibility of truth is a reason not to doubt it. Since by hypothesis the premises are supposed to be probable, there is more reason not to doubt than to doubt the conclusion. It does not follow that one should believe undoubtingly, for belief and doubt are subject to degrees. The rational conclusion is that one should believe tentatively. The real lesson of this Cartesian argument is that certainty is impossible, not that belief is always unjustified.

If Descartes is the father of the demand for indubitable premises, Aristotle is its grandfather. Although his explicit discussion is put in terms of explanation, it has often been applied to justification. Where he spoke of the causes or reasons why of things, we can think of the reasons for statements instead. 3) An ethical statement can always be challenged; one can always ask why one should accept it as true. The answer to this why question is a reason for the original statement. But now one can ask why one is to accept this reason as true. Presumably the answer would consist in giving a reason for the reason. Obviously we are generating a regress of reasons for reasons for reasons. What if there is no first or ultimate reason? Then the regress is an endless one, and everyone knows that an infinite regress is philosophically intolerable. Therefore, if there are no ultimate reasons, there are really no reasons at all.

But is an infinite regress always intolerable? Aristotle seems to have distinguished between vicious and benign regresses. He accepted the view that the world is eternal and drew the conclusion that the series of events goes back infinitely in time. On the other hand, he used the first-cause argument, which presupposes that there cannot be an infinite regress of causes.[3] If the temporal regress of events is acceptable, why is an infinite regress of causes unacceptable? Well, a cause is supposed to be the reason why of something; to give the cause of something is supposed to explain why that thing is as it is. But if each answer to the question why poses a new question why, then the why of things never gets explained. Only if at some point one can give an answer to the question why that does not raise the question why once more, can one really answer the question why at all. Therefore, explanation can be genuine only if it can appeal to first causes. Analogously, if every reason which can be given in reply to the question why one should accept some conclusion as true raises a new question why, then the question why never gets answered. Only if there are ultimate reasons, reasons whose truth cannot be challenged, can the truth challenge ever really be met. Although not every infinite regress is vicious, the regress of reasons why is intolerable.

So it would seem, but it is not so. It is true that, in the absence of ultimate reasons, every reason one can give to meet the truth challenge can itself be challenged. Every answer to the question why opens the way to a new why. But notice that it is a new why! It is not a question why which remains unanswered throughout the unending regress, but a series of different questions. Although every answer makes a new why possible, it also answers the original why. In fact, this is really granted by the infinite regress argument itself, for the difficulty is supposed to emerge from the fact that there is an infinite regress of reasons. It will not do to argue that because there are so many reasons, there are really none at all.

Perhaps my point could be clarified by giving a sample conversation:

> "You ought to be ashamed of yourself!"
> "Why?"
> "Because you are a cruel man."
> "Why?"
> "Because you beat your son."
> "Why?"

This conversation is a bit stilted because of the unnatural repetition of the "why?" But with sufficient imagination, I think that we can interpret this conversation as repeating the truth challenge on level after level. Now my point is that although there appears to be a single question reappearing on level after level, actually it is a new question on each new level. Thus the first "why?" means "what evidence is there to prove that I ought to be ashamed of myself?" while the second "why?" means roughly "what evidence is there to prove that I am a cruel man?" The fact that each answer can give rise to another question does nothing to prove that it is not an answer to the quite different question to which it is a reply. For every truth challenge there is a response. That this response can itself be challenged does nothing to show that it is not a response to the original challenge. That challenge, at least, has been met. The chain of reasons is real, with or without an end.

One need not assume that every possible chain has a first link in order to avoid an endless chain of actual reasons. On the other hand, the metaphor of a chain may not be a happy one. When one is pushed hard to justify some conclusion, he does not always, or even typically, move back indefinitely from reason to reason in a straight line. More often he moves around in a circle. Thus one may justify some conclusion C by premise P, justify P by Q, Q by R, and then, before long, justify R by an appeal to C. This is particularly apt to be the case when C is challenged on one occasion and R on another. It is not so much as though one premise hangs from another like a chain; it is more as though each statement supports every other like the stones in an arch.

Arches, alas, tend to be curved. And although "mutual support" sounds very impressive, "circular argument" sounds rather less reassuring. Hence there arises another argument to show the need for ultimate reasons. *4)* If there are no ultimate reasons, then the premises from which one argues in justifying any given conclusion always remain open to challenge, either now or on another occasion. As challenge follows challenge, the arguer trying to justify all his statements will eventually be driven round in a circle so that some of the same statements will occur as both premises and conclusions in his arguments. Clearly such circular reasoning is logically fallacious. Therefore, one cannot justify all one's statements if there are no ultimate reasons.

There does seem to be something fallacious about circular arguments, but just where does the fallacy lie? It consists in arguing that C is to be accepted only because it follows from P and that P is to be accepted only because it follows from C. The mere fact that C follows from P is no justification for accepting C unless one also accepts P. Justifying a conclusion by giving reasons is more than pointing out the logical relevance of premise to conclusion; it is appealing to some premise that is accepted independently of the reasoning. Unless the reason has some weight of its own, it cannot add weight to any conclusion. Imagine trying to construct a solid arch out of perfectly weightless stones.

What this argument really proves is that reasoning is justification only if it is more than circular inference. It follows that arguing in a circle does not in itself prove anything; it does not follow that proof can never circle back upon itself. Mutual support may be logically circular, but it must be composed of statements that have some credibility quite apart from the logical circle. In the end, one does not accept a set of statements because they support one another; they support one another because, in addition to their logical relationships, one has already accepted them. Once one has accepted the statements, however, one can go on to justify any one of them by appealing to the others.

But is it enough that the premises from which one reasons be in fact accepted? Brandt has argued that mere acceptance is not enough.[4] 5) Obviously, not every premise from which a conclusion follows justifies the claim that that conclusion is true. For example, appealing to premises known to be false does nothing to show that the conclusion is true. Nor does one show that some conclusion is true by appealing to premises about whose truth or falsity he knows nothing. Only if one knows that his premises are true does he have any justification for concluding that his conclusion is true also. Therefore, merely accepted premises do not justify the claim to truth; justification must begin with premises that are known to be true themselves. This would seem to imply that there are ultimate reasons because if justification must *begin* with known premises then these premises cannot require justification by any more ultimate reasons.

This argument does drive home an important truth about justification. It is certainly not possible to justify a conclusion simply by dreaming up some premise or set of premises from which it follows. Unfortunately, I cannot justify my conclusion that society ought to support me in luxury by asserting that philosophical writings are of immense value to society and that philosophers write best when they are relieved of all economic pressures, for these assertions are at least dubious and probably false. A reason is more than a premise from which the conclusion follows. A reason justifies the claim that the conclusion is true only because it has some prior claim to truth. To lend support to a conclusion a premise must have some weight of its own.

The question remains as to exactly what is required to give any premise weight. Brandt's suggestion is that the premise must be known to be true. I hardly know what to make of this suggestion until I know how he wishes to interpret the conception of knowledge. Still, he may have shown that something beyond mere acceptance, whatever it may be, is required. We often find that other people try to justify their conclusions by appealing to premises which we know, or at least suspect, to be false. Clearly we do not think that they have justified their conclusions simply because *they* accept the premises we find unacceptable. We can even go on to imagine ourselves accepting these dubious premises, but we do not imagine that this would transform the argument into a genuine justification. The only result would be that we would be fooled by the illusory justification which now misleads those others who accept false premises. Clearly, one is not always rationally justified in accepting the statements he does accept, for these are often false; and appealing to false premises does nothing to justify the claim that the conclusion which follows from them is true.

I suspect that this sort of reasoning does not prove what it is usually thought to prove. It does not show that something more than acceptance is required to make a premise a justifying reason; what it shows is that a premise is a reason only for the person who accepts it. When I reflect upon the attempts of others to justify their conclusions by appealing to premises which they accept, I find nothing wrong in these attempts as long as I also accept their premises. But when I reject, or at least doubt, their premises, then I judge that they have not really justified their conclusions. But to whom have they not justified their conclusions? Well, obviously not to me. But this can be explained by the fact that I do not accept their premises. Now suppose that I go on to imagine myself accepting these premises. Why do I still imagine that the premises would not justify me in drawing the conclusion from them? Because I also continue to be convinced that the premises are false. What I imagine is myself accepting false premises. But this is not to accept them. This is why the argument still does not constitute a real justification for me. All that this line of reasoning shows is that an argument, no matter how logical, does not justify its conclusion for one who does not accept its premises.

If more seems to follow, it is because we think of justification in purely impersonal terms. A statement is not true for me and false for you, nor is the validity of an argument relative to the arguer. What is more, we often do make impersonal claims about whether some conclusion is really justified or whether some argument really justifies without regard for who is doing the stating or arguing. Nevertheless, these impersonal claims arise from and are justified by the activity of justifying which is carried on by individual persons. Although these products of this process are impersonal in their way, the process itself is ultimately egocentric and first-personal. It will not be easy to explain how an impersonal and objective claim can arise from a personal and relative activity of justifying. For the moment I will simply point out that I can meet the argument intended to show that more than acceptance is required if I am willing to accept this awkward relativity. What the example of others arguing from false premises shows is really that their argument constitutes a justification only for them, not for me; it does not show that their argument is not a real justification at all.

At this point another argument for ultimate reasons becomes pertinent. 6) Whatever may be thought of a possible regress of reasons for reasons, any actual reasoning must begin somewhere. Obviously we can, and should, ask of these first reasons whether we are justified in accepting them. If we are not justified in accepting our first premises, then they hardly justify us in drawing any conclusion from them. If we are justified in accepting these first premises, what is it that justifies our acceptance? If they were ultimate reasons, we could justify our acceptance on the grounds that they are beyond challenge. But without such ultimate reasons, we can say only that they have not in fact been challenged. But to claim that the mere absence of a challenge justifies one in accepting the premises as true is to assume that the fact of acceptance in itself renders these premises worthy of acceptance. As Lewis put it, our various beliefs can support one another by their logical congruence only if each is assumed to have an initial credibility prior to their mutual support.[5] The present argument is maintaining that this shows that all such justification rests upon an arbitrary assumption that whatever is credited is credible, that whatever is accepted is, to some degree at least, to be accepted. Therefore, without ultimate reasons justification would turn out to be a sham resting upon a basic postulate which is itself without any justification.

Any actual justification rests upon certain first premises, reasons for which no further reasons are given. It is quite proper to ask whether we are justified in accepting these first premises. My answer is that we are entirely justified in accepting them. But what is it that justifies our acceptance? It is the mere fact of acceptance itself. That is, we are justified in accepting these premises just because they are not challenged. Nevertheless, our acceptance is not a reason for our acceptance; the mere fact of acceptance is not at all evidence to show that what we accept is true. Acceptance does not function as a reason but as making the giving of any reason unnecessary. In the absence of any challenge, one need not give reasons to support his statements or beliefs. The fact of acceptance justifies what is accepted only in that it makes the giving of reasons unnecessary by precluding any challenge.

It is, therefore, a misunderstanding to think of the problem of the epistemologist as giving reasons for accepting those statements we find ourselves accepting without reasons. As long as they are accepted and unchallenged they need no reasons. It is a distortion of the situation to say that the fact of acceptance is a reason for judging the statements acceptable; it is not in this way that acceptance renders these statements worthy of acceptance. Nor do we need any postulate of initial credibility, any general assumption that accepted statements are more likely to be true than unaccepted ones. We do not need to postulate any presumption of truth because as long as these first premises are accepted no question of their truth can arise. If the question does arise, then we do need to give reasons for thinking these premises true. But these reasons will not consist in the mere fact of acceptance, for these premises will no longer be accepted without challenge. As long as they are unchallenged, they need no justifying reasons.

Still, it might be thought that some sort of arbitrary postulate is required. If one need not assume that the fact of acceptance is some reason to accept, one must assume that the absence of any challenge is a reason why no justification is necessary. Now my reply to the question as to why one is justified in accepting his first premises does in fact presuppose my theory of justification. But this theory is not just an arbitrary postulate to be presupposed by any and all attempts to justify. It is an epistemological account of justification. As such it can be justified in the same way that any other philosophical theory can be justified by showing how well it can explain the facts it is intended to render intelligible. I do not arbitrarily postulate a theory of justification; I argue for it in various ways. Hence my claim that accepted premises need no justification as long as they remain unchallenged is not a pure postulate. It is an assertion to be argued for or against and to be accepted or rejected on the basis of philosophical reasoning.

When any statement is challenged, its claim to truth can be justified by appealing to reasons which are in fact accepted. It begins to look as though the Idealists were right in suggesting that coherence is the only test of truth, for one justifies the claim that any given statement is true by showing that that statement coheres with other accepted statements. This suggests another argument for ultimate reasons. 7) Given a set of accepted premises, it may be possible to justify some additional statement which follows from them. On this view justifying a given statement is nothing but showing that it belongs to a system of coherent statements. Unfortunately, it is logically possible to specify an equally coherent system of statements in which the statement in question proves to be false.[6] Therefore, whether one is justified in regarding a given statement as true or as false depends upon which system of premises one chooses to begin with. And since one system is as coherent as the next, coherence gives no basis for choosing one system to another. In the end justification must rest upon a completely arbitrary choice of systems of belief. Within any given system one can justify the choice of one statement by appealing to others, but there is no justification for choosing one entire system of beliefs over another. The only way to avoid this need for choice between systems of statements would be to find certain ultimate premises which need not be chosen because they are not open to doubt.

It seems to me that this argument hinges upon two confusions. First, it confuses actual with possible acceptance. It starts with the view that one justifies a given statement by appealing to a set of accepted premises. Then it claims that one can find another set of premises from which the contrary of that statement would follow. No doubt it is true that one could think up such a set of premises. But would appealing to such a set of premises show that the original statement was unjustified? Not in the least unless this other set of premises were also accepted. Specifying a set of logically possible premises which *might* have been accepted does not directly bear on the question of justification at all. Only premises which are in fact accepted can serve as reasons in justifying. What other sets of premises are logically possible is beside the point. If the premises which are actually accepted count for a statement, then they justify that statement as long as they are accepted.

Second, the argument confuses logical alternatives with alternatives in a choice situation. The argument points out that on the coherence theory of justification, justification always takes place within a system of accepted statements. It points out that it is logically possible to specify a very different system of statements which could (logically) have been accepted instead. It goes on to suggest that therefore one must choose between these logically possible systems and that there can be no justification for such a choice of entire systems. But I do not think that the logical possibility of constructing alternative systems of statements implies that one need ever choose between such systems. No normal human being ever is faced with a choice between entire systems of beliefs. As a rule he does not choose to believe, he just finds himself believing. It may be that when he comes to question some belief, he then has to choose whether or not to continue believing it, although even here one may wonder whether the notion of choice is quite appropriate. In any event, as long as most of his beliefs remain unquestioned, he is not confronted with any choice between them and their logical contraries. In fact, the choice between entire systems of beliefs does not arise. Therefore, it is a mistake to argue that everyone has made, or will soon have to make, an arbitrary choice between systems of belief.

It must be admitted that alternative systems of belief can be specified. This does imply that it is logically possible that one might have to choose between such systems of belief. This possibility would become actual if a person found himself confronted with two systems of beliefs, none or very few of which he accepted. That is, if a person ever found himself without a large core of unquestioned convictions, then he would have to decide (in some sense) between two entire systems of statements. But in such a situation, the unfortunate person could not justify his choice of one system over the other on the basis of some arbitrary choice of premises; he would have to give up the attempt to justify altogether. What the argument really proves, therefore, is not that our attempts to justify rest on an arbitrary choice of some set of premises. What it shows is that *if* a person had to choose his premises, he could not justify any conclusions. But this does not at all show that a person who accepts a set of premises, and therefore does not have to choose them, cannot justify his conclusions.

The sufficiency of dubitables

Thus far my tactics have been purely defensive. I have been trying to refute the main arguments intended to show that justification is possible only if there are indubitable premises to which we can appeal. I do not think that it has been proved that we must have ultimate reasons, reasons which are beyond any possible truth challenge. Now I wish to take the offensive. I will try to prove that dubitable premises are sufficient, that one can genuinely justify a conclusion by appealing to reasons that could be, but have not been, challenged. As long as the first premises are actually accepted by the parties concerned, they constitute reasons that justify the conclusion in question.

1) What is it really to justify some conclusion? The place to start in trying to answer this question is with instances of what seem to be justifications. Wherever he may end, the philosopher should begin by reflecting upon those occasions when someone seems to be successful in justifying some conclusion to another or to himself. I do not go so far as to claim that these paradigm cases define the very meaning of the term "justification" so that it is impossible by definition for a philosopher to deny that these are cases of genuine justification. Still, unless the philosopher begins with some preanalytic notion of what constitutes justification, it is hard to see how his eventual definition will be more than an arbitrary stipulation. The presumption is, then, that we really do justify our conclusions on those occasions we seem most successful in doing so. Now we normally regard a person as having justified his conclusion when he supports it by appealing to generally accepted premises, whether or not these could have been challenged. If the process of appealing to dubitable but undoubted premises is usually taken to be sufficient justification, the burden of proof would seem to be on any epistemologist who would assert that real justification requires more than this.

That one ought not to require more than mere acceptance might be argued on the basis of the inevitable consequence of such a requirement. There is a thought experiment which is as illuminating as it is sobering. Reflect for a moment on all the beliefs that you hold and that you feel rationally justified in continuing to hold. Now imagine yourself justifying them one by one by appealing to unchallengeable premises. Even granted the dubious assumption that self-evident principles and reports of immediate experience are beyond challenge, it is hard to imagine oneself fully justifying even a single interesting belief. At best, one's supply of indubitable premises is too small to justify one's conclusions. Even if there are self-evident truths, these are probably limited to a relatively few universal principles. Even if reports of immediate experience are indubitable, they remain so only as long as the experience is given and very little of one's total experience is given at any one time.

This thought experiment suggests a very simple argument for saying that merely accepted premises are sufficient to justify. 2) Most of my beliefs, even those that I do not seriously doubt, cannot be justified by appealing to indubitable premises. Thus either dubitable but undoubted premises are sufficient to justify or most of my beliefs are unjustifiable. It is not true that most of my beliefs are unjustifiable. Therefore, merely accepted premises are sufficient to justify.

The crux of this argument is that, since our supply of ultimate reasons, even on the most favorable interpretation, is insufficient to justify the beliefs to which we wish to adhere, either we must give up the demand for indubitables or we must accept skepticism. For my part, I find skepticism unacceptable. I am quite willing to admit that any one of my beliefs may be mistaken, but I am not willing to conclude that most of my convictions are unjustifiable. Others, of course, may be prepared to accept skepticism as the price of indubitability. But let them beware of pushing their skepticism too far. They can hardly be justified in claiming any rational justification for a view which undermines the very possibility of justification.

Another argument for the sufficiency of merely accepted premises arises from the nature of the claim to be justified. 3) At the moment we are considering attempts to justify the claim that some conclusion is true by giving reasons to support that conclusion. Now to claim that a conclusion is true is simply to claim that it will be accepted at the end of the reasoning process. But at any given stage in the reasoning process our primary test of acceptance in the end is acceptance so far. No matter how far the reason has progressed, the claim to truth is to be measured by acceptance. If acceptance is the primary measure of the truth of the conclusion, acceptance is surely sufficient in any reason advanced to justify that claim to truth.

This argument hinges on the relation between the terms "accepted" and "acceptable." Analogous pairs of terms are "desired" and "desirable," "enjoyed" and "enjoyable," "admired" and "admirable," "believed" and "believable" (in the sense of worthy of belief). I am suggesting that "true" means "acceptable" in the sense of to be accepted or worthy of acceptance. Words like "acceptable" have critical meaning; they are used to make a claim within the process of reasoning. To say that some statement is acceptable is to claim that its acceptance will be sustained by the give-and-take of reasoning. It is to challenge all comers to reason one out of his acceptance and to serve notice that one is prepared to reason others into acceptance. To make such claims is not to predict the outcome of any finite segment of reasoning or even of the infinite process of ideal reasoning. Therefore, "acceptable" cannot be defined descriptively as "will be accepted under such and such conditions." Critical terms do not function to predict the outcome of reasoning; they function to initiate, guide, and terminate the process.

Nevertheless, at each stage of the reasoning the claim to acceptability is to be judged in terms of what is accepted. The only test of what will be accepted at the ideal limit of reasoning is what is now accepted after the reasoning to date. It is not that the fact that some statement is accepted is a reason to accept it. The reasons for acceptance are the considerations advanced within the process of reasoning itself. But whether or not the critical claim has been made good is decided at each stage of the reasoning by whether or not the statement on whose behalf it is being made is accepted so far.

Now if being accepted is decisive of the claim to truth in the end, why not in the beginning? There is, of course, a difference between mere acceptance and acceptance after critical reflection, between that which is accepted prior to challenge and that which has withstood the ordeal of challenge. But this difference is not, as Dewey seems to suggest,[7] a difference in kind; it is a difference in degree. In both cases there is acceptance to date. The premises that are accepted without reasons because they have not been challenged have withstood the test of reasoning in one sense; they have presented themselves within reasoning and were thought not to need challenge. Besides, the fact that the premises were not challenged on this occasion does not prove that they have never been challenged. Many of our accepted beliefs have arisen from past experience and have passed through the ordeal of criticism on previous occasions. After all, the process of reasoning is a lifetime one, and the reason that goes unchallenged today may not be so immune on other days. Therefore, in its way the merely accepted premise has as good a claim to truth as the rationally supported conclusion. Both have done all that any statement can do to make good its claim to be acceptable; both have been accepted in the light of all the reasoning to date. No doubt the premise is vulnerable to challenge at any moment, but so is the conclusion. No matter how far the reasoning has been carried to date, the question of acceptability can always be reopened. The merely accepted premise can serve as a sufficient reason to justify the claim to truth because in the end the only test of that claim is what is accepted in the light of the reasoning to date.

That merely accepted premises are sufficient is also indicated by the nature of justification itself. *4*) As I conceive it, justifying is the process of meeting challenges. If this conception is granted, merely accepted premises are sufficient. To accept a premise is to concede its claim to truth. Once the truth of the premise is conceded, the premise is surely a reason for the conclusion and sufficient to justify its claim to truth. Hence, to advance an accepted premise is to meet the challenge to the truth of the conclusion.

Of course, the truth of the premise can be challenged in its turn. If it is, then one must try to meet this new challenge. But this would not be to meet a challenge to an accepted premise, for at that point the premise is no longer accepted. As long as the premise is accepted there is no need to give any justification for *its* claim to truth. If justifying is meeting challenges, then no justification is needed until after a challenge has been made. Merely accepted premises, since being accepted rules out being challenged, need no justification as long as they retain their status as accepted.

There are those, however, who may still feel that one cannot afford to wait until challenged to justify his premises. If the premises are merely accepted, they are open to challenge at any time. And if they were to be challenged, can one be sure that he could really meet all challenges? Unless one can be sure now that he is in a position to meet all the challenges that could possibly arise in the future, one can hardly claim now to be in a position to know that his conclusion, which rests on these premises after all, is really justified. Hence, it appears that one cannot rest his case until all possible challenges have been met.

If one insists upon certainty, one must indeed meet all possible challenges. Just for this reason, I am prepared to give up the claim to certainty. But the claim to truth, to rational acceptance, can be justified by less than this.   5) The demand that one meet all possible challenges confuses the potential with the actual. It amounts to demanding that one actually meet all possible challenges. Why demand an actual response to a merely possible challenge? Because until one has actually responded to a challenge, one cannot be sure that one can meet it. But all that this proves is that it is always possible that one may turn out to be mistaken in the end no matter how fully one has justified his conclusions. And this is surely so. It would be no great merit in a theory of justification to rule out the possibility of error, for that possibility is always with us. Any adequate theory of justification will accept this possibility of error and show how acceptance can sometimes be justified in spite of this possibility. To do this the theory must recognize the distinction between actual challenges and responses and merely potential ones. Justification, in the only form in which it does or possibly could exist, is an actual process of challenges and responses. The claim to have justified requires that every actual challenge be met with an actual response. But this process of actual challenges and responses is only a selection from the ideal series of all possible challenges and responses. If there is some possible challenge to which there is no possible response, then in the end the attempt to justify will fail. But it does not fail until that challenge is actually made on this occasion to this speaker and the justifier finds himself unable to meet it. To demand that every possible challenge be met with an actual response is to confuse these two very different series—the series of actual challenges and responses which makes up justification as it actually exists and the series of possible challenges and responses which makes up the ideal limit of justification. The point of this conception of an ideal limit of justification is not to show that actual justification is not justification at all, but to remind us that any actual justifying could have gone on further than it did and that, therefore, the claim to truth is always open to further challenge.

One of the favorite moves of the skeptic is to describe some possible challenge and then to claim that it is impossible in principle to meet such a challenge. Does not the skeptical argument show that it is sometimes necessary to meet merely possible challenges, those the skeptic alleges could be made whether or not he himself makes them? Not at all. It is the actual challenge presented by the skeptic's argument itself and not the merely possible challenge referred to in the argument that must actually be met. The skeptic is alleging that some challenge he describes, but does not actually make, cannot, for reasons he gives, be met. The pertinent reply is not actually to meet the possible challenge the skeptic merely describes but the actual one he makes. One does this by showing either that there is no challenge of the sort alleged by the skeptic or that it can in principle be met. But describing how in principle it could be met is not meeting it; it is meeting the claim that it could not be met. Therefore, although it is true that important skeptical arguments can arise from reflection upon merely possible challenges, it is not true that to meet the skeptic's arguments one must actually meet any challenges that are not actually made. To actually justify one need meet only actual challenges.

The confusion between actual and merely possible challenges and responses arises out of the fact that we think about justification in two very different ways. Each is legitimate in its own way; what is not legitimate is muddling the two together. The notion of justification first arises out of the give-and-take of challenge and response. One person challenges the statement of another who then tries to defend it with reasons, or one person comes to doubt one of his own convictions and to resolve his doubts by pondering the evidence. In this give-and-take of discussion or thinking, every challenge and response is actual. Thought of in this way justification is something one actually does, an activity in which one engages from time to time and in which one either succeeds or fails.

But there is a very different way of thinking of justification. Instead of thinking of an activity of challenging and responding carried on by oneself or others, one can think of a timeless logical relation between a conclusion and the premises from which it follows. Thought of in this way, it is not the speaker who justifies his statements or beliefs, but the premises which justify the conclusion by their timeless truth. Whether anyone actually asserts or even thinks of the premises is now beside the point. A statement is still justified or unjustified in the light of the impersonal facts by virtue of certain purely logical relationships. Thought of in this way, the give-and-take of discussion or thinking may reveal a justification which exists independently; the discussion or thinking cannot be said to *be* the justification.

Which way of thinking about justification is to be chosen? Although each seems to be correct in its own context, I hold that the former is more basic than the latter. It is better to think of logical relationships in terms of the give-and-take of discussion and thinking than to think of discussion and thinking as revealing independently existing logical relationships. Justification does involve certain impersonal and nontemporal claims, like the claim to truth and the claim to validity. But these claims arise out of and should be explained in terms of the actual processes of challenge and response which make up discussion and critical thinking. I have tried to show how this can be done when I explained my views of reasoning and of justification.

If the reader will entertain this approach for a moment, he will provide me with another basis for arguing that merely accepted premises are sufficient to justify the claim to truth.

6) My view is that any statement constitutes a justifying reason as long as it remains unchallenged. The fact that it could be challenged does not count against it; only actual challenges need be met. I am not, of course, contending that any challenges can be ignored. As soon as a challenge is made, it must be met. All I am arguing is that one need not meet the challenge now, that one may wait until it is actually made. My view is that justification is a piecemeal process in which each challenge is to be met when, and only when, it is actually made. To reject this view seems to be to require that all challenges be met right now, that everything be justified at once. To ask this is to fail to see that justification is an essentially temporal process. Justifying is an activity which takes place in time and which takes time. By its very nature it must be done one step at a time. At each moment the task is to meet the challenges that are being made at this time. Therefore, as long as some premise remains unchallenged it need not be justified.

To be sure, what is now unchallenged may be challenged at some other time. But at that time the challenge may well be met. Would we be any better off if we could appeal to unchallengeable premises, if we did have ultimate reasons? Not really. Let us suppose that there are a sufficient number of unchallengeable truths to establish some debatable conclusions. That there are such truths is of no avail to the person now trying to justify his assertion of that conclusion unless he is now in possession of all these truths. The fact that he could discover them by a lifetime of investigation is no real help to him now. So let us suppose that the person actually possesses all these indubitable premises. Can he state them all at once to someone else who questions his assertion? Can he even think them all at once to himself? Perhaps he could do this in a few very simple cases, but in most interesting cases it would take some time to run over, in speech or thought, all the relevant premises. This means that, even if there were indubitable premises, justification would still remain a piecemeal process in which not every challenge would be met in any single moment. That only actual challenges should be met by any actual response is primarily a function of the temporal nature of justification not of the dubitability of the reasons given. The existence of ultimate reasons would limit the potential challenges, but it would not enable one to meet all possible challenges at any one moment. As long as one must accept the fact that only some challenges can be met at any given time, why not admit that premises which could be but are not challenged can serve as justifying reasons? My conclusion is that there need not be any ultimate reasons to provide any indubitable basis for justification.

Other regresses

When the truth of some statement is challenged, the most satisfactory response is to give reasons in support of the statement. But the truth of any of these reasons can in turn be challenged. The obvious response is now to give reasons in support of one's reasons. In this way there arises a regress of reasons for reasons for reasons. The problem of this chapter has been whether justification requires that in the end one be able to give ultimate reasons, reasons which could not themselves be challenged with respect to their truth. My answer has been that one need not give ultimate reasons at any stage in the process of justification, but that sometimes we are able to do so.

There are, however, other regresses that develop in the course of justification. Suppose that some statement has been made and its claim to truth supported by some argument. Now suppose that the validity of that argument is challenged. One way, although not necessarily the best way, to meet this validity challenge is to present an argument to prove that the original argument is really valid. One might argue, for example, that the original argument is an EIO syllogism in the second figure and that all such arguments are valid. But the validity of this new argument could, conceivably, be challenged. In this way there arises a regress of arguments for arguments for arguments.

Is there any limit to this regress of arguments for arguments? It is not possible to stop this series of validity challenges by giving any ultimate argument, an argument whose validity is not open to challenge. There are no ultimate arguments for the same reason that there are no ultimate statements. By its very nature a statement makes a claim to truth, and this claim is always subject to the test of further reasoning. Similarly, the claim to validity is essential to any argument, and this claim has significance only so long as it can be supported by further discussion and reflection. But as long as the claim is subject to the test of further reasoning it could always fail that test. Therefore, every argument is necessarily open to the validity challenge. Since there can be no ultimate arguments, the possibility of an infinite regress of arguments for arguments is just as real as the potential regress of reasons for reasons.

Nor are these the only infinite regresses that threaten the justification of ethical statements. Another way of meeting a challenge to the validity of an argument is to reformulate it or describe its point so that its logical force can be brought out. Such an explanation, since it is not always an argument, may be immune to the validity challenge. However, it may be unclear and may require further explanation. In this way there can arise an infinite regress of explanations of explanations. In a similar fashion, anything one might say in reply to the charge that an ethical statement is meaningless could itself be challenged as meaningless. Thus an infinite regress of attempts to meet the charge of uttering meaningless noises could arise. The attempt to justify a single ethical statement can give rise to not just one but many infinite regresses.

Fortunately, the threats posed by all of these potential regresses can be met in the same way that I have met the regress of reasons. Since all these infinite regresses are merely potential, they do not need to be actually met. Justification consists in actually meeting every challenge that is actually made. Potential regresses in any form are only potentially dangerous. All that is required for justification to be genuine is that one actually meet each regress as its potential infinity be actualized, and any actual regress will necessarily be finite. The infinite more implies only that the process of justification is never final and infallible; it does not imply that the process of justification, because it is finite, fails to justify. Justification can be and is both tentative and genuine.

CONCLUSION

My view is that to justify something is to meet every challenge actually made to it. Perhaps the greatest virtue of my conception is that it takes seriously the question it is designed to answer, "what is justification?" Too often this question is brushed aside as requiring no extensive consideration because it is simply assumed that to justify something is to give reasons for it. This tempting identification of justifying with reasoning will not do because there are challenges that cannot be met with reasoning, and those challenges that can be so met can also be met in other ways. One can sometimes meet a challenge by asking a question or looking to see or explaining an argument, for example. Defending a statement with good reasons is only one way of justifying it.

But if not all justifying is reasoning, it is still essentially tied to reasoning. What is challenged and justified is some claim to rationality; only something that makes such a claim requires or is capable of justification. Since this claim is about the outcome of reasoning, justifying is to the point only where reasoning is also to the point. Justifying is tied to, but goes beyond, reasoning.

Moreover, justifying and reasoning are analogous in their ambivalent nature. They are psychological processes that actually take place on specific occasions and have actual outcomes. Reasoning arises from the process of persuading, and justifying arises from the process of upsetting and reassuring. Yet neither is merely psychological because both are defined by critical claims about an ideal outcome determined by an indefinite amount of criticism.

One advantage of thinking of justification in this way is that it reconciles human fallibility with justifiability. Human beings are often mistaken, and there is no way completely to remove every possibility of error. Also, human beings are sometimes justified in what they say or do, although perhaps not quite so often as they take themselves to be. The philosophical problem is to explain how these two are compatible. How can a man be justified in making a statement, even be truly said to have justified his statement, when that statement may still be false? My view allows for the possibility of error by incorporating within the process of justification certain critical claims that inevitably go beyond any actual justifying and criticizing. On the other hand it explains how these claims can be tested by limited criticism. Therefore, it allows for the possibility that someone may have justified his statement even though that same statement is not justified. In this way it can admit both the possibility of error and the reality of justification.

Although I do not pretend to have given any conclusive arguments for my conception of justification, it has enough advantages so that I believe that I am justified in accepting it, at least tentatively. In an area that has for so long received less than its share of attention, it is unlikely that I have found the final answer. What is important is that the urgent need to answer the question "what is justification?" be made clear and that my proposal have that tantalizing combination of plausibility and implausibility that provokes critical discussion and further exploration.

two

HOW CAN
ETHICAL STATEMENTS
BE JUSTIFIED?

7. truth

NOW that I have explained and defended my answer to the question "what is justification?" I am prepared to tackle the other question central to this study—"how can ethical statements be justified?" On the challenge-response model of justification, to explain how ethical statements can be justified is to explain how the various challenges to which they are subject can be met. This is the purpose of Part Two of this book. I make no attempt to mention, much less discuss, every possible challenge and response. What is required to clarify the methodology of ethics is to define the dimensions of justification, the fundamentally different *sorts* of challenge and response that are possible, and to give a few examples of each to illustrate the nature of the dimension and to show how these dimensions actually structure our discussion of and reflection on live ethical issues. Since justification consists of meeting challenges, the place to begin is with a classification of those challenges that are relevant to ethical statements.

The dimensions of justification

Let us imagine that one of the ladies playing cards says emphatically "Sally was a lewd and lascivious woman." The other ladies might challenge the speaker in various ways:
1. That's false.
2. How do you know?
3. She always dressed decently.
4. It's wicked to talk that way about the dead.
5. It's impolite to talk with your mouth full.

6. It's not pronounced laskivious.

This list could be continued indefinitely, but it is long enough to illustrate one important point; the first three remarks challenge the speaker in a way that the last three do not. Given an utterance, one should distinguish between what is said and the act of saying, in this case between the statement and the stating. Now the first three challenges are relevant to the statement, while the last three are not. Only the former need to be met in order for the speaker to justify her statement, although the latter must also be met if she is to justify her act of uttering the statement on this occasion.

What is it that determines whether or not a challenge is relevant to a given statement? The crux of the difference is that the first three challenges throw doubt upon the claim to truth implicit in what the speaker said while the last three, even if conceded, leave that claim untouched. To assert that a statement is false is obviously to deny its truth. To ask the speaker how he knows that what he said is true is usually to challenge his claim to speak the truth because it is to insinuate that he may not be able to give sufficient evidence for his statement, and, if he cannot, then he cannot defend his claim to truth. "She always dressed decently" challenges the truth of the statement because it presents evidence to show that Sally might not have been as indecent as the statement implies. But to assert that it is immoral or impolite to make the statement in no way challenges the truth of what was stated; the speaker could very reply "yes, but it's true anyway." Whether or not the speaker pronounces correctly has just as little relevance to the truth of his pronouncement. All and only those challenges that must be met to defend the claim to truth are relevant to the statement on whose behalf truth is claimed. If one is concerned with the justification of something other than a statement, of course, some other set of challenges will be relevant. Since my subject is the justification of ethical statements, I shall limit my attention to those challenges that bear on the truth of such statements.

How many types of relevant challenges are there? The most obvious and direct sort of challenge to any statement is a truth challenge—that is, a challenge aimed directly at the claim to truth implicit in the statement. To assert that a statement is false or even to ask insistently for evidence that it is true is to throw doubt upon its claim to truth. Until a speaker has met this challenge, the most common of them all, he clearly has not justified his statement. To meet this challenge, however, is not to justify fully, for there are several other challenges remaining.

A more radical sort of challenge is the truth-value challenge. While the truth challenge takes it for granted that the utterance is a genuine statement and questions only its claim to truth, the true-value challenge questions the utterance's status as a statement. To show that what appears to be a statement is really a disguised exclamation or command, for example, is to rule out of court the question of truth or falsity that the truth challenge raises. Moreover, to make good the truth challenge is to show only that the statement is false, but to make good the truth-value challenge is to show that the utterance lacks both truth and falsity. Although this more radical challenge is quite distinct from the truth challenge, it is relevant to the claim to truth. Obviously no speaker can admit that his utterance is without truth-value and continue to claim truth on its behalf. Therefore, the truth-value challenge is one that must be met by anyone concerned to justify fully his statements.

A still more radical challenge is the meaningfulness challenge. Not every noise is a word and not every combination of words is really a sentence. Surprisingly, a speaker can think that he is saying something when in fact he is saying nothing at all, and hearers can be fooled by forms of expression that appear to be perfectly good English but are actually without meaning. Therefore it is possible to challenge the claim of any noisemaker to be speaking, to be uttering a significant sentence. This challenge is even more radical than the truth-value challenge, for that challenge at least conceded what this one does not, that the utterance is a part of language, perhaps an exclamation or an imperative. This challenge suggests that the noise is without this status as a unit of language. Yet clearly a speaker must meet this challenge also if he is to defend his claim to speak the truth, for he can scarcely claim to speak the truth unless he is speaking in the first place.

Although there are several ways of meeting a truth challenge, in the end it must be met with reasoning. Ultimately, the way to defend the claim to truth is by presenting arguments to prove the truth of the statement in question. But as soon as the speaker starts to argue, he opens himself to a new set of challenges to which he was immune as long as he simply asserted his conclusion dogmatically. I do not refer to the suggestion that one or more of his premises is false, without truth-value, or meaningless; these are simply the same old challenges aimed at another statement. What I have in mind is the validity challenge. Even granted its premises, not every argument is a good one. It may be that the premises advanced in support of some conclusion are really irrelevant, that they only seem to lend support to the conclusion. Hence every argument claims validity, claims implicitly that it is correct to draw the conclusion at hand from the premises advanced. To challenge the validity of an argument is quite a different thing from challenging a statement. Still, this challenge must also be met by anyone who wishes to justify fully his statements, for one must use arguments to defend his statements. One cannot afford to admit that his arguments are invalid because an invalid argument does not really prove anything about the truth of the conclusion.

Just as the truth-value challenge is more radical than the truth challenge, so the validity-value challenge is more radical than the validity challenge; the difference is that the two former are directed at statements or purported statements while the two latter are directed at arguments or purported arguments. To challenge the validity of an argument is to concede that it is an argument but to suggest that it is an invalid one. To challenge the validity-value of a purported argument is to suggest that what appears to be an argument is not really an argument at all, that the bit of language is misinterpreted when it is thought of as claiming to support a conclusion with relevant considerations. Just as an apparent statement might turn out to be a disguised exclamation or imperative, so a piece of language that has the grammatical form of an argument might really be something quite different, perhaps a sermon or a poem. This validity-value challenge is far removed from the truth challenge, but it still must be met by anyone intent on establishing the truth of what he says, for eventually he will need to argue for his statement to prove it true, and he cannot admit that he is not really arguing while claiming that his arguments really do prove his conclusion.

The sixth sort of challenge, the competence challenge, is more personal than the others, for it challenges the competence of the speaker to assert or defend his utterance. At first glance this challenge would appear to be strictly irrelevant to the claim to truth, for surely the speaker could reply "yes, but what I say is true anyway." A person with no evidence to support his statement may make a lucky guess, and a drunken man may speak the truth upon occasion. To show that the speaker is incompetent is not to show that what he says is false. Still, it remains true that the speaker who wishes to justify his statements cannot admit his incompetence. A speaker may happen to speak the truth when he has no supporting evidence, but he can hardly defend his claim to have spoken truly if he has no evidence he can produce to prove his assertion. And if a speaker is judged incompetent to reason, then nothing he says need be taken as reasoning in support of his claim to speak the truth. Therefore, the competence challenge is, in a roundabout way, relevant to the claim to truth. Although an incompetent person may speak the truth occasionally, only a competent one can justify his claim to have spoken truly.

Finally, to turn from the speaker to what he has said once more, it is possible to challenge the knowability of a statement. In a way this is the weakest of the challenges that can be directed at a statement. It concedes that the utterance is meaningful, that it is a genuine statement, and that it might even be true. What it suggests is that no one can be in a position to know whether it is true or not. Although this knowability challenge admits that the statement might be true, although it admits the possibility of truth, it cannot be conceded by anyone who wishes to justify his claim to speak the truth. This is because to suggest that the statement is unknowable is to imply that all speakers are incompetent to know it. Therefore, to admit the unknowability of a statement is to admit one's own incompetence. Since no speaker can afford to concede his own incompetence, it follows that the knowability challenge must be met in order to justify completely the claim to truth.

How many fundamentally different kinds of challenge might a speaker be called upon to meet in order to justify fully his claim to speak the truth? I have been able to think of only seven—truth challenges, truth-value challenges, meaningfulness challenges, validity challenges, validity-value challenges, competence challenges, and knowability challenges. Each of these defines a dimension of justification, a whole set of possible challenges and responses with a common orientation. It is of some importance to distinguish these dimensions carefully, for to place some challenge on the wrong dimension is to misunderstand the nature of the challenge and to invite an inappropriate response. Therefore, I will discuss each dimension separately, beginning with truth challenges and responses.

Truth challenges

What is challenged by a truth challenge and what one is defending when one responds to such a challenge is the claim to truth implicit in the statement to be justified. Just what is this claim to truth? One could call it the claim to objective correctness, but this would explain little because the notion of correctness is as obscure as that of truth. I prefer to say that it is one form of the claim to rationality. To claim that a statement is true is to claim that the reasons that could be given for it outweigh whatever reasons could be given against it; the claim to truth is the critical claim that an indefinite amount of reasoning would support that for which the claim is made. This claim is clearly one to be made good, or to be shown mistaken, by the process of reasoning itself. More important, it is a claim that can be understood only in the context of the process of reasoning. The very word "true" loses its meaning when one tries to interpret it apart from the activity of giving reasons for and against that to which it is applied, for it makes a claim about the outcome of this process of giving reasons.

Recall the lady who asserted, seriously and with some

conviction, "Sally was a lewd and lascivious woman." There are several different ways in which the truth of this allegation could be challenged. The most obvious way is *1*) to deny its truth. If someone were to reply by saying "That's false" or "She was not," he would clearly be denying the claim to truth implicit in the original statement. But one need not go so far as this to throw doubt upon its truth. One could simply *2*) question its truth. One might ask "Are you sure?" or "What reason do you have to think that?" The obvious tactical advantage of this form of the truth challenge is that it does not commit the challenger to defending some counterassertion. It must not be assumed, however, that questions, at least in the context of justification, stand in need of no defense at all; there is a distinction between reasonable and unreasonable doubts. Another form of the truth challenge is *3*) to argue against the statement made. Some hearer could reply "Sally always dressed decently" or "She was brought up in Boston." These replies are evidence against the original statement; they are reasons, not conclusive to be sure, to reject its claim to truth. I do not pretend to have given a complete list of truth challenges. The point I do wish to make is that there are several different ways in which the truth of a statement can be challenged.

I have illustrated the various forms of the truth challenge by an imaginary situation in which a speaker is challenged by one of his audience, and the very word "challenge" immediately suggests such interpersonal situations. I welcome this suggestion and believe that the nature of justification is much clearer if one thinks first of one person trying to justify some statement to another. Such interpersonal justifications are clearer because it is easier to observe what people say to each other than what is going on in one's mind and because the process of justifying gets expressed in language more completely when it takes the form of public conversation. In the end, however, justification is a private thing. One often justifies to oneself, and conversation constitutes justification only when each person is thinking as well as speaking. Although I am happy to have the notion of a challenge suggest first of all public conversations, I do wish to claim that it need not be public. A person can challenge his own statements. A person may doubt what he said and come to the conclusion that it was false. In this way truth challenges may be made by the speaker himself, whether or not uttered audibly, as well as by his audience.

Meeting a truth challenge

Assuming that the truth of some statement has been challenged, either by the speaker himself or one of his hearers, how can the speaker, or anyone else, meet such a challenge? Clearly, the kind of response that is appropriate will depend upon the way in which the challenge was made. Suppose that someone denied the truth of the original statement. What kinds of response would meet this form of the truth challenge? The most obvious response would be to give reasons for the original statement. The arguments advanced to defend the statement might be deductive, inductive, or conductive depending on the statement being defended; the varieties of ethical reasoning have been discussed at length in the first part of this book. Other responses are possible, however. One might try to throw the burden of proof on the challenger by asking him what reason he has to deny the original statement; if he cannot support his denial with evidence, he may be forced to withdraw his challenge. The speaker might ask the challenger to assert some alternative statement. To deny that a given statement is true is to imply that one of its contraries is true instead. However dubious the original statement may be, the contraries may turn out to be even more questionable. To get the challenger to commit himself to some alternative statement is to make him vulnerable to attack and may be the first step in getting him to withdraw his challenge.

Enough has been said to drive home two important lessons. First, there are several different ways in which the truth of an ethical statement can be challenged and several possible responses to any truth challenge. Second, the kind of response that will meet any truth challenge depends upon the way in which the challenge is made. The process of justification has begun to reveal something of its complexity. This is, I fear, only a hint of the complications to come. As each new kind of challenge is brought in, each with its several ways of being made, justification becomes more and more complex. But this complexity of challenges and responses need not obscure the conception of justification it illustrates. The way to justify any ethical statement is to meet whatever challenges are made to it.

Ethics as illusion

The challenges and responses discussed in the last two sections were thought of as aimed at this or that statement, whether ethical or nonethical; and it is normally the truth of individual statements that we discuss. But philosophers love to generalize, and one might expect someone to challenge statements wholesale. To assert that all statements are false would seem to be self-defeating, if not meaningless, and it is hard to see on what grounds one could even doubt that any statements at all are true. But to assert that all ethical statements are false, since such a statement is not itself ethical, would seem to be more tempting. In fact, Mackie has asserted just this.[1] Let us see whether this wholesale challenge to the truth of ethical statements can be sustained.

One hopes that it cannot, for it would have awkward consequences for the logic of ethics. If all ethical statements are false, then statements that appear to be logical contradictories, like "all pleasures are good" and "some pleasures are not good," turn out not to be contradictory in the logical sense. In fact, it becomes impossible to contradict any ethical statement at all. If some moral reformer announces that breathing air is wrong, I cannot contradict him by saying "breathing air is not wrong," for my assertion is as false as his. This is surely peculiar. Any theory that thus flies in the face of appearances should be avoided if at all possible.

Fortunately Mackie's conclusion can be avoided, for the arguments he gives for it are hardly sufficient. His first, and most general, argument can be put quite simply. Moral statements assert the existence of moral facts, but there are no moral facts; therefore, all moral statements are false. The logic of this argument is impeccable and the second premise seems to me to be true. The first premise, however, is more debatable. Mackie accepts this premise because he accepts the nonnaturalistic analysis of ethical statements. To say that something is good is to say that it possesses the nonnatural property of goodness, and to say that an act is right is to assert that the act has the property of rightness. Therefore, all such statements assert the existence of nonnatural qualities and relations inhering in objects or acts. Although no such entities exist, we mean to assert their existence whenever we make an ethical statement. This is why all ethical statements are false.

Mackie's mistake is to accept the intuitionist's analysis of the meaning of ethical statements. Why did he think that he had to accept this analysis? Because he saw that ethical statements claim objective validity. Surely to claim objectivity is to claim that one's statement corresponds with objective fact. Perhaps, but even this does not require one to postulate moral facts; it is nonmoral facts that establish moral conclusions. For example, the fact that someone is in pain is a reason to conclude that I ought to help him and the fact that he is kind is a reason to conclude that he is morally good.

The world is real enough, but there is nothing in the world that is specifically ethical. What exists is one thing; what would be good if it existed is another. Not everything that ought to be done is done, and actions have no reality unless they are actually done. Must I, since I deny that there is any specifically ethical reality, concede that ethical statements are without truth? I do not think so. All that is required for the objective validity of ethical statements is the possibility of giving reasons for and against them. Ethical statements can continue to claim truth as long as there is a process of ethical reasoning by which this claim can be tested. To be sure, the regress of reasons ultimately terminates in experience. And since we are aware of reality through our experience, ethical statements, at least those that are not a priori, are ultimately grounded in reality. But this reality and our experience of it need not be specifically ethical. What we are aware of is reality as it is, not as it should be. From our knowledge of reality as it is we then infer what reality should be and what we should do. Because ethical statements can be supported or attacked by such reasoning, they are really true or false.

As far as I can see there are two main arguments against my contention that the truth or falsity of ethical statements can be grounded by reasoning from nonethical facts. The first hinges on the correspondence theory of truth. If there are no ethical facts, there is nothing in reality with which ethical sentences may correspond or fail to correspond. But truth consists in correspondence with reality. Therefore, if there are no ethical facts, no ethical sentences can ever be true. The difficulty with this argument is the notion of correspondence. If correspondence is thought of as resemblance or fitting, then the conclusion seems to follow from the premises. However, I would deny this version of the correspondence theory of truth; in no literal sense does a true sentence resemble or even fit the facts. Actually, correspondence consists in the relation of being a reason for. A sentence corresponds with a fact when that fact is a reason for the sentence; it fails to correspond when the fact is a reason against the sentence. If correspondence is thought of in this way, there is no need for the fact to be similar to the truth it establishes. Hence, there is then no reason to assume that an ethical sentence can correspond only with an ethical fact. Nonethical facts may well be reasons for or against ethical conclusions.

Here we arrive at the second argument against my contention. It is alleged that nonethical facts by themselves could not possibly be reasons for or against an ethical conclusion. Any valid reasoning to an ethical conclusion must have at least one ethical premise. This is because there can be nothing in the conclusion of a valid argument that is not contained implicitly in the premises. Why not? Because reasoning is thought to be nothing but making explicit what is already in the premises. If induction and conduction are really reasoning, as I have already argued, the conclusion of a valid argument can go beyond its premises. If I am correct in claiming that conduction is a valid form of reasoning, then ethical conclusions can be grounded in nonethical premises. Therefore, the denial of any specifically ethical facts in reality does not imply that ethical statements are without truth.

Mackie's other argument applies only to statements that express judgments of obligation. Obligation statements imply both determinism and indeterminism, but either determinism or indeterminism must be false; therefore, all obligation statements must be false. Again, there is no logical error in the argument. One might try to avoid the second premise by arguing that obligation statements imply determinism and indeterminism in different respects and that partial determinism is quite compatible with partial indeterminism. Mackie has anticipated this objection and argues that both determinism and indeterminism must apply at the same point if obligation is to be genuine. Unless character determines action, one cannot say that the *agent* ought to do the act, but one cannot say that the agent ought to do the *act*, unless it is free and not determined by his character. My own objections center on the other premise in the argument. First, I would agree that ought implies can. This seems to imply that freedom, in some sense, is presupposed by the existence of genuine obligation. I do not believe, however, that the sort of freedom required is indeterminism. I am not at all sure just what is required, but an element of chance in the universe really adds nothing to my freedom. Second, the sense in which ought implies can is not that required for Mackie's argument. He takes it for granted that the implication is logical, that the truth of ought statements logically presupposes the truth of can statements. But Strawson and others have shown that there are other kinds of presuppositions besides the logical. In the next chapter I will argue that can is a truth-value presupposition of ought. This means that when we say that someone ought to do an act, we presuppose that he can do it in the sense that, if he cannot, we regard our utterance as neither true nor false. Judgments of obligation are appropriate to the area of free action only; where there is no freedom, obligation statements are not so much false as inapplicable or beside the point. Therefore, if Mackie's argument really proves anything, it proves that what seem to be obligation statements are not really statements at all, that they are neither true nor false. This is quite a different conclusion from the one he tries to draw from the principle that ought implies can.

My conclusion is that Mackie has not proved his case. Nor do I know of any better arguments that can be advanced to prove that all ethical statements are false. If ethical statements are really statements, a point that can be argued at much greater length, then some of them are true and some are false. Thus they obey the same logic of contraries and contradictories as any other statements. While many ethical statements are false, their denials are true. Which is which is not easy to tell. This is why justification is so necessary when one would claim truth for one of his ethical statements. But at least one challenge can safely be ignored, the challenge that this statement must be false because all ethical statements are false. Such a universal challenge of ethical statements cannot be made good.

CONCLUSION

Since justification is meeting challenges, there are as many dimensions to justification as there are possible kinds of challenge. One kind of challenge to any ethical statement is the challenge to the claim to truth implicit in it. Although this challenge can be made in several different ways, there are a variety of possible responses to meet any such challenge. To meet truth challenges is not always easy, and sometimes it is impossible. In those cases where it cannot be done, the ethical statement cannot be justified because it is false. However, I see no reason to think that it is always impossible in principle and that all ethical statements are false. Some of them, at least the ones I make, are true. Hence the way to justify an ethical statement along the truth dimension is to meet piecemeal and individually whatever truth challenges may be made. Given time and imagination (and evidence) that can be done in the case of every true statement, and clearly there is no need to go on to explain how false statements can also be justified.

8. truth-value

THE truth-value of an utterance can be challenged in a variety of ways. Let us begin by noting a few of the ways in which this challenge can be verbalized.

It's all a matter of taste.

That's just the way you feel.

Aren't you simply expressing your emotions?

Show me that you are making a genuine statement!

That has no cognitive meaning.

That has no objective validity.

That's unverifiable.

It's all relative.

One is to imagine that in the last example the ambiguous term "relative" is used in the sense that rules out objective validity.

Some of these formulas are typically philosophical. One does not expect the man in the street to talk about cognitive meaning or even objective validity very often. But other forms of expression are of the sort that often occur in nontechnical discourse. The notion that rational dispute is quite beside the point in matters of taste is common property, and people say things like "that's just the way you feel" before they have been corrupted by any study of philosophy. The fact that we can easily imagine contexts for these sample remarks suggests that the truth-value challenge is not unknown and may even occur frequently. I wish to emphasize the fact that, although my terminology is new, I am not just dreaming up a barely conceivable challenge; I am here concerned with an important challenge that is often made.

To have truth-value is to be either true or false. Some utterances have truth-value and some do not. Since it is part of the meaning of any statement to make an implicit claim to truth that either is or is not justified, every statement is either true or false. Exclamations and imperatives, on the other hand, lack truth-value because they make no such claim. If it were always obvious whether an utterance made an implicit claim to truth, there might be no occasion for the truth-value challenge. But a statement can take the form of an exclamation; "wicked man!" might mean to assert that the indicated man is wicked even when uttered in an emotionally charged tone of voice. And "I want you to open the window," in spite of its indicative grammatical form, may have directive meaning rather than, or in addition to, its descriptive assertion about the speaker's psychological state. Hence, it is quite possible for an utterance to be taken for a statement when it is not or thought not to be a statement when in fact it is. For this reason it is quite in order to challenge any apparent or purported statement to show that it is a genuine statement, that it really does have a truth-value.

The truth-value challenge is more radical than the truth challenge. To challenge the truth of an utterance is to concede its status as a statement and to suggest only that it may be a false statement, but to challenge the truth-value of an utterance is to suggest that it may not be a statement at all because it may be neither true nor false. If this challenge can be sustained, it removes the utterance from the sphere of reasoned support or attack. Where the question of truth or falsity cannot arise, it is quite beside the point to try to give reasons to prove the utterance true. Therefore, any speaker concerned to justify the truth of his statement must meet any challenge to its truth-value, for one can hardly continue to claim truth for an utterance admitted to be neither true nor false.

Unverifiability

Logical positivists have sometimes maintained that ethical sentences are literally meaningless or mere nonsense. They are not challenging the right of ethical sentences to be taken as a significant form of discourse, but only the claim of such sentences to be statements. Like exclamations and imperatives, both respectable kinds of ordinary language, ethical sentences are said to be neither true nor false. Thus the logical positivist is really issuing a challenge to the truth-value of ethical utterances.

This challenge rests upon what is often thought of as a principle of meaningfulness, but which might better be thought of as a principle of having truth-value: a sentence has cognitive meaning (i.e., truth-value) if and only if it is either analytic or empirically verifiable. Is this principle to be accepted? It is not plausible, I believe, unless one takes it for granted that there are only two ways of establishing the truth of any statement, the analysis of its terms and checking it against experience. If I am correct about the validity of thought experiments, there is at least one method of establishing a priori truths besides analysis. On this basis alone I could dismiss the positivistic principle that only analytic or empirically verifiable sentences have truth-value.

But to dismiss positivism so soon would be to miss the very important truth implicit in it. Let us reformulate its central principle in this way: a sentence has truth-value if and only if it is verifiable. In this reformulation, the term "verifiable" is used in a very wide sense in which to be verifiable means to be capable in principle of being shown to be true or probably true by some sort of valid reasoning. It is not required that verification be completed or even possible in practice, but only that it be logically possible to give some sort of evidence for the truth of the sentence. Thus reformulated, I believe that the principle is correct. The claim to truth is the claim that acceptance will be sustained by the process of reasoning, that the reasons that can be given for the sentence outweigh those that can be given against it. Where there could be no such reasons, there can be no process of reasoning to test the claim to truth and the claim loses all significance. And where the claim to truth becomes empty, there is no truth-value. Therefore, ethical sentences have truth-value only if they are verifiable in this wide sense.

Is there any possible way of verifying ethical sentences? Well, sentences like "all good things are good" and "one ought always to do his duty" certainly seem to be analytic. Since their truth can be established by analysis, they clearly have truth-value. Even Ayer admits the possibility of a philosophical ethics consisting of analyses of ethical words.[1] Probably he does not regard this admission as qualifying his challenge to ethical sentences, however, because he believes that their tautologous nature robs them of any normative content. It is not clear whether he is correct until he gives us some clearer explanation of what he means by "normative content" and proves that tautologies are empty. Notice that he still calls the set of these analytic truths "philosophical ethics," indicating that he considers them to have some ethical import. For my part, I do not see why these should not be considered ethical sentences, but I shall not insist on this classification because most ethical sentences are not analytic.

The real challenge of positivism is directed at synthetic ethical sentences. These are declared to be without truth-value on the grounds that they are not *empirically* verifiable. Here verification is conceived of narrowly as checking the sentence or its implications against experience. Since synthetic ethical sentences neither describe present experience nor imply any predications about the nature of future experience, they are unverifiable and, therefore, without truth-value. Can this truth-value challenge be met?

That ethical sentences are empirically unverifiable is often taken as too obvious to require any extended argument. Sociological studies of the incidence of stealing are completely irrelevant to whether people ought to steal. What experiment could one perform to test the assertion that personality is precious? Clearly observation and experiment are irrelevant to ethical issues. On the other hand, it is often maintained that ethical words can be defined in terms of empirical characteristics. If ethical naturalism is correct, then ethical statements do describe experience. It would follow that they are empirically verifiable in a straightforward manner.

To my mind the claim that ethical sentences are not empirically verifiable is neither to be conceded without question nor rejected out of hand. Admittedly the fact that people do steal is irrelevant to whether people ought to steal, but it does not follow that all other facts are equally irrelevant. Granted that crucial experiments are hard to come by in ethics, it does not follow that experimentation is entirely out of place. We sometimes do appeal to observation or experiment to establish some ethical statement, some statement expressing a judgment of value or obligation. We test the assertion that roses always smell good by systematic sniffing, and we test the claim that castor oil tastes bad by trying some. Although these mundane judgments of smell and taste are not specifically moral, they are samples of value judgments. If they are empirically verifiable, then one cannot reject all evaluations as empirically unverifiable. Nevertheless, to explain how they are verifiable by defining ethical words in terms of experience is too simple a solution. Since I have argued against ethical naturalism at length elsewhere,[2] I will not repeat myself here. Let me just record my conclusion that ethical sentences do not describe experience. Hence, if they are empirically verifiable, it must be in some way other than that envisaged by the naturalist.

I believe that some, certainly not all, ethical statements are empirically verifiable even when verification is thought of as narrowly as the positivist does. The statement that some given experience like that of sipping this glass of sherry is or is not intrinsically good is verified or falsified by direct confrontation with the experience to which it refers. Some other evaluations can be verified or falsified by checking their consequences against experience. As an example, let us take the statement that *The Spy in the Sky* is a good book. If I care to do so, I can test the truth of this assertion by reading the book for myself. My experience of reading through the volume serves to confirm or disconfirm the reviewer's statement. Here is one value judgment that is empirically verifiable in much the same way that a factual judgment would be verified.

In spite of appearances, many will argue that the reviewer's evaluation is not really verified or falsified by my experience. Several arguments deserve some consideration. *1)* The sentence "*The Spy in the Sky* is a good book" cannot be directly verified. That is, one cannot look at the cover of the book, or even all its pages, and see its goodness as a book there. There is no single experience that will reveal what the evaluation asserts in the way that a single experience might reveal the color or the shape of the book. I would agree that the statement in question can only be indirectly verified. One tests its truth, not by direct confrontation with experience, but by inferring its consequences and confronting them with experience. But I doubt whether anyone would still restrict empirical verification to direct confrontation. Long ago positivists realized that indirect verification is both scientifically necessary and philosophically respectable.

2) Another difficulty is that "*The Spy in the Sky* is a good book" cannot be conclusively verified. Suppose I read the book and have a thoroughly unsatisfactory experience. This may indicate that I was too tired, in a bad mood, or just not open to that sort of book rather than that the book is bad. And if I like my reading experience, this may indicate that I am uncritical rather than that the book is good. Still, this inconclusiveness of any empirical test is just as characteristic of factual as of ethical statements. Conclusive verification is not required for having truth-value; all that is necessary is that experiences add to or subtract from the probability of the statement being tested.

No matter how inconclusive and indirect verification may be, a statement is empirically verifiable only if it implies something about present or future experience. 3) But "*The Spy in the Sky* is a good book" when taken alone implies nothing about experience. It does not imply that I will enjoy reading it unless we also assume that I like spy stories; it does not imply that I will laugh at it unless we also assume that I have a sense of humor. Only when the value statement is taken together with various other statements can one make any predication about the kind of experience that will ensue. Even so, this is as true of factual statements as of evaluations. Quine and others have rightly emphasized the fact that verification involves systems of beliefs rather than isolated statements. If the need for additional assumptions undermines the validity of verification, all of science is unverifiable. In this respect ethics and science seem to be on a par.

Some would argue that there is a difference, however. 4) When we examine the logic of the situation carefully we are supposed to discover that evaluations, unlike factual statements, play no essential role in the derivation of empirical consequences from a set of statements. To say that some statement plays no essential role in a derivation is to say that the same conclusion could have been drawn from the other premises without this one. If so, finding the conclusion true does nothing to verify the unused and superfluous premise. Let us grant that "*The Spy in the Sky* is a good book" does not by itself imply "Wellman will enjoy reading it." Now we try to remedy this difficulty by adding the assumptions that Wellman enjoys spy stories and that this is a spy story. Fine, we can readily derive the empirical prediction from the total set of statements. Unfortunately, we can just as easily derive it from the two factual asumptions without using the value statement at all. Therefore, finding the consequence true does nothing to show that the evaluation is also true.

In this particular case I would admit that the value judgment is not verified by my experience of enjoyment, but I doubt whether this case is typical. For one thing, is it plausible to asume that Wellman enjoys all spy stories, even the worst? Perhaps our additional asumption should be that Wellman enjoys good spy stories. If so, we would need the value statement that "*The Spy in the Sky* is a good book" to derive the prediction that Wellman will enjoy this spy story. In that case the evaluation would function essentially in the inference and would be verified by the experience of enjoyment. For another thing, there might be other consequences that could be drawn from the evaluation plus additional assumptions that could not be drawn without it. For example, we might infer that the experience of reading the book will be a good one from the value statement but not be able to infer this evaluative consequence from the set of factual assumptions alone. In this case also the evaluation would function essentially in any verification. Therefore, I do not believe that evaluation always functions vacuously in drawing empirical consequences from a set of assumed premises.

The last example requires further scrutiny. "*The Spy in the Sky* is a good book" together with certain assumptions about Wellman's competence as a reader implies that Wellman's experience of reading the book will be a good one. My suggestion is that the evaluation of the book is indirectly verified by the evaluation of Wellman's experience of reading it and that this evaluation in turn is verified by confronting it with the experience to which it refers. 5) It can be argued that the confrontation of an evaluation with the experience it evaluates is no real test of the truth or falsity of that evaluation because experience reveals no value characteristics. Goodness and badness are not given in experience the way that redness and sourness are. Therefore, what one finds in a given experience can never establish the truth or falsity of any evaluation of that experience. Now I agree that value and disvalue are not empirical characteristics in quite the way that sweetness and loudness are; we do not find any identifiable qualities or relations of goodness or badness in our experiences. But I do not concede that experiences are incapable of establishing or refuting evaluations of them. Such a denial seems to rest on the assumption that the confrontation between an experience and a statement about that experience is a test of truth only when the content of the experience corresponds to the content of the statement. If "corresponds" means "serves as evidence for," then the assumption is true by definition. But if "corresponds" means "is similar to" or even "is described by," then it is false. The taste of a cake is a direct confirmation of the statement "this taste of the cake is good," even though that statement does not describe any characteristic found in the experience of tasting. I appeal to the taste as a reason for my evaluation just as I would appeal to it as evidence for my statement that the taste is sweet.

6) Ethics seems to differ from science in that neither novelty nor controllability are essential to it. A scientific experiment is usually an attempt to construct a new experience, one that needs to be deliberately produced because it does not come along by itself. And ideally the experiment should be constructed in such a way that the variables are controlled so that one can know which variable is operating in any given situation. Observation in the field has similar characteristics. One goes into the field in order to extend the usual range of experience and have experiences that might not come to one

in the usual course of events. Although the events observed are not controlled as a rule, the observation is controlled in that certain procedures of selection and recording are carefully followed and the report is put into terms that allow the observations to be duplicated and checked by others. These characteristics of novelty and control do not seem typical of the verification of evaluations. To discover that pains are bad or that roses smell good one does not need to construct laboratory equipment or go very far into the field. Many evaluations are verified by everyday experience. Moreover, the element of control is usually not in evidence. Still, I would probably discount any smelling of roses I did in hay fever season, and I would have to extend my normal range of experience to test the assertion that fried snails are good. Perhaps some element of novelty and control are present even in ethics. In any event, neither novelty nor control are essential to verification. Although they extend the range of the verifiable and the precision of the verification, neither is logically required for the validity of verification.

It might be thought that control, at least, is essential for verification. Without controls verification loses its publicity; that is, it cannot be duplicated by others with the same results. Here, it is often argued, is the crucial difference between scientific verification and the appeal to experience to decide questions of value.   7) Whatever the logic of the situation, in practice observation and experiment settle scientific questions but leave ethical issues unsettled. Perhaps one should be able to decide whether *The Spy in the Sky* is a good book by reading it, but one cannot. Two people can each read the book carefully and come to quite different conclusions about its value. Thus even such simple cases of evaluation are not subject to empirical decision. The appeal to experience may be a decision procedure in science, but in ethics it decides nothing. This argument is a basic one because it raises the question of the relation between intersubjective agreement and objective validity. My answer to this question depends upon my conceptions of truth and validity. To claim that a statement is true is to claim that the reasons for it outweigh the reasons against it; to claim that an argument is valid is to claim that it would be persuasive after indefinite criticism. Both "true" and "valid" derive their meaning from an open-ended process of criticism. Therefore, the objectivity of these claims does not depend upon any actual agreement reached at any given time; all that is required is that the process of criticism lead to agreement at the ideal limit. We need not deny that the acceptance of a value judgment on the basis of the experience evaluated is valid reasoning simply because in actual practice considerable disagreement exists. In the end, this objection is no more conclusive than the others. I conclude that some ethical statements are empirically verifiable even in the fairly narrow sense envisaged by the positivist. Even here this truth-value challenge cannot be sustained.

If we return to verification in the wider sense in which it covers any way of establishing the truth of a conclusion by reasoning, we find another sort of empirical verification for ethical statements—conduction. Conductive arguments typically move from factual premises to ethical conclusions. Since these factual premises are in turn shown to be true or false by an appeal to experience, the ethical conclusions are grounded in and tested by experience. Thus the statement "John is a wicked man" is shown to be true or false by the facts established by observation of John's behavior under a variety of circumstances, and "you ought to enlist in the army today" is to be defended or attacked by appealing to empirical information. Conductive reasoning often constitutes a form of empirical verification overlooked by the positivist.

What, then, are we to say about the truth-value challenge to ethical statements on the grounds that they are unverifiable? We should admit that a sentence can have truth-value only if it is verifiable in the wide sense; this is the real insight in the challenge of positivism to ethics. But perhaps some ethical statements are analytic truths and surely some others are empirically verifiable even in the narrow sense admitted by the positivist. Moreover, it is a mistake to imagine that the only methods of verification are analysis of the terms used, inductive reasoning, and the direct confrontation of an empirical description with the experience it describes. In addition, the truth of a statement may be established by nonempirical induction and by conductive argument. Ethical sentences are verifiable in a variety of ways and, therefore, have truth-value.

Statements and pseudostatements

The truth-value challenge can be made wholesale or retail as it were. Philosophers typically challenge a whole class of utterances. Some logical positivists have charged that all normative ethical sentences are cognitively meaningless. A determinist might claim that no ought sentence has truth-value because obligation presupposes an ability to do otherwise ruled out by the fact of universal causation.

Ethical sentences appear to be genuine statements. Grammatically, they are in the indicative mood. We ordinarily speak of them as "true" or "false." In ethical disagreements we seem to be disagreeing about which ethical conviction is true. In trying to decide which statement to accept, the individual usually thinks of himself as seeking evidence for or against the truth of some tempting conclusion. And if he comes to change his mind about which ethical sentence to accept, he concludes that his former opinion must have been mistaken. These appearances themselves are seldom denied. However, it is sometimes alleged that they are deceiving. It is then asserted that ethical sentences are only pseudostatements, that they really have no truth-value. I have examined and rejected the most popular line of argument used to challenge the truth-value of ethical sentences.

Unless other evidence is forthcoming, the reasonable conclusion is that ethical sentences are what they seem to be. Simply to save the appearances, if for no other reason, the philosopher should grant that ethical statements have truth-value. So what? Stevenson now grants that ethical sentences are true or false but insists that nothing follows from this about the rational justifiability of such sentences.[3] He seems to think that he can abandon his truth-value challenge without giving up anything essential to his emotive theory of ethics. And he could do this *if* he were correct in his interpretation of the meaning of the words "true" and "false." In his interpretation these words simply reiterate, and possibly emphasize, any indicative sentence to which they are applied. In my own interpretation, these words function to claim rationality. If I am right, Stevenson cannot concede that ethical sentences are true or false without also granting that they have a genuine claim to rational justifiability. This is why it is so important to meet any truth-value challenge in ethics.

If no wholesale challenge to the truth-value of ethical statements as such can be substantiated, not all ethical sentences are pseudostatements. It does not follow, however, that none of them are. In particular cases, an utterance that appears to be an ethical statement may turn out to be neither true nor false. These cases seem to fall into two large classes.

The first class of cases are what might be called counterfeit ethical statements. Here a form of words typically used to make an ethical statement is used with a meaning that is quite different. These utterances are perfectly good bits of language, but not the kind of language they seem to be. "That was a wicked thing to do" looks and sounds like a statement of moral disvalue, but on some occasions it might be simply an expression of the speaker's disgust or even anger. If a fellow says "I really ought to be going now," his perceptive, or suspicious, girlfriend might interpret his remark as an expression of his desire to leave without offending. When I say "you ought to stop writing now" at the end of an exam period, I am probably issuing an order to my students under the guise of an impersonal statement of obligation. In examples such as these an utterance that is not a statement at all is given the linguistic expression usually reserved for ethical statements. In such cases a truth-value challenge would be quite in order.

The second class of cases can be labeled abortive ethical statements. Here the speaker attempts to make an ethical statement but fails because the context is not of the right sort. Although such utterances are meaningful, they are neither true nor false. Imagine that my back is soundly thumped with a snowball as I hurry across the campus and that I turn to the nearest smirking student and say "you ought not to have hit me with that snowball." Now if it was not he who threw the snowball, the student is unlikely to object to my utterance on the ground that it is false, for he hardly wishes to defend the truth of the contrary statement that he ought to have hit me. Rather he wants to object that the question of which ought statement about his act of hitting me is true is entirely out of place, for he did no such act. Again, it is quite out of place to say "he is wicked" of a child if he has not yet reached the age of even partial moral responsibility. Such utterances are neither true nor false because they are made in a situation in which some truth-value presupposition of that sort of ethical statement is false. Since this appeal to truth-value presuppositions plays an important and often misunderstood role in the discussion of concrete ethical issues, I would like to consider a few instances in some detail.

Truth-value presuppositions

One way to challenge the truth-value of an utterance is to attack one of its truth-value presuppositions. Although this conception owes much to Strawson,[4] it is different enough to require some explanation. The notion of a logical presupposition is common enough. To say that one statement P logically presupposes another statement Q is to say that if Q is false then P must be false. The "if . . . then" in this definition is stronger than material implication, for it requires that there be some sort of nonempirical connection between P and Q such that the truth of Q is a necessary condition for the truth of P. I define a truth-value presupposition in a precisely analogous way. To say that P truth-valuationally presupposes Q is to say that if Q is false then P must be neither true nor false. We can avoid the barbarous term "truth-valuationally" by putting the matter this way: to say that Q is a truth-value presupposition of P is to say that if Q is false then P must lack truth-value. The "if . . . then" in this definition also is stronger than material implication, for it requires a conceptual connection between P and Q such that the truth of Q is a necessary condition for the truth-value of P.

Although the notion of a truth-value presupposition is modeled on that of a logical presupposition, it is worth pointing out one way in which they are not analogous. When P logically presupposes Q, the falsity of Q entails both that P is false and that not-P is true, since the falsity of any proposition entails the truth of its contradictory. Moreover, the falsity of Q entails that one or another of the contraries of P is true. Clearly no analogous conclusions may be drawn when Q is a truth-value presupposition of P because in such cases the resulting lack of truth-value for P rules out any further relations of contradiction or contrariness. Substantially the same point can be put another way. In general the logical presuppositions of each of a set of contrary statements are different, but an entire set of contrary statements will always have the same truth-value presuppositions. For example, "the present king of France is bald," "the present king of France has thinning hair," and "the present king of France has a thick head of hair" all truth-valuationally presuppose that there is a king of France at present.

Why bother to coin this expression? My purpose is to make it clear that an utterance may presuppose the truth of certain statements in different ways. This very important fact about language has only begun to be appreciated. As an example take the factual utterance "the man in the moon eats green cheese." This utterance presupposes "the man in the moon eats cheese" and "there is a man in the moon," but in quite different ways. If it is false that the man in the moon eats cheese (of any color), then it must (logically) be false that he eats green cheese. Therefore, to deny a logical presupposition of an utterance is to give a reason against its claim to truth. Now, to say "but there is no man in the moon" is also to say something that counts against the utterance in question; but it does not logically imply that the utterance is false, for that would be to imply that its contradictory is true. Rather, the question of the truth or falsehood of purported statements about the man in the moon cannot arise because there is nothing for these utterances to be statements about. I coin the expression "truth-value presupposition" to indicate the way in which the falsity of "there is a man on the moon" implies that the utterance "the man in the moon eats green cheese" is neither true nor false.

Now let us apply this conception to a few examples of ethical statements. Many, but not all, judgments of moral value presuppose the existence of some particular act to which they refer. When I say "it was so good of you to send me those lovely flowers," I am assuming that you did in fact send me the flowers; when I tell my son "you were wicked to hit your little sister," I am taking it for granted that he actually committed an act of aggression. Whether or not such statements are justified will depend in part upon whether or not these presuppositions are correct. Hence, in defending my statements I may assert "the card that came with the flowers had your name on it" or "I saw you hit your sister." The common notion that justification is reasoning easily leads the unwary to regard these assertions as reasons for the statements, as evidence of their truth. But this way of looking at things misinterprets the nature of the challenge and the response involved, for it confuses two very different dimensions of justification.

Suppose someone says to me "it was cruel of you to laugh at him." I might reply "but I was laughing in sympathy with him" or "my laugh was intended to encourage him." These replies serve to show that the accusation of vice is false, that the speaker has misjudged my act of laughing. However, I might reply instead "but I did not laugh." This reply would also count against the accusation, but in a very different way. I am not trying to prove that my accuser's statement is false, for that would be to prove that some contrary statement is true. Surely, the fact that I did not laugh does nothing to show that my act of laughing was kind or morally indifferent rather than cruel. I am not claiming that my accuser has misjudged my act, but that there is nothing to judge. I am not trying to show that his accusation is false, but that it is out of place. If I did not laugh, then the question of the truth or falsity of any purported statement of moral value that refers to my act of laughing cannot arise. Thus "you laughed at him" is a truth-value, rather than a logical, presupposition of "it was cruel of you to laugh at him." The reason for insisting upon the difference between these two kinds of presupposition is that it brings out the very different ways in which considerations can count for or against an ethical statement.

The examples just given are relatively obvious, and therein lies their value. There can be no real doubt that such statements do presuppose the existence of the acts to which they refer, and it is clear that they do not logically presuppose these acts. Thus these examples reveal clearly the existence of truth-value presuppositions in ethics. To realize the importance of such presuppositions in the give-and-take of ethical debate it is necessary to look further. Statements that ascribe moral goodness or badness to some act truth-valuationally presuppose, not only that the act exists, but also that the doer is a moral agent. Debate about the conditions under which someone is responsible is as important in morality as in courts of law.

The lion is not wicked to live by tooth and claw, neither is he virtuous because of his excellence as a fighter. The road is not literally treacherous, and the dog is not literally faithful. Even the human infant, no matter what a good baby he may be, cannot be said to be morally good. Just what conditions must be fulfilled to qualify as a moral agent is a question as important as it is difficult. One of the conditions seems to be rationality. Since one can be more or less rational, it is not easy to draw any hard-and-fast line between moral agents and beings that are nonmoral. No infant is virtuous or wicked, but adults are normally morally good and evil. Precisely when does a child become morally responsible as he grows up? While the child is growing up he is gradually becoming responsible; it is not that he is completely nonmoral until he wakes up one morning a moral agent. Does this mean that he is less good and bad for each thing he does or that he is morally good or bad for some things and not for others? And to what extent and under what conditions can we judge the feeble-minded and the emotionally disturbed as moral agents? I do not raise these questions about moral responsibility to answer them, but to remind the reader of their importance in the discussion of live ethical issues. My contribution to this discussion is not to define the conditions of responsibility more precisely, but to clarify the way in which the appeal to such conditions enters into the challenges and responses that constitute the justification of ethical statements. The conditions of responsibility are truth-value presuppositions of statements that ascribe virtue or vice to an agent or his acts.

Ought implies can

To the statement that one ought to do something the agent can normally reply "but I can't"; to the statement that one ought not to do some act the agent can reply "but I can't help it." If true, these replies seem to be a complete rebuttal to the respective judgments of obligation. This fact about the logic of obligation is often put by saying that ought implies can. The principle that ought implies can is widely accepted and is probably true, but just what does it mean?

What sense of "can" is involved here? Mere logical possibility does not seem to be enough. Logically I can cure all the diseases in the world by merely snapping my finger, for there is no logical inconsistency in such an act. Yet I do not lose much sleep regretting that I have failed to fulfill my obligation to do this obviously beneficent act. Nor does my clear conscience result from the evidence I have that I ought not to do this act because of the suffering it would cause the doctors who would suddenly find themselves unemployed. Rather, I realize that in this case any judgment of obligation is out of place. It is less clear whether the sense of "can" involved can be explicated in terms of natural law. Is it sufficient that the act in question should be possible according to the principles of a perfected natural science? Would it be more accurate to say that the act is not ruled out by the laws of nature together with a complete statement of the initial conditions? Does possibility in this sense imply lack of complete causal determinism? The word "can" raises many difficult problems of philosophical analysis.

Philosophers have given a great deal of attention to the precise analysis of the word "can" in "ought implies can." Occasionally someone like Frankena has pointed out that the meaning ascribed to "ought" makes a difference, too.[5] But it seems to have been generally taken for granted that the word "implies" is unproblematic, that this word is used in its stand- ard logical sense in this principle of obligation. This is not so. If this were so, to say that ought implies can would be to say that ought logically presupposes can. But the replies "I can't" and "I can't help it" do not function as evidence that the ought statement is false. *1*) They are a radically different kind of consideration from the evidence for or against an ought state- ment. A utilitarian would appeal to facts about the evil or harm or possibly the lesser good done by an act to disprove the statement that one ought to do it. To say that the agent is un- able to perform the act is not to appeal to value considerations at all, but surely the utilitarian does not wish to rule it out as completely beside the point. One need not, of course, be a utilitarian. One might even adopt a pluralistic theory of obli- gation according to which there are a number of quite differ- ent ought-making characteristics. But no one has ever sug- gested that being unable to help it is an ought-making characteristic. Nor would such a suggestion be very plausible if it were made. Ability and inability are a very different sort of consideration. *2*) That these considerations are not one bit of evidence is indicated by the fact that they need not be weighed against the others. Suppose someone tells me that I ought to resign my teaching position and go to help the na- tives of Africa as Schweitzer did. I might give as evidence against the truth of this judgment of obligation the facts that my family would suffer, that I have a duty to my university, and that I would do harm in Africa by disrupting established patterns of life. This evidence against the judgment of obliga- tion must be weighed against the evidence for it—that my uni- versity could easily replace me, that it would be broadening for my family to live abroad, that my teaching skills are badly needed in Africa. And if enough evidence were presented for the judgment of obligation, I would be rationally forced to ac- cept it in spite of the evidence against it. Now suppose that someone tells me that I ought to cure all the diseases in the world by snapping my fingers. I can reply that I just can't do that. Notice that no amount of evidence that such an act would be beneficial, that I have an obligation to my fellowman, etc. could possibly prove that I really ought to do the act if I really cannot do it. I do not need to weigh the evidence for the ought statement against the fact that I cannot do the act, because "but I can't" is not evidence at all. *3*) "But I can't" counts against the ought statement in a very different way. This can be seen most clearly if we consider an ought statement made to an agent in a particular situation. The primary, although not the only function, of ought statements is to guide choice, to answer the question "what ought I to do?" asked by some person in a choice situation. Imagine that I have read the reports on the relation between smoking and lung cancer and now ask myself "ought I to give up smoking?" There seem to be only two possible answers to this question, "I ought to give up smoking" and "I ought not to give up smoking," unless it turns out that either action is equally right. Now "but I can't give up smoking" seems to rule out the conclusion "I ought to give up smoking." But it does not do this by showing that this conclusion is the wrong answer to my question and, therefore, that "I ought not to give up smoking" is the right answer. Rather it shows, if true, that my question is out of place. There can be no true answer to the question "what ought I to choose?" where there is no room for decision. And if there is no true answer, there is no false one, either. Appeals to the inability of the agent to do or not do some specified act count against the statement that the agent ought or ought not to do the act by showing that these sentences are neither true nor false. Can is a truth-value presupposition of ought. This is the sense of "implies" in which it can be maintained that ought implies can.

Even if all the difficulties in the interpretation of "ought implies can" were cleared up, the work would not be over. In addition to the need for refined linguistic analysis, there is a need for considerable factual inquiry to discover the kinds of cases that fulfill or violate the sort of possibility presupposed by our statements of obligation. In what ways and in what degrees can a person control his emotions? At what point does a habit become too strong to be broken and what sorts of remedy are available for addiction? Can a person change his personality in any but superficial ways?

As a combined result of this conceptual unclarity and factual ignorance, there is considerable doubt, both in particular cases and in general, as to just when statements of obligation are in order. We are tempted to assert "white people ought not to hate the Negro so," "you ought to give up taking dope," and "he ought not to lose his temper so often." More radical than the question of the truth of such utterances is the question of whether they have truth-value. Anyone who hopes to justify such a statement must be prepared to meet the truth-value challenge, for if his utterance is neither true nor false it can hardly be true. That this truth-value challenge is theoretically important is indicated by the frequency with which philosophers appeal to the principle that ought implies can; that it is practically important is indicated by the occasions on which replies like "but I couldn't help it" or "but he can't do that" are made in the discussion of concrete ethical issues.

CONCLUSION

I hope that by now it is evident that the truth-value challenge is not only possible, it is of considerable interest. The contention that all ethical sentences lack truth-value has often been made and has been supported by a number of plausible arguments. I have argued against some logical positivists that ethical statements are just what they seem to be, genuine statements. Although the wholesale truth-value challenge cannot be made out, the challenge can sometimes be made good on a retail basis. In particular cases, sentences that seem to be ethical statements may be neither true nor false. Some ethical utterances are, after all, only pseudostatements. Therefore, no one who wishes to justify an ethical statement can ignore the truth-value challenge if it should arise.

The truth-value challenge is, as it were, halfway between two other and more familiar challenges. To challenge the truth of a statement is to grant that it is a statement but to suggest that it may be false instead of true. The truth-value challenge is more radical than this. To challenge the truth-value of a sentence is to challenge its status as a genuine statement; it is not just to take sides on the question of its truth or falsity but to suggest that the very question is out of place. Thus the truth-value challenge does more than deny the claim to truth; it undercuts it and makes it beside the point. However, there is a still more radical challenge that can be made of an ethical sentence. The truth-value challenge insinuates that the sentence is without truth-value, but it throws no doubt upon its status as a sentence, as a significant linguistic utterance. The meaningfulness challenge questions the right of the utterance to claim that it is a part of language at all. It is not even as respectable as exclamations and imperatives which, although without truth-value, are still perfectly meaningful. In this way the truth-value dimension of justification stands midway between the dimension of truth and falsity and that of meaningfulness and meaninglessness.

9. meaningfulness

TO make an ethical statement is to invite a number of distinct challenges. Most obviously, the truth of the statement can be challenged. More radically, the truth-value of the sentence can be challenged. Beyond these two challenges is the meaningfulness challenge. To challenge the meaningfulness of an utterance is to suggest that it has no meaning at all, that it is not even a significant part of language. Exclamations and imperatives have no truth-value, and therefore no truth, but no one would wish to deny that they are perfectly respectable parts of language. There are cases, however, when one would wish to deny, or at least to question, the meaningfulness of some utterance. One can charge "that has no meaning" or "that's nonsense" or ask "what does *that* mean?" in a tone of voice intended to suggest that no answer is to be expected.

A survey of the recent philosophical literature would suggest that this challenge is a very common one. Assertions to the effect that ethical sentences are meaningless, mere nonsense, are now familiar to all. But one must not be led astray by the vocabulary used in these assertions. What is really being asserted is that ethical statements have no *cognitive* meaning, that they are neither true nor false. The challenge I have in mind in this chapter is a much more radical one; it is a challenge to meaningfulness of any sort. So far as I know, no one has seriously argued that ethical sentences are really meaningless in the strict sense of being completely without meaning. Still, such a challenge is clearly possible.

If made, a meaningfulness challenge would have to be met by anyone concerned to justify his ethical statement. A speaker can hardly admit that his utterance is meaningless and continue to claim that he has made a true statement. If his utterance has no meaning at all, it is not a statement, much less a true statement. This challenge is, therefore, relevant to my subject. One of the dimensions of justification is that of meaningfulness, the dimension of challenges and responses concerned with the claim of any utterance to be a significant part of language.

Category mistakes

Long before Ryle introduced the notion of a category mistake, Locke gave a paradigm case of this sort of absurd utterance. The question whether a man's virtue is square is, he suggests, altogether improper because it is without significance. It is absurd either to assert or deny that virtue is square because virtue is simply the wrong sort of thing to have any shape. Locke went on to argue that the traditional philosophical problem of whether a man's will is free is equally improper and lacking in significance. The words "free" and "unfree" may properly be predicated of a man or moral agent, but it does not even make sense to predicate them of a man's will.[1]

Since my interest is in the methodology of challenge and response in ethics, my interest is in the kind of argument that Locke presents to back up his meaningfulness challenge. His first line of argument is to show that the will is simply the power or ability to do or not do some action and that freedom is the power or ability to act or forbear as a man wills or prefers. It follows that to predicate "freedom" of the will is to predicate one power of another power. This is patently absurd because powers or abilities belong only to substances.[2] This sort of argument draws the line between different categories metaphysically, in terms of ontological categories. I do not find it convincing because it is not clear on what grounds the ontological distinctions are made and, more important, just why crossing ontological boundaries must result in absurdity rather than plain falsehood. Possibly Locke's argument could be filled out, but as it stands the absurdity in predicating one power of another is not as gross and obvious as he supposes.

His other line of argument is to show that predicating "freedom" of the will would lead to absurdities, not just obvious falsehoods but senseless questions and answers.[3] For example, if one could predicate freedom of one power, the will, then presumably it would make sense to predicate it of another power, freedom. It would then be meaningful to ask "but is freedom itself free?" just as Midas wished to ask the absurd question "but if riches make a man rich, are riches themselves rich?" Again, if one thinks of powers as substances, then a man becomes a mass of separate powers (like the power of walking, the power of thinking, the power of dancing, the power of digested food, etc.) that act on one another. But "anyone, who reflects on it, will easily perceive" that the power of singing does not act on the power of dancing or any power on another power. This sort of argument seems more promising. If this support to the meaningfulness challenge is to be sufficient, however, it is important that the absurdities that are drawn from the form of sentence be really meaningless rather than just obvious falsehoods.

Much later in the history of philosophy Ryle attacked "the bogy of Mechanism" by arguing that the problem of the freedom of the will arose from various category mistakes. Philosophers are bothered by mechanism because they confuse human actions with volitions (a sort of mental cause of overt behavior), laws of nature with governmental fiats, and explanations in terms of causes with explanations in terms of reasons. Thus it does not even make sense to speak of mechanical laws compelling human beings to act as they do.[4]

Here, and elsewhere, Ryle backs up his claims about category differences with a variety of detailed arguments. He often follows the lead of Locke in trying to draw out absurd consequences from a way of speaking, but there are two other sorts of argument that are particularly important in his writings. First, he suggests that sometimes a category may be defined by a set of terms that could supply answers to a given question.[5] Hence, one can distinguish categories by showing that the sorts of questions one may ask of one thing cannot significantly be asked of another. Thus to ask how long it took me to will the act of opening the window makes no sense, but it does make sense to ask how long it took me to open the window. Again, one can ask who passed a civil law and how long it has been in effect, but neither question can properly be asked of a law of nature. This technique, at least in the hands of Ryle, does seem very successful in revealing differences and bringing out confusions. What is needed, however, is some rationale of the practice. Is it always true that the absurdity of transferring questions from one area to another corresponds with a radical semantical gap? Might it not be that sometimes it marks only a distinction between two very different species of a genus? Perhaps not, but *why* not? In practice there is the additional problem of recognizing whether or not it is absurd to ask a certain question. There are those who maintain that acts of will do take place in time and last for a finite length of time. We are baffled when asked to specify how long an act of will takes only because we do not know, just as we have no very precise notion of how long it takes to wink.

Ryle's other sort of argument is to substitute one expression for another in various sentence frames. If such substitution reduces some of these sentences to absurdity, then the two expressions are of different categories.[6] Probably, but must they be of completely different categories? It might be possible for the two expressions to differ in such a way that in some sentences substitution does not affect meaningfulness while in others it does. Ryle seems to suppose that the fact that some substitutions produce obvious absurdity proves that in all other cases there is unnoticed absurdity. Again, some rationale is needed to explain just how this sort of argument works and why.

Unfortunately, I have no suggestions to make, either in the way of new sorts of argumentation or in the way of explaining the arguments now used. Still, I will venture two very tentative conclusions. Disputes about whether or not some utterance is senseless because it commits a category mistake do arise in ethics; and although it is not easy to establish the existence of any but the most obvious category mistakes, this sort of meaningfulness challenge is a legitimate one.

Incomplete sentences

Some sentences are incomplete as they stand. If taken as they are, they are meaningless because something essential to their meaning is missing. Usually it would be unfair to the speaker to take them as they stand. As a rule they are merely elliptical; they are incomplete verbalizations of complete thoughts. When pressed the speaker will fill them out to make sense of them. But if he refuses to fill them out, if he cannot see that they are incomplete, then he has not really said anything at all. Therefore, one can challenge the meaningfulness of an utterance by claiming that what is said, as opposed to the expression of it, is essentially incomplete.

Sometimes the incompleteness of an utterance is obvious. It is hard to imagine anyone saying "John is very good at" unless he has been interrupted in the middle of his utterance. Any competent speaker of English would realize that this must be filled out to specify *what* John is good at. But if some speaker, possibly a child, saw no need to complete the utterance, we would be justified in concluding that the utterance is meaningless. In other cases the incompleteness of the utterance is less obvious. Does "John is good" require filling out? Quite possibly, for it may well mean "John is a good man" rather than "John is a good golfer" or "John is a good philosopher."

Ross has distinguished between the attributive and predicative uses of "good" and "bad." [7] In "this is a good knife" and "John is a good man" the word "good" is used attributively. But in "pleasure is good" and "cruelty is bad" the value terms are used predicatively. One cannot always tell how the value term is used by inspecting the grammatical form of the utterance alone. I might hold up my knife and say "this is good," but in spite of appearances I have probably used the adjective attributively, for I probably mean good as a knife and not good as a paperweight or good as a screwdriver. Geach has gone a step further and argued that, in spite of appearances, the words "good" and "bad" are always attributive. [8] Since they are never used predicatively, utterances like "pleasure is good" and "cruelty is bad" are essentially incomplete; they necessarily pose the questions "good as a what?" and "bad as a what?" If the speaker refuses to answer these questions, then his utterance is not just elliptical; it is meaningless.

As it happens, many speakers, including Ross, refuse to fill out such sentences. They cannot see that there is anything incomplete about such sentences. Here we have a philosophical issue of some interest. In effect Geach has challenged the meaningfulness of certain ways of talking which other moral philosophers continue to use as completely meaningful. As far as I can see, Geach does not *prove* that these sentences, if taken as complete, are without meaning. Rather his test for distinguishing between attributive and predicative adjectives, that the former cannot be split from their nouns without destroying their meaningfulness, presupposes that "good" is meaningless when used as a complete predicate. My own language sense differs from that of Geach. I cannot see that "pleasure is good" and "cruelty is evil" are essentially incomplete as they stand. Therefore, I would agree with Ross that "good" and "bad" are often attributive but sometimes purely predicative. Nevertheless, this disagreement among moral philosophers is an interesting one for my purposes because it shows how the meaningfulness of a class of utterances can hinge on the question of their incompleteness. If Geach can produce arguments to back up his challenge, then he can show that certain utterances, usually taken as making perfectly good sense, are really without meaning unless they are filled out in a way which many speakers refuse to recognize as necessary.

There is another class of ethical sentences which have sometimes been challenged as meaningless as they stand. A moralist might assert sternly "polygamy is wrong." Such an utterance might well provoke a cultural relativist to ask "in what society?" It is often maintained that obligation is relative to the agent's society so that what is wrong in one society may be right in another. It would seem to follow that any statement of obligation that does not specify the society to which it refers is essentially incomplete. But the ethical absolutist is apt to reject this contention and reply "what I mean is simply that polygamy is wrong, period!" He refuses to see any relativity in his utterance that renders it essentially incomplete. Here again the claim that a large class of utterances are meaningless as they stand hinges on the alleged incompleteness of the utterances.

How might these sentences be shown to be incomplete? The relativist can appeal to at least two arguments. First, he can argue that the relativity of obligation is built into the definition of the terms "right" and "wrong." He may suggest that "right" means something like "is demanded by the mores of ——— society" and that "wrong" means "violates the mores of ——— society." There seem to me to be two difficulties with this argument. *a*) How is the blank to be filled in? Often the proposal is that it is the mores of the agent's society that determine the rightness or wrongness of an act. But if so, the speaker need not specify which society he is speaking about. The statement that an act is right or wrong invariably refers to the agent's society. No doubt different agents belong to different societies, but this relativity cancels itself out because of the way it is built into the definitions. If, on the other hand, it is assumed that the blank is to be filled in in different ways for different utterances, then statements of right and wrong are incomplete unless they specify how the blank is supposed to be filled in. But now it becomes hard to defend the definitions, for there is no good reason to think that the meaning of "right" and "wrong" varies in *this* way, and the reasons to suppose that obligation varies with the agent's society are no longer applicable. *b*) I would not try very hard to find reasons to defend the definitions, however, because they seem to me completely implausible. Quite apart from the general considerations that rule out any naturalistic definition, there is the fact that any given set of mores surely may conflict with what we take to be right or wrong. Therefore, the notions of right and wrong cannot be defined in terms of any set of mores.

Second, the relativist can appeal to the truth or falsity, rather than the meaning, of judgments of obligation. He may argue that "polygamy is wrong" may well be true when applied to our society but false when applied to another society. I would agree in principle, although I am not sure about the specific case of polygamy. Still, it *might* be that polygamy is wrong in our society where there is roughly a balance between men and women of marriageable age and right in another society where there are four or five women for every man. But notice that it is not the mores of the society, but the circumstances in which the agent finds himself, that make a difference to the rightness or wrongness of his action. I am quite prepared to admit that the rightness or wrongness of an action depends upon the circumstances and is, in *that* sense, relative. I am even prepared to admit that a sentence like "polygamy is wrong" *may* be incomplete. It may be that the speaker means to assert only "polygamy in our society is wrong." If so, he will probably be quite prepared to fill out his elliptical utterance and admit that he has not meant to assert that polygamy in all cases is wrong. On the other hand, it is very likely that he meant to assert "polygamy in all cases is wrong." If so, he may be mistaken, but there is nothing meaningless about his utterance. There is no relativity built into the predicates "right" and "wrong" that requires that one specify which society is involved in their predication. What is required is something else, that the speaker make clear what the subject of his statement is. It makes a difference to the truth of his utterance whether he is referring to all cases of polygamy or to some limited subset of such cases. But this is not at issue between the relativist and the absolutist, for the absolutist is happy to admit that he is talking about all cases wherever they may occur. True or false, his assertions are not essentially incomplete. Therefore, their meaningfulness cannot be challenged on that ground at least.

CONCLUSION

When a person makes an ethical statement, he opens himself to a number of challenges. In addition to the truth and truth-value challenges there is the more radical meaningfulness challenge. To challenge the meaningfulness of an utterance is to question its status as a bit of significant language. Although I have emphasized statements, a more complete discussion would have to give equal consideration to questions and arguments as well, for these can also be meaningful or meaningless. Prichard seems to be arguing that the question "why should I do my duty?" is one that, no matter how tempting it may be to certain philosophers, is ultimately without meaning.[9] It would be helpful if we could know when the questions we are tempted to ask need no answers because they have no meaning. Again, since arguments are meaningful bits of language, they are also in danger of the meaningfulness challenge. What seems to be an argument might turn out to be senseless for some reason. Anyone attempting to use arguments to justify his ethical statements would like to know when his arguing ceases to have any real meaning. However, since I pretend only to open up an area deserving of much more exploration and study, I will omit any discussion of questions and arguments.

At least it should be clear by now that the justification of ethical statements does have a meaningfulness dimension. On this dimension wholesale challenges do not seem to take place. I do not know of any philosopher who has seriously challenged the meaningfulness of all ethical statements, and it is hard to see on what grounds such a challenge could be made. There is much room for debate as to just what kind of meaning ethical statements have and whether their meaning is compatible with their having truth-value, but it can hardly be doubted that ethical sentences are a genuine part of language. Nor is the meaningfulness of any species of ethical statement, like ought statements or judgments of value, especially in doubt. Retail challenges, on the other hand, are quite in order and do take place. Speakers sometimes do use ethical language without following the rules for its use, or make category mistakes, or utter incomplete sentences as though they were essentially complete. Nor is it always obvious to either speaker or hearer when significant language lapses into insignificance. Therefore, there is room for meaningfulness challenges and responses on particular occasions. In the more difficult cases there may be considerable debate about whether or not some utterance is meaningful. Therefore, although it is probably less important than truth and truth-value, meaningfulness does play an essential role in the justification of ethical statements.

10. validity

TO make an ethical statement is to open oneself to a variety of challenges. If the truth of his statement is challenged, the speaker will often try to defend his assertion with arguments; that is, he will give reasons in support of his statement. Although in the end this is the only satisfactory way to defend the claim to truth, this appeal to ethical reasoning does have its dangers, for now the speaker is doubly vulnerable. Not only can the truth of his original statement be challenged, but the soundness of the argument he gives to defend it can also be challenged, and in two quite different ways.

To argue is to give reasons for some conclusion. These reasons are the premises of the argument and, within the argument, they are taken for granted. But usually the truth of these premises can be challenged, just as the truth of the conclusion was denied or questioned. It follows that the more premises one asserts in defense of one's conclusion the more statements one is committed to defend. By far the most common sort of attack on ethical arguments is precisely of this kind; in most cases the question of how sound an argument is revolves around the question of whether its premises are true. However, it is not this sort of attack on ethical arguments which concerns me here, for truth challenges and responses have received their share of attention already.

What does concern me is another way in which an ethical argument can be challenged. Instead of questioning the premises of the argument one can throw doubt upon the transition from the premises to the conclusion. Ignoring any doubts about the premises themselves, one can challenge the correctness of the inference from the premises to the conclusion. Every argument makes an implicit claim to validity; it claims that, *if* accepted, the premises are good reasons for the conclusion. This claim that the inference is logically correct can be challenged. Let us see how, if at all, such validity challenges can be met.

Meeting the challenge

There are several different ways in which one can defend the validity of a challenged argument. The most obvious defense is simply to counter whatever charge has been made by the challenger. If the meaning of the argument has been "clarified" to reveal confusion, one may object to the proffered analysis of the argument. If it is alleged that the argument commits some specified fallacy, one may either try to show that it is not of the sort covered by the fallacy or even deny that the specified sort of argument is fallacious. For obvious reasons, the way one counters a charge depends upon the nature of the challenge made.

According to military tradition, the best defense is a good offense. The best way to meet the charge of invalidity is to prove that the argument is actually valid. Often one can do this by appealing to the discipline of logic. Logic can be of help in at least three ways. First, it supplies a number of principles of the form "all arguments of kind K are valid." If one can subsume the argument in question under such a principle, one can readily deduce its validity. Second, logic provides a number of rules of inference specifying which sorts of logical transitions are permissible. An example would be "from a disjunction together with the negation of one of the disjuncts one may infer the truth of the other disjunct." If one can find an applicable rule of inference, one can use it to show that one's argument is a permissible one. Third, logic offers a variety of test procedures such as Venn diagrams or truth tables. Where some such procedure exists, one can show that a challenged argument is valid by going through the procedure and obtaining a favorable result.

Frequently the question of whether or not an argument

is valid cannot be settled by any such appeal to logic. It does not follow that validity challenges and responses must cease at this point. In the end one may have to judge the validity of an argument by thinking it through for oneself, but before that end comes, there is a great deal to be said about the argument. Often the challenger cannot see the validity of the argument because he does not fully understand it. The way to defend the argument is then to explain its meaning so that the argument will become persuasive. To explain an argument one may have to make explicit something that was unexpressed originally, one may have to define some key expression used in the argument, one may need to break the argument down into steps and reorganize the steps, one may just have to indicate the point of the argument. Any sort of explanation is legitimate provided it does not distort the meaning of the argument in question.

The importance of this move of explaining an argument in meeting a challenge to its validity shows that defending an argument is not always supporting one argument with another. Sometimes it is; we often do show that one bit of reasoning is correct by another bit of reasoning. This reasoning about reasoning is a second-order argument. Appealing to a logical principle or a principle of inference illustrates the way in which a person may use one argument to defend the validity of another argument. The importance of this second-order reasoning should not be denied; what must be added is that one need not, and probably cannot, always appeal to such reasoning. In the end some argument must be accepted simply because everyone concerned recognizes its validity by thinking it through. Explanations of the argument designed to clarify its meaning may play a decisive role in enabling one to recognize its validity or invalidity. Reasoning may or may not be defended with more reasoning, for there are several ways of meeting a validity challenge.

The naturalistic fallacy

A challenge to the truth of some ethical statement is to be met ultimately by giving reasons for the statement, but the validity of this ethical reasoning can in turn be challenged. We have examined briefly some of the ways in which an argument can be shown to be valid. Let us now look at a few of the more common and interesting validity challenges in some detail. Perhaps the most common charge is that some argument commits the naturalistic fallacy. Just what is the naturalistic fallacy and is it really fallacious?

The expression "the naturalistic fallacy" is applied to several alleged errors. Attempting to define an indefinable word, defining an ethical word in terms of empirical characteristics, reducing a synthetic proposition to a tautology, treating an a priori principle as though it were an empirical generalization—all of these have been called the naturalistic fallacy. But none of these are fallacies in the logical sense of the term; none of these are errors in reasoning. The one alleged error that is relevant to our topic is that of inferring an ethical conclusion from purely factual premises. That this is actually a logical error follows from a widely accepted logical generalization: no argument all of whose premises are factual statements and whose conclusion is an ethical statement is valid. Although this logical principle is sometimes accepted as obviously true, it is also often vigorously denied. Clearly, here is one place where there is serious doubt about the validity of a certain kind of ethical argument.

Why is it thought that no argument all of whose premises are factual statements and whose conclusion is an ethical statement is valid? Although explicit arguments for this logical principle are surprisingly difficult to find, there seem to be several of them. *1*) One very common way of defending this principle is by giving examples of arguments from factual premises to ethical conclusions. "I like it, therefore it is good"; "polygamy is thought wrong, therefore polygamy is wrong"; "many people do steal, therefore it is all right to steal." These obviously invalid arguments are supposed to show that all arguments that, like them, go from factual premises to ethical conclusions must be invalid. In principle there is nothing wrong with this reasoning. It infers the truth of a logical generalization by induction from examples of individual arguments. This is exactly the way I would argue for or against a logical principle myself. However, the range of examples is far too narrow. Only a few examples, and these the most implausible, are considered at all. Of course some, and probably many, arguments from factual premises to ethical conclusions are invalid. What is to be shown is that each and every such argument is invalid, and to do that one must examine the most plausible, rather than the least likely, candidates. What is one to say of the following examples? "It is pleasant, therefore it is good"; "it is acutely painful, therefore it is bad"; "you promised, therefore you ought to do it"; "it would cause unnecessary suffering, therefore you ought not to do it." Although some or all of these may be invalid, these are not obviously so. Only if we can somehow know that examples like these are invalid, can we infer inductively that all arguments from factual premises to ethical conclusions are invalid. My own view would be that some, at least, of these arguments are in fact valid. Therefore, a careful induction shows that the logical generalization in question is false not true.

2) Another very common argument for the fallaciousness of inferences from facts to ethical conclusions is hard to put precisely. Ethical statements are of a fundamentally different kind from factual statements. But reasoning cannot bridge the gap between different kinds of statements. Therefore, any argument from purely factual premises to an ethical conclusion is invalid. This is a cogent argument, but it is hard to know what to make of either premise. Are ethical statements of a fundamentally different kind from factual statements? Sometimes this is based upon an alleged difference of subject matter. Facts are one thing; values or norms are quite another. The realm of nonnatural characteristics is clearly different from the world of nature. Unfortunately, positing such nonnatural or nonfactual realms seems to raise a large number of metaphysical and epistemological problems. Moreover, the difference between factual and ethical sentences

seems to be more basic than any difference in subject matter. Hence others base their difference upon a difference in function or meaning of the utterances themselves. I would agree that there are such differences, although I doubt that either factual or ethical sentences constitute a homogeneous class. There are many differences to be noted, not just one vast gulf. It is less easy to know how fundamental each of these differences is, for there are also similarities to be noted. But what of the other premise? Is it true that reasoning cannot bridge the gap between different kinds of statements? One hardly knows what to say until one knows more about the nature of reasoning and what constitutes a difference in kind. This premise would seem to be false. Occurrence statements would seem to be different in kind from disposition statements, but the argument "this is dissolving, therefore this is soluble" would seem to be valid. At the very least, the assertion that one cannot validly infer one kind of statement from statements of another kind is as much in need of defense as the assertion that one cannot infer an ethical conclusion from factual premises. Therefore, this argument needs further development before it can show that the naturalistic fallacy is indeed fallacious.

3) Hare has presented an argument to bring out what he thinks is the crux of the naturalistic fallacy. A factual statement is properly formulated in the indicative mood. Any ethical statement implies at least one imperative. Hence, if a set of factual premises implied an ethical conclusion, a set of indicative premises would imply an imperative conclusion. But no set of purely indicative premises can imply an imperative conclusion. Therefore, no set of factual premises can imply an ethical conclusion.[1] Although this is a very plausible argument, there are two serious difficulties with it. First, it is not clear that every ethical statement does imply an imperative. Perhaps "you ought to open the window" implies "open the window" in some way, but "these poisoned cupcakes taste good" hardly implies "taste them." Hare argues that ethical statements *must* imply imperatives because the function of ethical statements is to guide conduct, to answer the question "what shall I do?" Admittedly, one way to guide conduct is to tell someone what to do, but there are other ways to guide

conduct as well. One might even guide a man's conduct by giving him information about the situation in which he is to act. Therefore, I doubt that ethical statements must imply imperatives. Second, is it true that no set of purely indicative premises implies any imperative? As long as Hare sticks to examples like "the door is shut" and "open the door" and "if the door is shut, open the door," he seems to be on safe ground. The trouble is that ethical statements do not seem to be purely indicative or purely imperative on Hare's analysis. Unlike genuine imperatives, they have a past tense and can apply to everyone; on the other hand, they are not supposed to be factual statements either. Now Hare insists that ethical statements *do* imply imperatives. This appears to be a counter-example to the principle that no set of indicatives can imply an imperative. Perhaps ethical statements are not indicatives, but they are not really imperatives either. Thus it is hard to see how the claim that ethical statements do not follow from factual ones can be supported by any appeal to a principle in the logic of imperatives. In fact, if ethical statements are somewhere between pure indicatives and genuine imperatives, then the gap between indicatives and imperatives cannot be as radical as Hare suggests.

Doubtless the most widely accepted justification for the claim that it is a logical error to infer ethical conclusions from factual premises is based upon a theory of reasoning. *4)* Valid reasoning is simply making explicit what is already contained in the premises of an argument. But no ethical statement is contained in any conjunction of purely factual statements. Therefore, one cannot validly infer any ethical conclusion from any set of purely factual premises. This argument also presents two serious difficulties. First, in precisely what sense is the conclusion of a valid argument contained in its premises? *a)* Hume and others occasionally talk as though the notion of containment is to be taken literally, at least as applied to ideas. The idea of a black square literally contains the idea of black in that the images which make up the idea of a black square include images of black. Accordingly one can discover what is contained in some idea by looking at the images in his mind and noticing the parts of which they are made up. But it is very doubtful whether concepts are images or constructs of images or whether they are introspectable items in which the thinker can observe the parts contained in the whole. *b*) A less dubious notion of containment hinges on the notion of a definition rather than what is contained in a concept. A conclusion is contained in a premise when it can be derived from that premise simply by substituting *definiens* for *definiendum* or vice versa in the premise. Although the notion of a definition is far from precise, it is clear enough to make this a relatively clear notion of containment. Moreover, when the conclusion is contained in the premise in this sense, the argument is clearly valid. But a great many arguments are also clearly valid when the conclusion is not contained in the premise in this sense. For example any of the valid syllogisms. These do not conform to this notion of containment because substitution by definition allows one to transform any given statement, but it does not allow one to put together two or more statements to give a single conclusion. Therefore, a wider conception of containment is needed. *c*) The obvious extension is to say that a conclusion is contained in a set of premises when it can be derived from those premises by substitution in accordance with definitions plus manipulation according to the principles of formal logic. Since we have a tolerably clear notion of what constitutes a definition and have well-developed systems of formal logic, this is quite a workable conception of containment. Moreover, it covers a very wide range of cases of valid reasoning so that it is fairly plausible as a theory of reasoning. And if all naturalistic definitions of ethical terms are rejected, then it is hard to imagine how ethical conclusions could be derived from purely factual premises. But what is hard is not always impossible to persistent and imaginative logicians. Recently several respectable logicians have advanced plausible arguments to show that certain arguments from purely factual premises to an ethical conclusion are valid by the principles of formal logic alone. They probably have not shown this beyond any shadow of a doubt; it may be that the real moral of their tale is that the distinction between factual and ethical statements is far from clear. But at least they have shown that it cannot be taken for granted that ethical conclusions are not contained in factual premises in this sense of containment. Nor is it clear that all valid inferences are formally valid. There seem to be arguments in which the conclusion follows necessarily from the premises even though it cannot be derived from them by appeal to definitions plus the principles of formal logic. This suggests an even wider conception of containment. *d*) A conclusion is contained in a set of premises when it follows necessarily from those premises. A conclusion follows necessarily from a set of premises when it is impossible for the premises to be true and the conclusion to be false. Now ethical conclusions do not seem to be contained in factual premises in this sense. It might be true that you promised to play golf with me yet false that you ought to do so because some new and more stringent obligation has arisen that requires you to be somewhere else at the time. It might be true that the dentist's act of drilling causes avoidable suffering yet false that he ought not to do it because in the long run proper care of the tooth will avoid even greater suffering. This does show, I think, that these arguments are not deductively valid, for in a valid deductive argument the conclusion must follow necessarily from the premises. However, one cannot argue that these ethical conclusions do not follow from these factual premises *because* their conclusions are not contained in their respective premises, for containment has now been defined in terms of following necessarily. That is, when the conception of containment is defined in terms of following necessarily, it can no longer serve as an independent criterion of what sort of conclusion follows from what sort of premises. Moreover, it may be that in a few cases ethical conclusions do follow necessarily from purely factual premises. Recently von Wright has proposed a version of the practical syllogism that seems to go from factual premises to an ethical conclusion,[2] and Black has suggested one way to infer a should statement from factual premises.[3] Certainly it is far from obvious that they are mistaken. Therefore, it is not clear that in no case is an ethical statement contained in a set of factual premises in this sense. It seems to me that two conclusions emerge from this brief survey of the various senses in which a conclusion might be said to be contained in a set of premises. First, that the notion of containment is far from clear and needs to be spelled out in precise detail. Second, that the obvious ways of spelling it out are either too narrow or too broad. If containment is thought of in terms of one idea being a part of another or one term being included in the definition of another, then there are many valid arguments in which the conclusions are not contained in the premises. If containment allows for manipulation according to the principles of formal logic or drawing any conclusion that follows necessarily, then probably some factual premises do contain ethical conclusions. Therefore, these last two conceptions of containment are too wide for anyone who wished to defend the fallaciousness of the naturalistic fallacy.

On the other hand, they are too narrow for anyone who wishes to formulate an adequate theory of reasoning. Even the last and widest conception limits reasoning to deductive arguments. Since inductive and even conductive arguments are valid, one should reject the theory that reasoning is simply making explicit what is contained in the premises. Reasoning sometimes goes beyond the premises with which it begins. Therefore, showing that an argument is not deductively valid is not the same as proving it invalid. "You promised to do it, therefore you ought to do it" is not a valid deduction, for the conclusion does not follow necessarily from the premise. Still, it is a valid conductive argument. Likewise, the fact that his drilling will cause avoidable suffering is a valid, although not conclusive, reason for the conclusion that the dentist ought not to drill into that tooth. If I am right about the validity of conductive reasoning, then in some cases ethical conclusions can be validly inferred from purely factual premises. Since I have given what seem to be good arguments for the existence of conductive reasoning, I conclude that the naturalistic fallacy, however mistaken it may be in its other forms, is not a logical fallacy. It is just not true that every argument all of whose premises are factual and whose conclusion is an ethical statement is invalid. In this sense of the term, there is no naturalistic fallacy.

Ethical egoism

Ethical egoism is often formulated as a deontological principle: one ought always to do the action that contributes most to one's own welfare. But it can also be formulated as a thesis about the grounds of obligation: the only reason one ought or ought not to do an action is that it will or will not contribute to one's own welfare. Although these two formulations are not identical, they are closely related. If the only reason why one ought to do anything is self-interest, then it follows that one ought always to pursue self-interest; and in fact philosophers who hold the deontological principle usually defend it by appealing to the thesis about the grounds of obligation. Therefore, I shall regard that thesis as the more basic form of ethical egoism.

On this interpretation ethical egoism is primarily a logical or epistemological position. It is a thesis about the range of considerations that are logically relevant to judgments of obligation. It implies that all inferences from the impact of an agent's action on others to his obligation to do or refrain from doing that act are invalid, unless they take the welfare of others to be relevant only as it bears on the welfare of the agent himself. Hence ethical egoism challenges the validity of a large class of ethical arguments quite common in the discussion of questions of what one ought to do. Can this validity challenge be made good?

At first glance, ethical egoism is obviously mistaken, for we often appeal to the effects of one person's action upon others in our ethical reasoning. We argue "you ought not to kick your little sister because it hurts her" or "I ought to give him first aid because it may save his life." Any theory that brands inferences like this as invalid must surely be rejected.

However, ethical egoism need not imply that all such arguments are invalid, for some of them are enthymematic. It is well known that, just as the action of one agent may affect others, so their actions will in turn affect him. And in judging how one ought to treat others, even an ethical egoist can take into account how those others will probably react to him. Perhaps the first argument should be stated "you ought not to kick your little sister because it will hurt her and if you hurt her she will retaliate by hurting you." This is a respectable egoistic argument in which the real reason not to kick little sister is that she will kick back. Thus the fact that one's action will benefit or harm another person may be indirectly relevant to a judgment of obligation; all the egoist is denying is that they are directly relevant. He is committed only to saying that the arguments in the last paragraph are invalid if taken as they stand.

How can ethical egoism be defended? The traditional argument for ethical egoism is probably the appeal to psychological egoism. If the welfare of others is relevant to what one ought to do, then in many cases one ought to act against his own self-interest because in many cases the interests of others will outweigh one's own interest. But since it is human nature to pursue self-interest, no one can choose to act against his own self-interest. And since ought implies can, it follows that we cannot say that one ever ought to act against his own self-interest. Therefore considerations regarding the welfare of others must be irrelevant to judgments of obligation. This argument is not very persuasive. For one thing, psychological egoism seems to be false. As Butler pointed out, the fact that one always acts on his own desires does nothing to show that the only object of desire is one's own welfare.[4] And as Hume argued, the simplest hypothesis to explain the appearance of benevolent action is that human beings do care about one another; any theory that can explain away every case of apparent unselfishness will be too complicated to be plausible.[5] For another thing, it is far from clear that the appeal to human nature in this way determines anything about obligation. I suppose that everything any human being does he does because of his human nature. In some sense he could not do otherwise, but we do not wish to say that judgments of obligation are always out of place. Therefore, the sense in which human nature makes it impossible for one to do otherwise cannot be the sense of "can't" that undermines an ought judgment.

Although Hobbes is less explicit than one could wish, one can construct an argument for ethical egoism from the hints he drops along the way.[6] If the way in which one's action benefits or harms others is relevant to judging whether one ought to do it, then in extreme cases one ought to do something that will result in death. Extreme cases might include the suicide mission of a soldier or the airline pilot's staying at the controls to allow more passengers to parachute from a burning plane as well as acts performed in a state of nature. But every human being has the right of self-preservation. Now if it is not wrong for any man to refuse to sacrifice his life, then no one has an obligation to do anything that will result in his own death. Therefore, the welfare of others cannot be relevant to judging what one ought to do. This is a very interesting argument, but it does not establish its conclusion. Although it may be that every human being has a right to preserve his own life, one would like some evidence in support of this key premise. Even if there is a human right to self-preservation, it does not follow that it is always right for a human being to preserve his own life. That someone has a right to do something does not necessarily imply that his act of doing it is right, for one can have a right that one ought not to exercise. For example, one may have a right to free speech when one ought not to speak freely because this is not the time or the place; one may have a right to demand that he be repaid when it would be wrong to force a husband with a sick wife to give up the money at the moment. Thus the soldier or pilot may have a right to save his own skin even though he ought to sacrifice himself for the welfare of others. But even if one never is under an obligation to sacrifice oneself for others, it may not be true that the welfare of others is completely irrelevant. The assumption of Hobbes' argument is that in extreme cases the welfare of others may outweigh the welfare of the agent by so great an amount as to require the agent to lay down his life. But if life is so very precious, then this situation never occurs. One can always justify the act of self-preservation, no matter how great the interests of others, by ascribing sufficient value to the agent's life. Therefore, this appeal to the supposed right of self-preservation does not prove that ethical egoism is correct.

Probably the strongest argument for ethical egoism is

the fact that self-regarding reasons seem to be ultimate in a way that other-regarding reasons are not. If it is said to anyone "you ought to do act A," he can always ask "why should I?" It is not just that this demand for reasons is barely possible, it is both legitimate and sensible to ask for justification of any judgment of obligation. Suppose that the reason given is that act A would alleviate Suzy's toothache or make Bill happy. John can always ask "so what?" or "why should I care about Suzy's toothache?" or "why ought I to make Bill happy?" Somehow, other-regarding reasons do not seem to be ultimate, for one can always challenge their status as reasons for the ethical conclusion. Moreover, the only sort of reply that would be likely to satisfy the man who challenges other-regarding reasons is an appeal to his own welfare. To point out that Suzy would probably be so grateful that she would bake a batch of cookies for John might well satisfy him that he ought to alleviate her toothache. Self-regarding reasons do not seem to need any such support, however. Suppose that the reason given for doing act A is that A would alleviate John's own toothache or make John happy. It is hard to imagine John asking "why should I care about my pain?" or "why should I make myself happy?" Thus other-regarding reasons seem to require some further justification to establish their practical relevance, and the only sort of justification that seems possible is an appeal to self-regarding reasons. Self-regarding reasons, on the other hand, seem immune to the question "why?" and to stand in need of no further reasons. The obvious conclusion is that other-regarding reasons are only indirectly relevant to judgments of obligation and that in the end only self-interest is a reason for action.

Now if it were true that self-regarding reasons were ultimate in a way that other-regarding reasons are not, then I think that one would have to accept ethical egoism. But this appearance of disparity is illusory. There is a difference here, but it is a difference of degree and not a basic difference in epistemological status. It is true that an agent can always challenge the relevance of any other-regarding reason; but it is also true that an agent *can* always challenge the relevance of any self-regarding reason. Every argument claims validity, and it is always possible to challenge this claim. It is hard to imagine anyone asking "why should I care about my tooth-ache?" or "why should I make myself happy?" This is because most people take a fairly keen interest in their own welfare. But not everyone does; a very despondent person may not care very much about doing anything to alleviate a present pain or produce some new pleasure. And all of us are less than per-fectly rational in pursuing our long-range or difficult goals; it is not so hard to imagine someone asking "why should I worry about the aches and pains of my old age?" or "why should I bother to ensure a happy retirement?" If what I said about infinite regresses in justification is correct, there are no ulti-mate arguments. Although we normally do not challenge the relevance of self-regarding reasons, it is always possible to do so. On the other hand, although we always could challenge the relevance of other-regarding reasons, we often do not do so. If John is in love with Suzy or is friendly with Bill, he will not ask "so what?" or "why should I make Bill happy?" Any appeal to their welfare will be accepted as a valid reason; and in the end this is as close to ultimacy as any reasoning can get. Therefore, the ethical egoist is wrong in contending that self-regarding reasons are ultimate in a way that other-regard-ing reasons are not. Neither sort of reason is ultimate, but both sorts are usually accepted as good reasons. Probably other-regarding reasons are more often challenged than self-regarding reasons. But when they are challenged, their valid-ity can usually be defended; and when they are not challenged, they need no further justification.

If the arguments for ethical egoism are insufficient, are the arguments against it any more satisfactory? Well, let us see. There is one argument which, although it does not really disprove ethical egoism, may make it less attractive. This is the appeal to the generality of reasoning. If some considera-tion is a good reason for me here now, then it must be a good reason for everyone in any similar situation. Now as long as the ethical egoist thinks only of himself and his own actions, he may find egoism attractive because it justifies his pursuit of his own self-interest without regard for the interests of others. But it can be pointed out to him that the claim that only his interests are relevant to his actions implies the same for each and every rational agent. Now is he really prepared to admit that other agents are rationally justified in pursuing their respective interests without regard for his interests, particularly since there are so many more of them than of him? Ethical egoism is apt to be attractive to the philosopher who cares most about his own self-interest. If in the end it is seen to justify many actions that would conflict with his own self-interest, ethical egoism may seem less attractive. Another way of putting the point is this: ethical egoism seems very attractive when one thinks of situations in which one might be asked to sacrifice one's own welfare for the sake of others, but it seems less attractive when one applies it to situations in which others are wondering whether it might be rational to sacrifice their welfare for one's own sake. Yet the claim to validity is universal in a way that will not allow the egoist to apply his theory to the former and refuse to apply it to the latter. If he tries to assert "everyone ought to consider only my welfare," then he can be asked to justify selecting himself as the only agent whose welfare is to be considered. Clearly none of the arguments we have considered support this version of egoism, and it is hard to see how any speaker could justify such a position. Any rational egoism will be universally applicable to all agents, and may turn out to be less than satisfactory in terms of the self-interest of any given moral agent or moral philosopher.

Strictly speaking, however, this is not a disproof of ethical egoism. The only refutation I can think of is an appeal to thought experiments. Ethical egoism implies that, apart from direct or indirect rewards, there is no reason for me to save a drowning man It implies that it is more reasonable for me to keep five dollars which I do not need very much rather than give it to a charitable organization that can use it to feed the starving or clothe the poor. It implies that if I were to choose between relieving the physical suffering of all mankind at the cost of a temporary mild discomfort in my hand and preserving my comfort at the cost of continued widespread suffering, I ought to refuse to accept the discomfort. When I perform thought experiments such as these, I find that I cannot accept the implications of ethical egoism. I conclude that it is not true that one ought always do that act which will contribute most to his own welfare and that the effects of one's actions upon others are directly relevant to any judgment of what one ought to do.

It may be thought that this argument begs the issue, for the ethical egoist will disagree with my thought experiments. It is quite possible that someone will disagree about the proper conclusion to draw from these, or similar, thought experiments. Such a person, of course, need not accept my conclusion. But it is always possible that someone may reject the premises of any argument. What I am contending is that no reasonable person will disagree on these thought experiments. This is because a thought experiment is a conductive argument. In effect, I am arguing that the results of these thought experiments disprove ethical egoism; and indeed they do, if the results are what I claim. However, these thought experiments are themselves ethical arguments in which the premises include other-regarding reasons. Thus my argument is essentially inductive. I am arguing that the general principle that other-regarding reasons are irrelevant to judgments of obligation is false because in these cases we can see that such considerations are clearly relevant. Anyone who sees the relevance in these cases must reject ethical egoism. In the end this is how I think that the logical issue between ethical egoism and ethical universalism must be decided, by confronting our logical generalizations with clear cases of valid ethical arguments.

CONCLUSION

When the truth of some ethical statement is challenged, the obvious move is to give arguments in support of the statement. But now one is open to a new sort of challenge, the validity challenge. Every argument claims that its conclusion follows validly from its premises, and this claim can always be questioned or denied. It is hard to imagine any grounds for challenging the validity of all ethical arguments, and as far as I know this wholesale challenge has never been made. On the other hand, certain species of ethical arguments have often been questioned. I have discussed arguments from factual premises to ethical conclusions and arguments from other-regarding considerations to judgments of obligation. I hope that the reader will agree with me as to the validity or invalidity of these kinds of reasoning, but at least I will have illustrated how one can go about discussing validity challenges. Validity challenges are most common in the case of individual ethical arguments; one is often called upon to defend some ethical argument one has used. Clearly validity challenges and responses are an important part of the process of justifying ethical statements.

11. validity-value

THE claim that any ethical statement is true is primarily defended by argument, by advancing considerations in support of the statement. But as soon as a speaker gives reasons for his ethical statement, he is open to several new challenges. The last chapter was concerned with one of these, the validity challenge. It may be suggested that what is advanced in support of the conclusion is not a good reason because, quite apart from any question of its truth or falsity, it is logically irrelevant to the conclusion it is intended to support. This challenge concedes that the speaker has advanced an argument but suggests that the argument is an invalid one.

There is, however, a more basic challenge that can be made at this point. The challenger may suggest that what the speaker advanced as an argument is not really an argument at all. It is not just that the consideration advanced is not a good reason, it is not a reason at all. Hence, what purports to be or is taken to be reasoning is not reasoning but something else like persuading or rationalization. It is not simply that the speaker's claim to be arguing validly is mistaken, it is entirely out of place. His linguistic performance is just not the sort of language that can claim validity. He has presented only a pseudoargument without any validity-value.

The term "validity-value" is intended to be an obvious analogue of the term "truth-value," for the parallel between arguments and statements is highly illuminating. Every statement makes an implicit claim to truth, and this claim to truth can always be challenged. But more radical than this truth challenge is the truth-value challenge, for this challenges the right of the utterance to even claim to be true. An utterance that is neither true nor false is not a genuine statement, much less a true one. Similarly, every argument makes an implicit claim to validity, and this claim to validity can be challenged. If the validity challenge is made good, the utterance is shown not to be an argument at all. It cannot even be mistaken in its claim to validity, for it is incapable of making any such claim. The utterance is neither valid nor invalid; it is some sort of utterance to which logical criticism is entirely inappropriate. No matter how much it may look or sound like an argument, at best it is a pseudoargument.

This validity-value challenge is clearly relevant to our subject. If a speaker is to justify his claim to have made a true ethical statement, he must be able to present arguments to support his statement. When he is trying to justify his statement by giving reasons for it, he can hardly admit that he is not really reasoning. Unless he can defend the validity-value of his arguments, he cannot claim that they give any logical support to his conclusions. Therefore, any speaker who would justify his claim to speak truly must also be prepared to meet any validity-value challenges that may be directed at his ethical arguments.

Wholesale and retail challenges

It may be well to give a few examples to show that this challenge is a real one. Although the term "validity-value" is new, the validity-value challenge is at least as old as Hume. He tried to show that induction should be analyzed in psychological rather than logical terms. Inferences from past to future cases are not rational arguments subject to a special logic of induction by which valid inductions can be distinguished from invalid ones. Properly understood the movement of belief from past to future cases is a habit of the mind produced by the impact of past experience upon the imagination. Extrapolation beyond past experience is to be ascribed to the imagination not to reason.[1]

More recently ethical arguments have been subject to the validity-value challenge. At one time Ayer thought that the emotive theory of ethics implies that there can be no dispute about ethical issues. If ethical sentences merely express emotions, then there is no logical incompatibility between "it is good" and "it is not good" said by two different speakers. In fact, since neither utterance is either true or false, there can be no such thing as proving either of them true. In ethical discussions, all the genuine reasoning concerns factual issues; there is no such thing as ethical reasoning.[2]

It should not be thought that the validity-value challenge is issued only by the overscrupulous philosopher. The man in the street or the student in his first philosophy course may challenge the status of whole classes of ethical arguments. It is often suggested that values are all a matter of taste or that everything is relative when it comes to social obligations. Although these suggestions are often poorly defined and incompletely worked out, they are usually taken to imply that reasoning is out of place in these matters. Wholesale validity-value challenges, challenges directed at all ethical arguments or some entire class of ethical arguments, are not uncommon.

Considerably less common, but not unknown, are retail validity-value challenges, challenges directed at some individual argument. Surprisingly enough, a speaker may take himself to be reasoning when he is not, and a hearer may take some remark to be an argument when it was not meant to be such. In these cases the validity-value challenge is quite in order. Let us look at a few examples of such pseudoarguments, bits of language that may seem to be arguments but which really are neither valid nor invalid.

Children learn to argue at a remarkably early age. It is not uncommon for a three-year-old to come out with things like "I don't want to go to bed because it's no fun being in bed" or "you should give me a piece of candy because you gave Billy a piece and it is no fair giving him a piece if you don't give me one." At other times the attempts of the child to argue are more suspect. He may say "this food is icky" or "you ought to give me a birthday present, too." When pressed for a reason, the three-year-old is likely to say "because" in an emphatic tone of voice. When asked "but why, because of what?" the usual reply is "just because." What the child takes to be a perfectly respectable argument is not an argument at all. It is not just that the reasoning is invalid; no reason has been given at all.

It is not only children who take themselves to be reasoning when they are not. In spite of their allegiance to the ideal of rationality, parents may become impatient with the need to justify their ethical statements to their children. All day long mother may explain patiently just why lying is wrong and why kindness is a virtue. But by the time the child asks "but why should I go to bed?" for the third or fourth time, the reply may be "because I tell you to, that's why!" This reply may be a genuine argument consisting in an appeal to the child's obligation to obey its parents, or it may be a naked threat of dire consequences to follow disobedience. But at times a mother or father may take himself to be arguing when he is only clothing a refusal to give reasons in the language of reasoning.

Pseudoarguments are not limited to conversations between parent and child. Consider the person who says heatedly "unnatural sexual acts are wrong because they are loathesome and disgusting." Probably the speaker wants to reason on this matter and takes himself to be advancing powerful considerations in support of his conclusion. What he is actually doing is using powerful emotive language to express his feelings and give psychological support to his moral conviction. On ethical issues where people feel deeply, particularly if the subject is either traditional or taboo, it is common for speakers to lapse into emotive language when they take themselves to be giving reasons for their ethical statements. When they do this they are not giving reasons in any logical sense, much less valid ones. It is not that the consideration advanced happens to be irrelevant, there is no premise to consider. On such occasions the validity-value challenge is quite in order.

Finally, it will be illuminating to consider a more colorful example of pseudoargument. Try to imagine that I am philosophical enough to say to the bear about to devour me "you ought not to eat me because I have a wife and children to support." My utterance seems to draw an ethical conclusion from a factual premise, but this appearance is misleading. The difficulty is not simply that this brute lacks the rationality to understand my argument or guide his conduct by its conclusion; futile reasoning is still reasoning. Rather, I have not really presented any argument because I have drawn no ethical conclusion. Although "you ought not to eat me" sounds like an ethical conclusion, it is not a genuine statement when "you" refers to a bear. It is a truth-value presupposition of any ought statement that the subject be a moral agent. Thus my attempted argument is left without any conclusion, and where there is nothing to prove there can be nothing like proof. This example may seem more picturesque than important, but it illustrates a principle that applies to more ordinary situations. We often find speakers trying to prove that little children, the feebleminded, or insane or emotionally disturbed people ought or ought not to do some action or, having done it, that they are or are not wicked. Now if it should turn out that these classes of people are not really moral agents, then these attempted arguments will be shown to be without conclusions. At this point the validity-value challenge could have a real bearing on our discussion of live ethical issues.

I hope that I have convinced the reader that the validity-value challenge is actually made in ethical discussions and that sometimes it is of both theoretical and practical interest. It is probably much less common than either truth or validity challenges, but it is not unknown. Pure emotivism seems to imply that there can be no such thing as a genuine ethical argument. Various philosophers have debated the existence of a kind of reasoning that draws ethical conclusions from purely factual premises and which can be reduced to neither deductive nor inductive inference. And in the case of this or that individual utterance there may be real doubt as to whether the utterance should be taken to be an argument or not. In such cases the validity-value challenge is very much to the point.

Ultimate ethical arguments

Sometimes the validity-value challenge is directed not at some individual argument offered by some particular speaker on some given occasion, but at all ethical arguments or an entire class of ethical arguments. Although Stevenson admits both deductive and inductive reasoning into ethics, he denies that either is applicable to ultimate ethical arguments. If ethical disagreement is pushed far enough, the only reasons a person can give for his ethical conclusion are the facts of the individual case, and these facts are related psychologically, not logically, to any ethical conclusion about that case.

Stevenson presents his argument to show that there can be nothing like logical validity in ultimate ethical arguments in chapter 7 of *Ethics and Language*. Baldly stated, his argument is the following. Since ethical sentences express attitudes and attitudes are neither true nor false, ethical sentences themselves lack truth-value. Therefore, logical validity, which is defined in terms of truth, is inapplicable to ethical arguments.

One difficulty with this line of reasoning is that it proves too much. If all ethical sentences lack truth-value and if truth-value is required for logical validity, then no argument leading to any ethical conclusion could ever be logically valid. Stevenson, however, wishes to insist upon the applicability of deductive and inductive logic to ethical argument. Let us see whether we can save Stevenson from his own validity-value challenge by examining the assumptions he makes.

Is it true that ethical sentences lack truth-value? Clearly if the *only* reason for asserting that ethical sentences are neither true nor false is that any such claims would be empty in the absence of ethical reasoning, then it would be logically circular to go on and use their lack of truth-value as the only reason for asserting that there can be no genuine reasoning to ethical conclusions. However, Stevenson avoids this vicious circle by offering an independent reason for denying truth-value to ethical sentences. They are incapable of being either true or false because they express attitudes, and attitudes are neither true nor false.

I must admit that attitudes are lacking in truth-value. Certainly we never apply the words "true" or "false" to desire or aversion, admiration or contempt, liking or disliking, or any other attitudes. Nor can I see any reason to claim that our ordinary language is misleading in this respect. On the other hand, we do ordinarily speak of attitudes as "reasonable" or "unreasonable," "appropriate" or "inappropriate" to their objects. I would insist that attitudes like desire and aversion, approval and disapproval do make a claim to rationality, a claim to be supported by the weight of relevant considerations. I have argued this point at some length elsewhere.[3] Because this claim to appropriateness is precisely analogous to the claim to truth, the sentences that express attitudes and claim implicitly that the attitudes expressed are reasonable can be said to make a claim to truth. Therefore, although it is true that attitudes are without truth-value, it does not follow that the ethical sentences that express them are similarly devoid of truth-value.

But even if they were, I could not admit that there can be no genuine ethical reasoning. The core of Stevenson's argument is that the claim to validity is essential to genuine reasoning and that the validity of an argument is defined in terms of the truth-value of its conclusion. I grant that reasoning is necessarily tied to validity, but I do not concede that validity is defined in terms of truth-value. Admittedly, logic texts usually say that to call an argument valid is to say that it is impossible for its premises to be true and its conclusion false. No doubt many, perhaps most, logicians do use the word "valid" in this limited sense. Quite possibly this is the most useful conception for the deductive logician to use. It is not, however, entirely satisfactory to the philosopher trying to understand the nature of reasoning in general or deduction in particular. The main difficulty with this definition is that it uses the notion of logical impossibility, and this notion is at least as obscure as that of validity. While it is entirely proper for the logician to take the notions of logical necessity and logical impossibility as undefined terms, the responsible epistemologist will want to give some sort of an explanation or analysis of these concepts. This is one reason I have tried to analyze the claim to validity in chapter 4.

Be that as it may, when I speak of validity I am not using the term in the restricted sense current among logicians, for I intend the word to apply to all kinds of reasoning. If it is granted that inductive and conductive arguments cannot be reduced to deductive form *and* that they are subject to logical criticism, then it must be admitted that there is a genuine sense in which these arguments are valid or invalid. By logical criticism I mean the judgment of correctness or incorrectness as inferences, as drawing a conclusion from one or more premises, quite apart from any question of the truth of the premises. Once deductivism is abandoned, the need for this broader conception of validity becomes apparent.

It may still be thought that, whatever the correct definition of "valid" turns out to be, it is bound to contain the notion of truth. Why? Why should it be assumed that one must define validity in terms of truth? Probably because we use reasoning primarily to justify the claim to truth. If validity were not defined in terms of the truth of the conclusion, it is hard to see how the validity of an argument from true premises could be any guarantee, or even support, for the truth of the conclusion. This does show, I believe, that we want some tie between validity and truth, but it does not prove that the notion of truth is the basic one. Instead of defining validity in terms of truth, we might well define truth in terms of validity. This is just what I would suggest. To say that a statement is true is to claim that it is supported by the weight of the valid reasons.

No doubt there are problems with my definition of truth, but there are even stronger reasons to reject the definition of validity in terms of truth. Recent developments in formal logic indicate that there may be a logic of imperatives. Although there is considerable controversy about the formal structure of any such logic, and even about its legitimacy, there is enough analogy between the formal relations among imperatives and those among indicatives to suggest that further investigation is promising. Now imperatives quite clearly are neither true nor false. Therefore, if imperatives can function as conclusions in logical arguments, logical validity can hardly be limited to proving truth.

Moreover, we speak of emotions and attitudes as reasonable or unreasonable. Although this could be a mere figure of speech, I have argued that it is not. Strange as it sounds when put this way, emotions can be the conclusions of arguments. This is implied by the way in which we criticize emotions and attitudes by factual information. Once more, reasoning is not limited to establishing the truth.

If ethics is genuine, reasoning must not be so limited. The central ethical problem is the problem of choice. Decision constitutes a problem, something calling for a solution rather than a purely psychological discomfort to be lived through, only because reasons are relevant to the choice between alternatives. To ask "what ought I to do in this situation?" is to presuppose that there are reasons for and against the practical alternatives presented by the situation. Any theory that circumscribes reasoning so narrowly that it is limited to true and false statements may satisfy the logician, the scientist, and even the moral philosopher who merely talks about action, but it can never satisfy the man who has to act. The practical problem is to discover the right action, not the right way to talk about action. For this reason it is not sufficient to look at ethical reasoning as leading to ethical statements that apply to action. Ethical reasoning must, at least sometimes, go beyond establishing the truth of a statement; it must sometimes be practical in the literal sense of leading to practice. Since actions are neither true nor false, valid reasoning must not be defined in terms of the truth of the conclusion.

In the end, then, one cannot deny that ethical sentences are statements, that they make a claim to objective truth, on the grounds that they express attitudes and, therefore, cannot be the conclusions of valid reasoning. Although attitudes are neither true nor false, sentences that express them can have truth-value. Even if they could not, there is a broad sense of logical validity applicable to arguments leading to conclusions that are neither true nor false. Thus, the analysis of the notion of validity cannot serve as a basis for denying that justification is appropriate to ethics.

Rationalization

Contemporary psychology presents a different challenge to the reality of ethical reasoning. The psychoanalyst can explain why a person values power or condemns "unnatural" sexual acts so violently, but the reasons the person himself gives to justify his ethical convictions fail really to explain why he holds them. And what is true of ethical convictions is also true of moral action. The reasons one gives, to others and even to oneself, to justify one's actions turn out not to be one's real reasons for acting at all; human action is primarily the result of unconscious desires and hidden goals. Therefore, what seems to be reasoning to reach an ethical conclusion is merely rationalization of some commitment already made on quite different grounds. The real function of such rationalization is not to determine whether or not the ethical judgment is correct but to conceal or make respectable one's desires and deeds.

The philosopher should not quarrel with the psychologist, at least not on matters of empirical psychology; but he may properly object to the conceptual confusions in this validity-value challenge. First, discoveries about the psychological function of ethical arguments are irrelevant to their logical status. No doubt the modern psychologist has discovered some surprising and even embarrassing things about our motives for giving ethical arguments and the ends we achieve by so doing. We are not always motivated by any pure desire to reach the objective truth; we are much more concerned to hide certain truths and to gain the love or avoid the censure of those around us or of ourselves. By so doing we may avoid personal conflicts, manage to continue to pursue our selfish ends, and even dominate those around us. But all this fascinating information about our motives in and the results of ethical discourse has no bearing on the logical status of our ethical arguments. The issue here is whether we make a genuine claim to validity that can be correct or incorrect in any strict logical sense. Why we argue is one question; whether we argue is quite another.

Second, there is a confusion in saying that ethical utterances are not really conclusions in ethical arguments. The contention is that to say that an ethical utterance is a conclusion of reasoning is to imply that it either was arrived at by reasoning or at least is corrigible in the light of subsequent reasoning. But ethical convictions are not the product of reasoning;

they arise from causes deep within the subconscious. Nor can
the reasons given ever put any ethical conviction in question,
for they are selected by the reasoner precisely to put a respectable face on his prior commitment. In reply, I would argue
that, within the context of justification, the origin of an ethical
conviction is irrelevant. The issue is not whether it was arrived
at by reasoning but whether, however it may have arisen, it
can now be justified by valid reasons. Still, the contention is
that the considerations advanced are not really allowed to
count for or against the conviction; rather the conviction is the
fixed point and the considerations are simply adopted to defend
it. Now even if it were true that an ethical arguer never gave
any reasons but those which put a good front on his conviction,
it might still be that they did this just because they were also
logically relevant. However, it is not true that reasons are never
allowed to count against an ethical conclusion. We often recognize the relevance of considerations advanced by those who
disagree with us and correct our ethical convictions in the light
of these considerations, and we sometimes go so far as to give
reasons against our own statements. Therefore, it is not shown
that ethical utterances are not really conclusions of logical
arguments.

Third, there is a confusion in arguing that the reasons
we give to justify our ethical conclusions are not really reasons because they are not the real reasons. When a psychologist talks about the reason for an action, he usually means
either the agent's motive in doing the action or the factor which
will explain why he did the action. A motive is a very personal
thing; my reasons for teaching may be very different from
those of another teacher. Something does not become my reason for acting just because it is logically relevant to my action;
only if I guide my action by that consideration do I make it
mine by adopting it. In addition to penetrating to my reasons
for acting, the psychologist may discover the reasons that explain my action. These reasons are the causes that explain in
terms of some theoretical structure why I do what I do. Now
what the psychologist has discovered is that the reasons that a
person gives when he is asked why he does something, or why
he accepts some ethical statement, are not the real reasons in

either of these two senses. They are not the person's real motives for doing what he did and they do not really explain why he did what he did. His real motives and the real explanations are usually hidden from the agent within his subconscious. But the fact that the stated reasons are not the real reasons (motives or explanations) does not imply that they are not really reasons (logically relevant considerations). The epistemologist is using the word "reason" in quite a different sense. In this sense it is not required that a reason for an action be the agent's motive for doing the action or a psychological explanation of the action; all that is required is that the consideration be logically relevant to the action and that it count for rather than against it. It is a mistake to confuse this logical sense of a reason with either of the psychological senses of the term.

There is, therefore, no need to deny the findings of empirical psychology in order to save ethical reasoning. Let us admit that much, perhaps most, possibly all ethical reasoning is rationalizing. Still, the fact that our motives in arguing are not purely rational and the results of our arguing may be to conceal the truth does not prove that we are not giving logical arguments for these motives and with these results. The fact that we often argue for conclusions that were not arrived at by reasoning does not prove that we are not now justifying them by reasoning. And the fact that the reasons we state may not be our real motives or any adequate psychological explanation of why we do what we do or believe what we believe does not prove that they are not logically relevant to our actions and ethical convictions. Ethical argument may be rationalization and genuine reasoning, too. Rationalizing is an empty show from the psychological standpoint, for it lacks motivating power and even disguises the real springs of action. But the power of justification is not identical with motivating force. Therefore, to show that certain considerations are psychologically ineffective does not in itself show that they are logically irrelevant.

CONCLUSION

When a speaker wishes to show that some ethical statement is true, he will usually present an ethical argument to support it. But something may seem to be a logical argument when it is not a bit of reasoning at all. Just as there are pseudo-statements, so there are pseudoarguments. These bits of language may seem to claim logical validity, but in reality they are neither valid nor invalid. Fortunately, there are ways in which a speaker can defend his claim to have given a genuine argument should its validity-value be challenged. In addition to such challenges of individual arguments, there are challenges directed at whole classes of arguments. I have examined the main validity-value challenges to all ethical arguments and to conductive ethical arguments and have tried to show that they cannot be sustained. Ethical arguments, even conductive ethical arguments, are a genuine form of reasoning. Reassured that rational justification is possible in ethics, let us continue our explanation of how ethical statements can be justified—that is, of how the possible challenges to them can be met.

UNLIKE that traditional American hero, the self-made man, ethical statements do not make themselves. Ethical statements are made by some person who utters them to others or to himself. This fact that stating is a linguistic act requiring someone to do the stating opens the way for a kind of challenge quite different from any we have discussed, the competence challenge. This is a challenge to the competence of the speaker, to his epistemological right to speak as he does. Heretofore we have usually considered statements and arguments as disembodied entities that claim truth or validity respectively; now we must take into account the fact that these claims to truth or validity are made on behalf of these forms of utterance by those who utter them. To make an ethical statement is to claim implicitly that it is true. Therefore, any speaker who makes an ethical statement opens himself to the charge that he is incompetent to make such a claim for his utterance. This is the competence challenge, which I will consider in this chapter.

There are, of course, many kinds of competence, but most of these are irrelevant to the justification of ethical statements. The speaker need not defend his competence as a golfer, doctor, typist, or even public speaker in order to justify his ethical statements. However, even within the relevant kinds of competence there are many varieties. There is competence as an ethical judge, as a judge of the truth or falsity of ethical statements. Then there is competence as an ethical reasoner, as one who uses or follows ethical arguments. There is also competence as an informed man, as a scientist, as a rational man, as a judge of the validity of arguments, or even as a clarifier of obscure statements and arguments. I shall focus my discussion on competence as an ethical judge, for this seems most central to the justification of ethical statements.

The relevance of the challenge

Why bother? Why is it necessary for the speaker to defend his competence? After all, the speaker's competence is not directly relevant to the truth of his statement. That is, one does not necessarily prove that the statement is false by showing that the speaker is incompetent, for there is such a thing as a lucky guess or an accidental assertion of the truth. Little as I know about horses and racing, I am sometimes fortunate when I try to predict the winner of the next race, and my drunken friends sometimes happen to utter true statements. Conversely, one does not ordinarily establish the truth of a statement by showing that the speaker is competent to make it. The reasons that show a statement to be true are the various premises that could be given to establish it, not the fact that this or that speaker happens to know these premises and grasps their relevance.

Therefore, a speaker can sometimes dismiss a challenge to his competence without attempting to meet it. He can either ignore the challenge or concede it without retracting his statement. A speaker might say "whether or not I am drunk is beside the point" or perhaps "I admit that I cannot prove it, but I still think that euthanasia is sometimes right." Just how long and under what circumstances it is legitimate to go on claiming to speak the truth while admitting that one is unable to support this claim is a nice question, but at least this move can sometimes be made and I believe that it is not always unreasonable.

Still, there is some connection between the competence of a speaker and his claim to speak the truth; in fact, there seem to be three ways in which competence is relevant to truth. First, we learn by experience that competent speakers are more likely to make true statements than incompetent ones. Therefore, the fact that a given speaker is competent is evidence for the truth of what he says and, similarly, the incompetence of a speaker is evidence against the truth of his statements. This argument from authority is a perfectly valid one, but it is necessarily indirect and secondary. This is so because we can establish the authority of a speaker only by showing that he is usually or always correct, and to do this requires that we have some prior and independent way to judge the correctness of his statements.

This appeal to authority is not only theoretically legitimate, it is of considerable practical importance in ethics. When trying to decide whether a new movie is worth seeing, one would do well to consult someone, either a friend or a reviewer, who has already seen the film. In picking a doctor or automobile mechanic upon moving into a new town, one should ask the advice of someone who is familiar with the town and, if possible, knows something about medicine or motors. If one is wrestling with a serious moral problem with which he is deeply involved, one will do well to consult someone who can take up a more dispassionate stance. The rational justification for seeking and following advice lies in part in the fact that, even when one may be unable to determine the truth or falsity of an ethical statement directly by weighing the relevant considerations, one may be able to infer its truth indirectly from the fact that it is accepted by one or more competent speakers. Normally, an authority is expected to be more competent in the matter at hand than the person who consults him. It is helpful to consult authorities because competence is a matter of degree and because it varies from subject to subject. Therefore, even a knowledgeable and reasonable man can often find an authority to consult on any given occasion.

The value of advice is not simply a matter of the greater competence of the adviser, however. One may reasonably seek advice from one who is no more competent than himself. Advice is sometimes justified because two heads are better than one, not because one head is better than another. A friend who is no better informed than myself may still know some things of which I am ignorant; a thinker no more rational than I may still not make exactly the same mistakes in thinking through some complex ethical issue. Therefore, the judgment of one person is apt to be better if he engages in discussion with other people, whether or not they are authorities. This is because the give-and-take of public debate supplies information and criticism that enables a man to think things through better for himself. In this way advice may be an aid to a direct knowledge of ethical statements as well as a basis for indirect knowledge of their truth. In any event, here is one way in which the competence of the speaker is relevant to the truth of his statement; the competent speaker is more likely to utter the truth.

Second, only a competent speaker is in a position to defend his claim to speak the truth. To make a statement is to claim implicitly that it is true, that it can be supported with reasons which will outweigh any reasons that can be brought against it. Now it is quite possible for this claim to be correct even though a given speaker is unable to produce these reasons because he has never learned them, he has forgotten them, he does not recognize their relevance, or he is rendered incoherent by emotional stress. On the other hand, neither speaker nor hearer has any reason for accepting the claim to truth as long as it is unsupported with evidence. Of course, someone other than the speaker could defend his claim to speak the truth, but such defenders are not always handy. Therefore, for a speaker to admit his incompetence as an ethical judge is for him to admit that he has no adequate basis for his claim to speak the truth and that he is not able fully to defend it in the give-and-take of discussion. This is tantamount to admitting that his claim to speak the truth is an empty gesture, a stab in the dark which may be lucky but on which there is no reason to bet. To admit this is to rob one's statement of any reasonable claim upon the acceptance of one's audience.

Third, an incompetent speaker has no vote on the truth of his statement. To judge a statement true is to render a critical verdict to be sustained or overruled by the process of criticism. Strictly speaking it is the various persons who engage in the thinking and discussion which is criticism who render verdicts of true or false. To claim that a statement is true is to claim that it would be accepted after an indefinite amount of reasoning for and against it by everyone who thinks in the normal way. At this point the respect in which the speaker is supposed to be incompetent becomes of some importance. Certain defects can be remedied by the very process of discussion itself. If the speaker is uninformed, the additional facts of the case can be brought to his attention; if the speaker is confused, the reasoning can be explained to him more clearly. But if the speaker is drunk or irrational, it may be that no amount of discussion can make him into a competent ethical judge. It is where the process of discussion cannot hope to remove the incompetence that one is most justified in breaking off discussion with an incompetent speaker and discounting his opinion as mistaken.

Another way to put this point is this. Normally disagreement is the occasion for discussion, for the giving of reasons for and against the statement in doubt. Out of this debate it is hoped that some degree of unanimity can be achieved; the aim is to produce agreement out of disagreement. If this can be done, the verdict of the process of reasoning is clear. But what if disagreement persists? Well, if one party can be shown to be incompetent, then his opinion can be dismissed as not warranted by the discussion. Therefore, any speaker who wishes to maintain his claim to speak the truth in the face of those who deny his statements will wish to defend his competence as an ethical judge. For only then can he claim that the fact that his conviction has withstood the test of criticism is any support for its correctness.

In sum, it appears that there are three ways in which the challenge to a speaker's competence is relevant to his claim to speak the truth. The incompetence of a speaker is indirect evidence of the falsity of his statements because incompetent speakers are less likely to speak the truth than other speakers. Although an incompetent speaker can claim truth for his statement, he is not in a position fully to defend this claim. And the opinion of an incompetent speaker cannot represent itself as the verdict of the process of criticism. For these three reasons one who makes an ethical statement may find that he must meet a challenge to his competence as an ethical judge in order to justify his ethical statements.

Defining competence

Although I do not accept the ideal-observer analysis of
ethical statements, I agree that competence does play an important part in the justification of ethical statements. It is,
therefore, incumbent upon me to give some sort of definition
of the competent ethical judge and some account of the way
this concept functions in justification. It is quite possible, I
fear, that there is no such thing as *the* competent ethical judge.
It may be that the sort of man who is a good judge of character
is not exactly the same as the sort of man who can size up a
practical situation and decide what is to be done. However, I
propose to ignore these complexities and consider only those
aspects of the subject that bear on the justification of ethical
statements.

What sort of a man would be competent to judge ethical
issues? Perhaps a man who is *1*) a sane *2*) adult *3*)
who understands the issue,   *4*) knows all the relevant facts,
5) is entertaining them all vividly *6*) and sees clearly their
relevance to the issue at hand,   *7*) has experienced similar
things himself,   *8*) has the sympathy to understand and care
for others,   *9*) is impartial with respect to everyone involved,
10) has a nervous system of the human type, and   *11*) is not
overexcited, tired, drunk, or drugged. This list of characteristics may strike the reader as either redundant or incomplete
or both; for my purposes this does not matter. What does
matter is that each have some plausibility and that the entire
list be something like the list that a more careful analysis would
produce.

Now one might be tempted to define the competent ethical judge as someone who fulfills all of these conditions. Something like this is often done in the ideal-observer theories. This
would be a mistake, however. For one thing, it trivializes some
very important questions. A person may reasonably ask "why
does a lack of sympathy render one incompetent to judge ethical issues?" or "how do you know that drugs do not sharpen a
man's ethical insight?" To incorporate being sympathetic and
undrugged in the definition of competence is to make the an-

swers to these questions analytic and to make the questions serious only for the person who does not fully understand the meaning of his question. But surely these are legitimate questions that do not arise from any confusion or lack of understanding. For another thing, such a definition misrepresents the justification for asserting that being sympathetic or sober are conditions of competence. To offer the definition as an analysis of what we ordinarily mean by a "competent ethical judge" is to suggest that the connection between such conditions and competence is established simply by reflection on what we mean. To offer the definition as a proposed redefinition is to suggest that the connection is not discovered at all but created by stipulation. In fact, however, conditions such as being sympathetic and sober are not contained in the very meaning of "competent ethical judge" as we now use these words, and the philosopher who proposes to include them in his redefinition does so because he finds them associated with competence in the prephilosophical sense. We know that being sympathetic and sober are conditions of competence because we find that people who lack sympathy or are drunk also lack the ability to make correct ethical judgments. We find this out, not by thinking about what we mean by "competence," but by observing the judgments of the unsympathetic and drunk and finding them frequently mistaken. Because our justification for asserting that being sympathetic and sober are connected with competence is in part empirical, it is misleading to make this assertion true by definition and thereby nonempirical. Another way of putting my point is that it is misleading to pack all the conditions of competence into the definition of "competence" because this obscures the very different ways in which one must justify his assertion that they are conditions of competence. How different these sorts of justification are we will see below, in the section titled "Justifying the Standards."

But if one is not to define the competent ethical judge in terms of the various conditions of competence, how can this notion be defined? I suggest that what we *mean* by the "competent ethical judge" is simply one who has the ability to judge an ethical issue correctly. Three points call for comment here. First, competence consists in a certain ability. One cannot define the competent judge as the one who does judge correctly; for someone may be competent to judge when he is not actually judging, and an incompetent judge may happen to make a correct judgment by accident. An ability, in the sense required by this definition, is a sort of capacity. It is not a capacity in the sense that salt has the capacity to dissolve in water, for then accidental success would establish the capacity to judge correctly. It is a capacity that can be exercised at will, one that will not fail because of external circumstances. The man with the complete ability to judge correctly can do so whenever he wishes; his ability protects him from trying and failing. Second, competence as an ethical judge depends upon what is to be judged. A person who is competent to judge one issue may well be incompetent to judge another with which he is unfamiliar or more personally involved. Thus competence can have a wider or narrower range. Competence is a relative notion, for it is always competence with respect to this particular or those few ethical issues. It is too much to expect any person to be universally competent. Third, competence as an ethical judge is an ideal which actual judgers can only approximate. Although we may distinguish very roughly between competent and incompetent judges in ethics, no man has the complete ability to judge ethical issues correctly, for ethical infallibility is beyond the human level. Still, some men are good, if not perfect, judges of ethical issues, and on any given issue quite a number of men may be able enough to reach the correct conclusion. All we normally ask of any speaker is that he be reasonably competent, not too obviously or seriously incompetent. If he can approximate the ideal of competence, then his judgment and the responses he gives when his judgment is challenged are worth taking seriously. "The competent ethical judge" can be defined, then, as one who has the ability to judge ethical issues correctly.

Standards of competence

If competence as an ethical judge consists in the ability to judge ethical issues correctly, how does one establish the competence or incompetence of some individual speaker? Occasionally by direct induction from his performance as an ethical judge over a period of time. A person can estimate the degree of practical wisdom of each of his close friends or associates by observing whether or not they usually come to correct conclusions about ethical issues. This inductive inference takes one's own ethical judgments as correct and really appeals to the extent to which others agree with one. It is not quite as arbitrary as it seems, however, because it can avail itself of hindsight and corrected insight. I may recognize the ability of my friend to predict values or disvalues by finding out, after the fact, that his predictions are usually confirmed by the course of events. Here I am not taking my own precarious prediction as the measure of his prediction, but my judgment of what has come about as the test of his guess as to what will come about. Again, I need not take my first opinion as the criterion of correctness. I may measure his judgments before much discussion or investigation against my conclusions informed by additional facts and extended criticism. Still, this way of estimating the competence of a speaker has serious drawbacks. It can be used only where one is thoroughly familiar with the person being judged, and it does take one's own competence for granted to an alarming degree.

Usually when the competence of some speaker is in question, the question is decided by appealing to some standard of competence. The person accused may say "you are in no position to judge me because you did not see what happened"; a speaker may assert "but I am sober as a judge." In challenges and responses like these being informed and being undrunk are used as standards of competence as an ethical judge. Thus the charge of incompetence and the defense of competence are normally supported with reasons, and each reason takes for granted some standard of competence. Discussion usually centers upon whether or not the speaker fulfills the standard to which the appeal is made.

What sorts of standards are available? In this respect, the definition of the competent ethical judge I have given is not very helpful. One cannot appeal very often to the ability to judge ethical issues correctly because this ability is not an occurrent property that is readily observable in any given case. In fact, when the question of competence arises, it is the existence of this ability that is at issue. To appeal to this ability or its absence to establish competence or incompetence is to beg the question. The best one could hope for would be a set of necessary and sufficient conditions universally correlated with this ability.

It seems to me that there are two conditions which are each necessary and jointly sufficient for competence as an ethical judge, that one have all the relevant information and that one recognize its relevance to the case at hand. In what sense must one have all this information? It is not enough that one be able to recall it bit by bit, for it must all be held together in the mind to be properly weighed. Yet only a very limited amount of information can be in the mind in the sense of being attended to or thought about at any single moment. What seems to be required is that all the relevant information be active in the mind, that it be informing the judgment even though the judger may not be paying attention to it all at once. In what sense must one recognize the relevance of all this information? Not just that one would acknowledge the relevance of each bit of information if it were suggested to him. One must be according to each and every bit of information its due weight in drawing the valid conclusion from it. Unless one has all the relevant information and recognizes its relevance in this sense, the correctness of his judgment is accidental; he cannot be sure of judging correctly. If these two conditions are fulfilled, no room for possible error remains. Therefore, these constitute a set of necessary and sufficient conditions of competence. But it is also very difficult to ascertain whether or not any given speaker fulfills these conditions. Hence, they are not very useful criteria of competence.

It might be easier to discover a necessary *or* a sufficient condition of being a competent ethical judge. If it can be shown that being sober is a necessary condition of competence, one can argue "you are incompetent because you are drunk." If it can be shown that knowing the facts plus recognizing their relevance is a sufficient condition of competence, one can argue "I am competent because I know all the relevant facts and recognize their relevance." In this way debate about the competence of this or that speaker to make a given ethical statement can proceed by appealing to certain accepted standards of competence, standards which are accepted because they are known to be conditions of competence.

It is very hard, however, to identify sufficient conditions of competence. I have suggested that having all the relevant information plus recognizing its relevance is one sufficient condition. However, it is so hard to show that one satisfies this condition that it is not a very useful standard for a speaker to use to establish his competence. There may be other, more easily identifiable, sufficient conditions of competence, but I find it impossible to think of any. On the other hand, there seem to be a great many necessary conditions of competence. Hence there are many standards to which one can appeal to challenge the competence of some speaker. Moreover, many of these conditions are empirical characteristics which are relatively easy to identify in any given case, such as being sober or being impartial. And in the case of critical predicates, such as "having all the relevant information," it may be much easier to show that this condition is absent than to show that it is fulfilled. The result of all this is that standards of competence function negatively for the most part. It is seldom if ever possible to establish one's competence as an ethical judge by appealing to any standards of competence, but it is often possible to establish incompetence by such standards. This means that any speaker who could defend his competence as an ethical judge is confined to meeting this or that challenge, to showing that he is not incompetent in this or that specified way. To go beyond this and show that one is completely competent in every respect is hardly ever practical.

Justifying the standards

Any attempt to establish the competence or incompetence of any speaker normally accepts certain standards of competence and applies these to the case at hand. But it is quite possible, and sometimes reasonable, to challenge some alleged standard of competence as an ethical judge. How, then, is it possible to justify a standard of competence? How can one show that it genuinely is a measure of competence as a judge of ethical issues? In many different ways, as a survey of a few standards reveals.

1

The correctness of past judgments in similar cases is one obvious standard of competence. That this is a legitimate standard can be seen by analyzing the notion of competence itself. By a competent ethical judge we mean one who has the ability to judge an ethical issue correctly. Since an ability is the ability to do something, the defining criterion for the existence of any ability is success in doing that thing. Just as the primary test of whether a person has the ability to play golf is whether he does play golf well when he tries, so the primary test of whether a person can make correct ethical judgments is whether in fact he does make correct ones when he tries to do so. Therefore, past success as an ethical judge is the primary basis for determining the competence of any speaker as an ethical judge. This conclusion is justified by an analysis of the very conception of competence as an ability.

2

Having all the relevant information and recognizing its relevance are also standards of competence. How do we know that these are each necessary and together sufficient to competence as an ethical judge? Primarily by an analysis of the notion of correctness. The competent ethical judge is one who has the ability to judge ethical issues correctly. Now what determines the correctness of his judgment? Well, to say that his judgment is correct is to make a critical judgment to be tested by the process of criticism, primarily by the presentation of reasons for and against his judgment. Now clearly, if the judge has all the relevant reasons and has given them their proper weight, then the verdict of the critical process must endorse his judgment; but if he lacks some of the relevant information or has not reasoned validly from what information he has, there is at least the logical possibility that he may turn out to be mistaken. Thus an analysis of the notion of correctness justifies the contention that having all the relevant information and recognizing its relevance logically guarantee that one is in a position to judge correctly.

3

Being reasonable, being willing and even inclined to reason, is also a standard of competence. It cannot be claimed that it is necessary to recognizing relevance on any given occasion, for even an unreasonable person may reason upon occasion. Still, the reasonable man is more likely to fulfill the condition of reasoning than the unreasonable man. This is shown by appealing to the definition of "reasonable." What is interesting about this case is that here we have a standard that establishes only the probability of competence, but a probability established by definition rather than by a correlation like that between being rested and judging correctly.

4

Being undrunk is another standard of competence. I say "undrunk" rather than "sober" because I think that this standard is a negative one. We do not hesitate to judge a drunken person incompetent as an ethical judge, but we do not regard soberness as any real assurance of competence. What justifies us in setting up undrunkenness as a standard of competence is in part that we find drunken judges tend to make incorrect judgments. But in part being undrunk can also be justified as a condition of reasoning, of recognizing relevance. Sober reasoners are more likely to reason validly than drunken ones. We know this because we find that drunken reasoners in fact often reason invalidly, and this finding can be explained to some extent by our psychological theories. In this way we can justify the standard of being undrunk.

But this justification hinges upon our judgment that in many cases the drunk is arguing invalidly. For if the invalidity of his reasoning is not established, then no correlation between drunkenness and invalidity can be established. Now suppose the drunk insists that he is not reasoning invalidly in any given case; after all, he cannot see anything wrong with his argument. We can reply that he is too drunk to recognize the invalidity of his reasoning, but he can counter with the charge that we are too sober to recognize its validity. How is this dispute to be settled? Certainly not by pointing out that we are sober and he is drunk. Our contention that being undrunk is a condition of reasoning validly can be established only after we have established the invalidity of many cases of drunken reasoning. Since to claim that an argument is invalid is to make a critical judgment, this judgment is to be established by the process of criticism. We must thoughtfully discuss the argument in question with the drunk and anyone else who happens to be interested and can make all of the moves appropriate to the validity dimension of justification. If we can convince the drunk that his argument is invalid, well and good. If we cannot, two possibilities remain: either we have not carried on the process of critcism far enough to reach a verdict or no amount of criticism could reach agreement because the drunk just does not think in the normal way. In the first case, we can only make a tentative critical judgment subject to correction in the light of more criticism; in the latter case, the drunk can be excluded from the critical community for which the critical judgment is applicable. The fact that he is not persuaded does not matter because the claim to validity is the claim that when subjected to indefinite criticism the argument will be persuasive for everyone who thinks in the normal manner, and when drunk he does not think in this manner. The moral of this tale is that if drinking causes a basic change in the way in which a person thinks, then *we* may be justified in judging his reasoning invalid even though there is no way of showing *him* that it is such.

5

Being undrugged is a very similar standard of competence. The reader may have wondered why I mention cocktail parties and drunkenness so often in this chapter. This is not so much a reflection of my way of life or standard of values as a reflection of my theoretical interests. The problems involved in justifying the claim that being drunk renders one incompetent are particularly interesting because they parallel the difficulties involved in justifying the contention that being undrugged or unmystical are also standards of competence. The drugs that particularly interest me are not aspirin, which might make one better able to reason if one was distracted by a pain, or morphine, which might make one incapable of reasoning at all, but drugs like LSD, which appear to alter the consciousness of the person radically without necessarily rendering him inarticulate. Thus it is quite possible to imagine someone who has taken LSD reasoning very differently about some ethical issue. He might dismiss or give too little weight to utilitarian considerations and give far too much weight to present feelings of exhilaration and intensified experience. Or so it seems to me, but he might argue lucidly that it is I who place too much weight on pragmatic considerations and underestimate the value of euphoria. Now I want to justify my contention that being undrugged is a standard of competence on the grounds that being undrugged is required for recognizing the relevance of the factual information, that it is a condition of ethical reasoning. But to do this I must justify my claim that the drugged person reasons invalidly. How can I show that it is he, and not I, who is reasoning invalidly?

At this point the comparison and contrast with being drunk is revealing. To the drunk I can say "you will agree with me when you sober up." He may reply "you will agree with me when you drink up," but the former is more likely than the latter. That is, drinking does not so much change the way one thinks as make one incapable of thinking very much or very well. This is reflected by the fact that drunkards do not tend to agree on statements and arguments different from those found acceptable by the sober; they disagree with one another as much as with their sober critics. Therefore, as long as the drunk is not too drunk, it may be quite possible to reason with him about the validity of his arguments and so establish the charge of invalidity to his satisfaction. If he is very drunk, it is not so much that reasoning with him is unavailing as that one can no longer reason with him. In this respect the taker of LSD seems to be in a different position. He seems to be articulate and capable of something like reasoning, and he can appeal to the fact that all or most takers of LSD think the way he does. There is something like a consensus of drug takers that utilitarian considerations are irrelevant or unimportant and that present euphoria outweighs everything else. Nor does this logical judgment give way before criticism. It may change when the drugs wear off, but our logical standards change in the opposite direction when our undrugged state wears off (that is, as soon as we take LSD). What this indicates, I think, is that people under the influence of LSD really think in a different way from the normal person. If so, they are excluded from the process of criticism; whether or not they find an argument persuasive has no bearing on the claim that under criticism it is persuasive for everyone who thinks in the normal way. We can condemn their thinking as invalid on the grounds that the verdict of the critical process is against it. Their disagreement can be dismissed as irrelevant. In this way we can justify our contention that being undrugged is a standard of competence as an ethical judge.

6

Being unmystical is a related standard of competence. There is a clear similarity between the way the mystic thinks about value and obligation and the thinking of someone who has taken LSD. Moreover, the mystic is apt to come to radically different ethical conclusions because he considers the mystical experience so all-important and ignores or underestimates the individual facts of the case. These differences are often expressed in ethical theories that hold that one ought to die to this world or that the good of man lies in some mystical experience. But the mystic's way of thinking cannot be traced to the influence of anything like a drug. It may be a relatively rare way of thinking, but in an important sense it is natural rather than artificial. The mystic has simply abandoned himself to a way of thinking open to almost everyone and into which most people slip from time to time. Therefore it is not quite so clearly abnormal and not so easily dismissed on that ground.

In fact, there should be no need to dismiss the mystic's way of thinking, to show that his way of thinking lies outside the critical process. The genuine mystic loses himself in given experience and refuses to notice distinctions or articulate relationships. The process of criticism involves analysis and explanation, stating premises and formulating arguments, making distinctions and tracing relevancies. In rejecting these the mystic is rejecting the very process of criticism which gives meaning to the claims that some judgment is correct or some argument valid. If the verdict of criticism goes against the mystic, he has no right to complain. We are justified in judging his reasoning invalid and his conclusions incorrect by the verdict of the critical process he rejects. He cannot disagree with our verdict, for he has removed himself from the critical process within which alone words like "valid" and "correct" have meaning or justification. Paradoxically, just because the difference between the mystic and the critical thinker is more radical than that between the drug taker and the normal man, it is easier to justify the claim that he is mistaken. While we must give some grounds for excluding the drug taker from the process of criticism, the mystic voluntarily withdraws from that process himself. But because competence is itself a critical notion to be defined in terms of the notion of correctness, we can appeal to that process in establishing the standards of competence. In this way we can justify our requirement that the competent ethical judge be unmystical.

What this all adds up to is that standards of competence can be justified, but that there is no one way of justifying all such standards. Most standards of competence are derived from more primitive ones. There seem to be two main ways in which one standard is derived from another. Sometimes the relation is purely analytic; being reasonable or willing and inclined to reason is by definition a condition of actually reasoning or recognizing relevance. Sometimes the connection is discovered by finding a correlation, as when being sober is found to be associated with judging correctly. There seem to be two sets of primitive standards from which all the others are derived. Success in past ethical judgments is the defining criterion of the ability to judge correctly, and having all the relevant information and recognizing its relevance are the epistemological conditions which alone can logically guarantee the ability to judge correctly.

CONCLUSION

Although I have rejected the ideal-observer analyses of ethical language, I have tried to show how competence as an ethical judge does enter into the justification of ethical statements. Since the incompetence of a speaker is indirect evidence against the truth of his assertions, since an incompetent speaker is not in a position fully to defend his statements, and since the opinion of an incompetent speaker cannot represent itself as the verdict of the process of criticism, a speaker who wishes to justify his claim to speak the truth may need to meet any challenge that may be made to his competence as an ethical judge. Such challenges and the responses to them usually take for granted one or more standards of competence, but these standards can themselves be questioned. I have illustrated some of the ways in which, granted my interpretation of our critical vocabulary, various standards of competence can be established. My conclusion is that it is possible, although not always easy, to justify the claim that a given speaker is or is not competent.

ONCE competence is admitted to be relevant to justification in ethics, knowability also becomes relevant. Knowability challenges are not at all uncommon. For example, some contend that we can never know what we ought to do because moral obligation is derived from God's command and we have no reliable way of ascertaining the will of God. It might easily be argued that we can never be sure whether Hitler was as wicked as he is usually pictured because we have very limited information about his real motivation and, since he is dead, little prospect of getting additional information. Again, it can be said that we cannot know whether welfare legislation is beneficial on the whole because so many imponderables, like the indirect economic consequences and the effects on human character, are involved. Such knowability challenges are, I suppose, the traditional weapon of ethical skepticism.

To say that an ethical statement is unknowable is not, of course, to deny its truth, for a statement may well be true even though nobody is in a position to know that it is true. Much less is it to deny either the truth-value or the meaningfulness of the statement, for only a meaningful sentence can have truth-value and only a sentence with truth-value raises any problem of knowledge. To know is to know whether or not some statement is true. Where there is no possibility of truth or falsity there can be no question of truth and, therefore, no problem of knowledge.

Still, knowability is relevant to the claim to truth, although in a doubly indirect way. We have seen that to question or deny the competence of a speaker is indirectly to challenge his claim to speak the truth. Now if a statement is unknowable, then clearly no speaker can be in a position to know it, and only the man who knows is in a position to justify his claim to speak the truth. In this way to challenge the knowability of a statement is to challenge the competence of the speaker, whoever he may happen to be, and therefore to undermine his claim to speak the truth. It follows that a part of any complete justification of an ethical statement will be meeting any knowability challenges that may arise.

The nature of the challenge

Since the knowability challenge is easily confused with two others, it is important to be clear on its precise nature. Compare three sorts of views holding that something cannot be known. *1*) No one could possibly know that because it is logically impossible to know that sort of thing. *2*) No one can know that because of limiting factors which no human being is able to overcome. *3*) You cannot know that because of your particular situation, nature, or condition.

The first denial seems like a knowability challenge, but it is not. It is put in a very misleading way because while it suggests that there is some knowledge that is unfortunately unobtainable, it actually implies that there is nothing to be known. Any considerations that could show that knowledge is logically impossible must show that there is no possible evidence for or against the claim that the statement is true. But thus deprived of all *possible* evidence, the claim to truth loses its very significance. Therefore, this first challenge is really a form of the truth-value challenge. If it can be sustained it proves that there is nothing to be known and, therefore, nothing to be unknowable either. What this reveals, besides the eternal need to avoid misleading language, is that the knowability challenge cannot be made too strong and still remain what it is. The obstacle to our gaining knowledge must remain something contingent, something that could conceivably be different.

It thus appears that some challenges that have been thought to be skeptical are really the reverse of this. Although they are sometimes taken to prove that something is unknowable, they really prove, if they are sound, that no question of knowledge can arise. For example, some logical positivists argue that there is no method of verification in ethics, no way to establish the truth or falsehood of any ethical sentence. This is not so, but if it were so it would lead to no skeptical conclusion. It would not prove that we are unable to know the truth in ethics. What it would prove is that there are and could be no truths in ethics which we do not know because there are no truths, or falsehoods either, in ethics. The argument of the logical positivist presents a truth-value and not a knowability challenge.

The third denial is not a knowability challenge, either. To deny that a given speaker can know something because his particular situation, nature, or condition prevents him from gaining this knowledge is not to contend that this matter is unknowable but only that this particular person cannot know it. This is a competence challenge of the sort discussed in the previous chapter. But to establish the incompetence of this or that speaker is not at all to show that the statement is such that no human being can know it.

The knowability challenge is a more general one, one that implies that no possible speaker, at least no human speaker, is or can become competent on the matter at hand. For this reason it is more embarrassing from an epistemological standpoint than any competence challenge. Although an incompetent speaker can always hope that some more competent ethical judge will come to his rescue and defend his statement for him, the knowability challenge rules out this reassuring possibility. The knowability challenge leaves open the logical possibility of knowledge, but it questions or denies that any speaker has the ability to attain it. It holds that there are certain insurmountable limitations in human nature or the world in which we live which prevent our gaining this knowledge. This is a more general and final challenge than the competence challenge because it is aimed at all men at all times and implies that no merely human effort can remedy the ground of the challenge. Yet it is a less radical challenge than the truth-value challenge because it does not touch the claim that the utterance is really a statement, that it is either true or false. Here on this middle ground ethical skepticism traditionally takes up its stand.

One variation in knowability challenges, that in strength, deserves to be mentioned. Traditionally knowledge was contrasted with opinion. Knowledge was certain truth. No matter how much evidence there might be that some belief was true, if the possibility of error remained it could be nothing more than opinion. More recently knowledge has been thought of as rational belief. The mere possibility of error does not rule out the claim to know as long as the belief is rationally justified. Hence, to claim to know something may be to claim certainty or only to claim probability; it may be to claim that one could not be mistaken or only that there is reason to think one is not in error. Correspondingly, to challenge the knowability of a statement may be to contend that no one can be certain of its truth or that no one can have any reasonable evidence of its truth. The former is a relatively weak claim that can probably be made good quite often; the latter is a much stronger claim that, let us hope, can be substantiated less often. To show that no man could have reason to believe some statement is completely to undermine the claim to truth implicit in asserting it, but to show that no man could be certain is only to require the speaker to moderate his claim to assurance.

Balanced arguments

One of the main weapons of classical skepticism was the argument from balanced arguments.[1] It was contended that one cannot know any ethical statement by reasoning because to reason is to present and consider arguments for or against some conclusion. Unfortunately, equal arguments can be advanced both for and against any ethical statement; each argument to prove the statement true can be balanced with an equal argument to prove it false. Therefore, rational argument can never enable us to know whether or not it is really true.

It must be admitted at the outset that in ethics there usually are reasons both for and against any statement. The evidence is seldom, if ever, all on one side. But granted the existence of opposed arguments in ethical reasoning, the question remains as to whether they are equal and, if so, in what sense they are equal. The skeptic may mean that the opposed arguments are equally valid and weighty or only that they are equally plausible.

Since most ethical issues arise from a conflict of pros and cons, it may well be that opposed arguments are both valid. But since some consideration weigh more than others, it does not follow that they are equally strong. It is logically possible, I suppose, that for every ethical argument there happens to be an equally strong one on the other side, but this seems a priori improbable. Moreover, reflection on the arguments for and against a few sample ethical statements will show, I think, that the pros and cons are seldom of equal weight. To be sure, occasionally the reasons for an ethical conclusion do seem to balance the reasons against it, but even here skepticism is not the proper conclusion. If, for example, the reasons for and against doing act A are really of equal logical force, one need not conclude that one cannot know what one ought to do; one should conclude that one ought either to do A or not to do A, that the alternatives are equally right. Therefore, ethical reasoning seldom reveals equally valid and strong arguments on opposite sides of an issue and, where it does, this does not justify skepticism.

It is quite possible, however, that the skeptic means only to assert that ethical reasoning reveals equally plausible arguments. With a little imagination it seems possible to advance plausible arguments for or against almost any ethical statement, and the classical skeptic was fond of inventing such arguments. The question raised by the existence of balanced arguments in this sense is whether it is possible to distinguish between the argument that only seems valid and strong because it is so plausible and the argument that really is valid and strong. The answer is that we can do this by subjecting the arguments to the process of criticism. The valid argument is the one which is persuasive when subjected to indefinite criticism, and the strong argument is the one which is highly persuasive after criticism. Since not all plausible arguments can stand up to this test of critical examination, the fact of equal initial plausibility does not imply any equality of rationality. Hence one could admit that ethical arguments are balanced in plausibility without conceding that reasoning is unable to determine the truth of an ethical statement. But why admit even this much? To be sure, the imaginative arguer can produce arguments of some plausibility for almost any ethical statement. Still, plausibility is a matter of degree, and it may be doubted that all these arguments are equally plausible prior to criticism. Some strike the listener as strained and forced even before he has thought them through carefully and discovered their fallacies. The skeptic is on no stronger ground when he appeals to psychological plausibility than when he appealed to logical validity and strength.

There is a lesson in all this. The moral of this skeptical argument is that it is very difficult to distinguish the valid ethical argument from the merely plausible one and that it is even more difficult to estimate the relative weights of the pros and the cons. Because of these very real difficulties, the invalid or weak argument can often masquerade as a strong and valid one. But there is a difference and this difference can in principle be discovered by human reason because the distinctions between valid and invalid, strong and weak are defined in terms of the thoroughly human process of criticism. Therefore, the difficulty of ethical knowledge does not indicate its unattainability.

Personal bias

Truth is impersonal; to claim that a statement is true is to claim that it would be accepted by any normal person who objectively considered all the evidence. But any actual speaker is some particular person standing in very special relations to other persons. It has been suggested that each of us lives in a sort of psychological space in which distances are measured by degrees of interest in other people. No one is completely disinterested, for he is too near some people and too far from others. One is too near someone when one loves or hates, admires or distrusts him strongly; such personal attachments make it very hard to arrive at any true ethical conclusion concerning the person to whom one is thus attached. One is too far from a person when one does not care enough about him to take his value or disvalue experiences seriously; it is not easy to recognize one's obligations to a stranger. To make any objective ethical judgment one would have to become completely disinterested, free oneself from all special and personal interests without losing all interests in the people involved. The skeptic can argue that since no man can achieve a completely disinterested state of mind, no man can know the impersonal truth in ethics.

Perhaps, but remember that neither personal attachments nor lack of concern are givens fixed beyond all control. In particular, interests can be modified in large measure by reasoning itself. When I come to know more about the starving Chinese or the uneducated in our own slums, I may come to care about people to whom I was indifferent before. When I come to know my friends and enemies better or reflect in a cool hour on what I already know about them, I may admire them less or stop being so annoyed with them. If personal interests often distort ethical judgments, it is also true that they are often modified by additional reasoning.

But can any human being become so perfectly rational as to become *completely* disinterested? To this skeptical question I would pose another question: need one become completely disinterested? It may be that one can make an impersonal judgment in spite of his personal interests. For one thing, a person can recognize value with only a minimal amount of love for the person whose value it is. This ability to put oneself in the other man's shoes is very important for ethical reasoning. To do this one must understand the nature of the other person's situation and respond to it imaginatively as though one were in that situation oneself. I do not pretend that our insight into the lives of others is infallible or that we respond to imagined situations as fully as we respond to actual ones. What I do contend is that human beings are capable of putting themselves in the other fellow's shoes and that this enables us partially to overcome the limitations of our individual perspectives and interests. Since we can often recognize the existence and degree of value by this imaginative displacement of ourselves, it is not necessary for us to achieve any perfect charity in which each person cares about all mankind as much as he cares for himself.

There still remain those loves and hates, desires and aversions that prejudice one's judgment of objects and persons near to oneself in psychological space. One cannot completely rid oneself of such personal interests. This is probably a good thing for living the good life, but it is a handicap to good ethical judgment. Nevertheless, one may be able to allow for such interests in various ways. To the extent that one can exclude them and their objects from consciousness, they tend to lose their persuasive efficacy. Knowing oneself and one's biases, one may be able to modify one's conclusions to take into account the probability that one is being led astray. And one can often ask the advice of someone who is less interested than, or at least has different interests from, oneself. Thus one may be able to correct one's judgment and overcome one's personal limitations.

Even if it is humanly impossible fully to allow for personal interests, the skeptic's conclusion does not quite follow. Given any situation, object, or person to be judged, many judgers will be personally involved because of their special interests. But many other potential judgers will not be personally involved at all; they will have no special interests in this matter, although they are deeply involved in other matters. Therefore, for any given subject of ethical judgment there will be many ethical judges who have no special interests to overcome. At most what follows from the fact of personal involvement is that any given judge will be incompetent to judge certain ethical issues impersonally and rationally, and this may well be so. But this implies no limitation upon ethical knowledge because there will be others who are not thus incompetent on this particular issue. On another issue the line between competent and incompetent judges will shift somewhat. But the fact that some may be incompetent to know any given ethical statement does not prove that that statement is unknowable. It is at least possible that some human being

is or can become disinterested enough to now whether or not
it is true.

Knowing the consequences

Any theory of obligation that holds that the rightness or
wrongness of an action depends wholly or in part upon its
consequences provides an opening for skepticism. This is because any action fits into a causal sequence that goes on until
the end of time, or at least until the end of our world. Since the
effects of any action are infinite, it is hard to imagine how anyone could know all the consequences of a given act before, or
at any finite length of time after, it is done. It seems to follow
that one can never really know whether the action is right or
wrong; the best one can do is to guess on the basis of those
relatively few consequences one is able to predict or discover.

It must be granted that no one can know all the consequences of any act. This is not because any of its consequences
is intrinsically unknowable but because the totality of consequences is infinite. Given an infinite length of time, there is no
reason one might not come to know an infinite number of
consequences. It is simply that no mortal man can know all
the results of any act. But does one need to know all the consequences of an act in order to determine its rightness or
wrongness? The teleological theory of obligation would seem
to imply this, for how can one know the value produced by an
act without knowing what things it brings into existence?
And if one cannot know the total value or disvalue brought
into existence by an action, one cannot know whether it is
right or wrong.

Before giving up let us remark that on most teleological
theories of obligation any conclusion about the rightness or
wrongness of a given act hinges on the comparative value
produced by this act as opposed to all other acts open to the
agent under the circumstances. Act-utilitarianism, for example, requires that one ought to do that action which produces
the most value or the least disvalue among all the alternative
actions which the agent could do given the situation. What

one needs to know, then, is the *difference* in value between the consequences of this act and the consequences of each of the other possible acts. At first glance this appears only to compound our difficulty, for now we have several infinite sets of consequences to know instead of just one. But although the consequences of any act may go on forever, the difference they make to the value or disvalue realized in the world as a whole usually becomes rapidly less and less. Not many of the acts I perform each day will make much difference, even to me, next year; much less will they materially change the lives of the next generation. Therefore, one can usually ignore the remoter consequences of any act in estimating its value compared with the value produced by other possible acts. If one knows the consequences for those most directly affected for the foreseeable future, one usually knows enough to reach a sound judgment of obligation. One's evidence can be sufficient without being complete. The possibility of error remains, of course; it is always possible that some remote or unexpected consequence will turn up that materially affects the value produced by the act. But I have already admitted that certainty is unattainable in ethical judgments; what I will not concede to the skeptic is that knowledge in the sense of rationally justified belief is likewise unattainable.

Glancing back

There it is, my answer to the question "how can ethical statements be justified?" Like anything else that stands in need of justification, ethical statements can be justified by meeting every challenge that is actually made to them. There are seven different sorts of challenge that are directly or indirectly relevant to the claim to truth implicit in any statement—truth, truth-value, meaningfulness, validity, validity-value, competence, and knowability. Each of these defines a dimension of justification, an orientation of challenge and response. In Part Two of this book I have described and illustrated each of these dimensions; I have explained how ethical statements can be justified.

My answer presupposes an answer to a prior question: what is justification? In the first part of this book I argued that justification is not to be identified with reasoning, much less with deductive reasoning. The best way to conceive of justification is in terms of challenge and response; to justify is to meet all challenges actually made.

Looking ahead

It is often held, and I am inclined to agree, that the central problem of ethics is the problem of choice. There are other ethical problems, of course, but they all revolve around and are subsidiary to the problem of deciding what is to be done in the situation in which the agent finds himself. Now an action is quite different from a statement, even a statement about an action. It may seem, therefore, as though my extended discussion of the justification of ethical statements is almost beside the point, at best a mere preliminary to justification in ethics. For surely justification in ethics is primarily the justification of doings and not of statements.

I willingly concede that it is the justification of actions that is central to ethics, but it does not follow that the justification of ethical statements is a mere preliminary to this because the problem of choice and the answers to it can be put into words, into the critical language we ordinarily use for discussing such issues. The problem of choice is the problem of what to do and not simply what to say, but one can pose this problem of doing by saying "what ought I to do?" The practical solution to a problem of choice is an action and not a mere statement. Still, if the action calls for justification, this is because it makes an implicit claim to rationality, which can be formulated "I ought to do that act," an ethical statement. To be sure, justifying this ethical statement is not the *same* as justifying that action, but there is no *more* to justifying the action. In fact, there is less; for the statement is open to challenges, like the truth-value challenge, to which the action is immune. Since the statement puts into words the claim to rationality implicit in the action, there is no way of challenging this claim of the action that would not also be a challenge to the statement. Therefore, the justification of the statement contains within itself everything that would be contained in the justification of the action and more. For this reason my discussion of the justification of ethical statements is no mere preliminary to the justification of actions.

In some theories of justification, genuine justification is limited to propositions. Such a theory might plausibly explain how ethical statements can be justified but clearly could never explain how actions, which are nonpropositional, could be justified. Even worse, such theories imply that actions or doings are entirely beyond justification. They thereby make the central ethical problem, "what ought I to do?," unintelligible. Such theories are no mere preliminary to justification in ethics; they are the end of ethics. On the other hand, my theory of justification does not explain the problem of choice out of existence. In trying to develop a theory of justification that would be adequate to statements, I have found a theory that is readily applicable to actions as well. Since actions are persuadable, since one's choice is modified by discussion and thinking, actions make an implicit claim to rationality. This claim can be challenged and such challenges met just as statements can be challenged and these challenges met. Therefore, on my theory actions can be justified in precisely the same sense and in much the same way that statements can be justified. Once more it is apparent that my account of the justification of ethical statements is no mere preliminary to an explanation of the justification of actions so central to ethics.

In another way, of course, my account, long as it is, is a mere preliminary. To discuss the nature of justification in ethics is not to justify any particular ethical statements or to justify any actions either. These tasks, justifying definite ethical statements and justifying chosen actions, lie ahead. The task of deciding what to do and of justifying one's doings to oneself and others is not a specifically philosophical one; it is the constant, unavoidable, demanding, and rewarding task of living as rationally and responsibly as one can. It calls for a life, not a book. The task of making and justifying ethical statements, at least if these are unusually general or fundamental, is a philosophical one. It might call for a book or several books. But that would be another discussion, a treatise in ethics, to which this treatment of the justification of ethical statements is a preliminary. This preliminary task of trying to solve the philosophical problems arising from the justification of ethical statements is now complete. One measure of its success will be whether or not it makes the next task an easier one.

notes / selected bibliography / index

1 deduction

[1] W. D. Ross, *The Right and the Good* (Oxford, 1930), pp. 28–29.

[2] Richard M. Hare, "Universalizability," *Proceedings of the Aristotelian Society* 55 (1954–55): 295–312.

[3] Kurt Baier, *The Moral Point of View: A Rational Basis of Ethics* (Ithaca, N.Y., 1958), pp. 191–95.

[4] Richard M. Hare, *The Language of Morals* (Oxford, 1952), pp. 46–49.

[5] Karl R. Popper, *The Logic of Scientific Discovery* (London, 1959), pp. 78–111 and 251–81.

[6] D. C. Williams, *The Ground of Induction* (Cambridge, Mass., 1947), pp. 105–30.

2 induction

[1] Plato *Philebus* 21C.

[2] William James, *Essays on Faith and Morals* (New York, 1947), p. 188.

[3] William Savery, "A Defense of Hedonism," *Ethics* 45 (October 1934): 14–15.

[4] James, *Faith and Morals*, pp. 189–91.

[5] John Dewey, *Human Nature and Conduct: An Introduction to Social Psychology* (New York, 1930), p. 190.

[6] Ludwig Wittgenstein, *Philosophical Investigations*, trans. G. E. M. Anscombe (Oxford, 1953), p. 94.

[7] Sir W. David Ross, *Foundations of Ethics* (Oxford, 1939), pp. 168–70.

[8] Immanuel Kant, *Critique of Pure Reason*, trans. Norman Kemp Smith (London, 1929), p. 44.

3 conduction

[1] Stephen Toulmin, *An Examination of the Place of Reason in Ethics* (Cambridge, 1950), pp. 132 and 144–52.

[2] Max Black, "The Gap Between 'Is' and 'Should'," *Philosophical Review* 73 (April 1964): 169, 173.

[3] Carl Wellman, *The Language of Ethics* (Cambridge, Mass., 1961), chap. 10.

4   reasoning

[1] For a detailed discussion of the distinction between descriptive and critical meaning see Carl Wellman, *The Language of Ethics* (Cambridge, Mass., 1961), chaps. 6 and 10.

[2] Charles Sanders Peirce, "How to Make Our Ideas Clear," in *Collected Papers of Charles Sanders Peirce*, ed. Charles Hartshorne and Paul Weiss, vol. 5 (Cambridge, Mass., 1934), pp. 266–70.

5   justification

[1] Charles Sanders Peirce, "The Fixation of Belief," in *Collected Papers of Charles Sanders Peirce*, ed. Charles Hartshorne and Paul Weiss, vol. 5 (Cambridge, Mass., 1934), pp. 233–35.

[2] W. K. Clifford, "The Ethics of Belief," in *Lectures and Essays by the Late William Kingdom Clifford, F.R.S.*, ed. Leslie Stephen and Sir Frederick Pollock, vol. 2 (London, 1879), p. 186.

[3] Peirce, "The Fixation of Belief," *Collected Papers* 5:231–33.

[4] J. L. Austin, "Other Minds," *Proceedings of the Aristotelian Society*, supplementary vol. 20 (1946), pp. 148–87.

6   infinite regresses

[1] René Descartes, *Rules*, in *Philosophical Works of Descartes*, ed. E. S. Haldane and G. R. T. Ross (Cambridge, 1931), pp. 3, 7.

[2] Descartes, *Meditations*, in *Philosophical Works of Descartes*, ed. E. S. Haldane and G. R. T. Ross (Cambridge, 1931), pp. 145–47.

[3] Aristotle, *Physics*, bk. 8, chap. 1 and bk. 7, chap. 1.

[4] Richard B. Brandt, *Ethical Theory: The Problems of Normative and Critical Ethics* (Englewood Cliffs, N.J., 1959), pp. 46–51.

[5] Clarence Irving Lewis, *Analysis of Knowledge and Valuation* (LaSalle, Ill., 1946), pp. 353–58.

[6] Ibid., pp. 340–41.

[7] John Dewey, *The Quest for Certainty: A Study of the Relation of Knowledge and Action* (New York, 1929), pp. 99, 243.

7 truth

[1] John Mackie, "A Refutation of Morals," *Australasian Journal of Psychology and Philosophy* 24 (September 1946): 77–90.

8 truth-value

[1] A. J. Ayer, *Language, Truth, and Logic* (London, 1946), p. 103.
[2] Carl Wellman, *The Language of Ethics* (Cambridge, Mass., 1961), chap. 2.
[3] C. L. Stevenson, *Facts and Values: Studies in Ethical Analysis* (New Haven, 1963), pp. 214–20.
[4] P. F. Strawson, *Introduction to Logical Theory* (London, 1952), pp. 175–79.
[5] William Frankena, "Obligation and Ability," in *Philosophical Analysis*, ed. Max Black (Ithaca, N.Y., 1950), pp. 157–75.

9 meaningfulness

[1] John Locke, *Essay Concerning Human Understanding*, bk. 2, chap. 21, secs. 14–26.
[2] Ibid., secs. 15–16.
[3] Ibid., secs. 16–26.
[4] Gilbert Ryle, *The Concept of Mind* (London, 1949), pp. 62–82.
[5] Gilbert Ryle, "Categories," in *Logic and Language*, ed. Antony Flew (Oxford, 1966), p. 66.
[6] Ibid., pp. 68–70.
[7] W. D. Ross, *The Right and the Good* (Oxford, 1930), p. 65.
[8] P. T. Geach, "Good and Evil," *Analysis* 17 (December 1956): 33–42.
[9] H. A. Prichard, "Does Moral Philosophy Rest on a Mistake?" *Mind* 21 (January 1912): 21–37.

10 validity

[1] Richard M. Hare, *The Language of Morals* (Oxford, 1952), pp. 28–31.
[2] G. H. von Wright, "Practical Inference," *Philosophical Review* 72 (April 1963): 159–79.

[3] Max Black, "The Gap Between 'Is' and 'Should'," *Philosophical Review* 73 (April 1964): 169 ff.

[4] Joseph Butler, *Sermons*, in *British Moralists*, ed. L. A. Selby-Bigge, vol. 1 (Oxford, 1897), pp. 227–28.

[5] David Hume, *Enquiries concerning the Human Understanding and concerning the Principles of Morals*, ed. L. A. Selby-Bigge (Oxford, 1902), pp. 298–300.

[6] Thomas Hobbes, *Leviathan*, introd. A. D. Lindsay (New York, 1950), chaps. 14 and 15.

11   validity-value

[1] David Hume, *A Treatise of Human Nature* (Oxford, 1888), pp. 86–94.

[2] A. J. Ayer, *Language, Truth, and Logic* (London, 1946), pp. 110–12.

[3] Carl Wellman, *The Language of Ethics* (Cambridge, Mass., 1961), pp. 117–27.

13   knowability

[1] Sextus Empiricus, *Outlines of Pyrrhonism*, in R. G. Bury, *Sextus Empiricus*, vol. 1 (Cambridge, Mass., 1933), pp. 119–21.

Aiken, Henry. "The Levels of Moral Discourse." *Ethics* 62 (July 1952): 235–48. Quite a different approach to a pluralistic theory of justification in ethics.

———. "Moral Reasoning." *Ethics* 64 (October 1953): 24–37. Argues that some, but not all, ethical reasoning is deductive.

———. *Reason and Conduct.* New York, 1962. Chapter 8: Argues that moral objectivity is different from scientific or logical truth.

Alston, William P. "Linguistic Acts." *American Philosophical Quarterly* 1 (April 1964): 138–46. Outlines a theory of linguistic acts in which the speaker must recognize the relevance of rules to his speech act.

Austin, J. L. "Other Minds." *Proceedings of the Aristotelian Society.* Supplementary vol. 20 (1946), pp. 148–87. Claims that one should accept a statement unless there is some special reason to doubt it.

Ayer, A. J. "Demonstration of the Impossibility of Metaphysics." *Mind* 43 (July 1934): 335–45. Supports the verifiability theory of meaningfulness by an appeal to examples.

———. *Language, Truth, and Logic.* London, 1946. Pages 20–22 and 102–13: A pure form of the emotive theory of ethics.

Barker, S. F. *Induction and Hypothesis.* Ithaca, N.Y., 1957. Discusses several views of induction and proposes a modified method of hypothesis.

Black, Max. "The Gap Between 'Is' and 'Should'." *Philosophical Review* 73 (April 1964): 165–81. Argues against Hume's contention that there is a logical gap between "is" and "ought."

Brandt, Richard B. *Ethical Theory.* Englewood Cliffs, N.J., 1959. Chapter 3: A criticism of the view that we can justify by appealing to merely accepted premises. Chapter 10: Proposes the qualified attitude for testing ethical beliefs.

Brown, D. G. "Evaluative Inference." *Philosophy* 30 (July 1955): 214–28. Argues that the principles of evaluative inference belong to morals rather than logic.

Brown, Patterson. "Infinite Causal Regression." *Philosophical Review* 75 (October 1966): 510–25. Interesting interpretation of the Aristotelian argument against infinite causal regresses.

Burke, T. E. "Methods of Inquiry." *Mind* 73 (October 1964): 538–49. Suggests that validity is more basic than truth.

Clifford, W. K. "The Ethics of Belief." *Lectures and Esays*, vol. 2, pp. 177–212. London, 1879. Contends that the burden of proof is on one who accepts any belief.

Cooper, Neil, "Some Presuppositions of Moral Judgments." *Mind* 75 (January 1966): 45–57. An interesting suggestion about how presuppositions work in ethics.

Demos, Raphael. "Is Moral Reasoning Deductive?" *Journal of Philosophy* 55 (February 13, 1958): 153–59. Argues that moral reasoning is more like induction than deduction.

Descartes, René. *Discourse on the Method of Rightly Conducting the Reason and Seeking for Truth in the Sciences.* In *The Philosophical Works of Descartes.* Edited by E. S. Haldane and G. R. T. Ross. Cambridge, 1931. Page 92: Accept only the indubitable.

———. *Rules for the Direction of the Mind.* In *The Philosophical Works of Descartes.* Edited by E. S. Haldane and G. R. T. Ross. Cambridge, 1931. Classic statement of the view that knowledge must begin with indubitables.

Dewey, John. *The Quest for Certainty.* New York, 1929. Rejection of the view that justification must rest on unchallengeable premises. Also contends that certainty is neither possible nor necessary.

Earle, William. "The Standard Observer in the Science of Man." *Ethics* 63 (July 1953): 293–99. Argues that only the exceptional man has the insight to understand fully his fellow human beings.

Edel, Abraham. *Method in Ethical Theory.* Indianapolis, Ind., 1963. Suggests some of the variety in the ways ethical theories can be challenged.

Edwards, Paul. *The Logic of Moral Discourse.* Glencoe, Ill., 1955. Chapter 3: A critical account of the error theory.

Empiricus, Sextus. *Outlines of Pyrrhonism.* In R. G. Bury, *Sextus Empiricus.* Vol. 1. Cambridge, Mass., 1933. Contains a wide variety of knowability challenges.

Ewing, A. C. "Meaninglessness." *Mind* 46 (July 1937): 347–64. Attempted refutation of the verification theory of meaning.

Falk, W. D. "Action-guiding Reasons." *Journal of Philosophy* 60 (November 7, 1963): 702–18. Claims that ethical reasons must cause action when properly held in mind.

Feigl, Herbert. "De Principiis Non Disputandum . . . ?" In *Philosophical Analysis*, edited by Max Black, pp. 119–56. Ithaca, N.Y., 1950. One attempt to extend justification beyond deduction from first principles.

Findlay, J. N. "Morality by Convention." *Mind* 53 (April 1944):

142–69. Interesting attempt to explain how emotions can be challenged and justified.

Firth, Roderick. "Ethical Absolutism and the Ideal Observer." *Philosophy and Phenomenological Research* 12 (March 1952): 317–45. An analysis of ethical words in terms of the ideal observer.

Fodor, J. A. "On Knowing What We Would Say." *Philosophical Review* 73 (April 1964): 198–212. Discusses an interesting parallel to thought experiments and argues that they prove nothing.

Frankena, William. "The Naturalistic Fallacy." *Mind* 48 (October 1939): 464–77. Puzzles over which alleged error is the naturalistic fallacy.

——. "Obligation and Ability." In *Philosophical Analysis*, edited by Max Black, pp. 157–75. Ithaca, N.Y., 1950. Unravels some of the senses in which "ought" might imply "can."

Garver, J. N. "On the Rationality of Persuading." *Mind* 69 (April 1960): 163–74. Analysis of the verb "to persuade" and discussion of when persuasion is rational.

Gauthier, David. *Practical Reasoning*. Oxford, 1963. Chapter 5: Classifies the main challenges that can be made of advice.

Geach, P. T. "Good and Evil." *Analysis* 17 (December 1956): 33–42. Contends that "good" is always attributive.

Gewirth, Alan. "Positive 'Ethics' and Normative 'Science'." *Philosophical Review* 69 (July 1960): 311–30. Suggests that contrasts between ethics and science often beg the issue of objectivity.

Glassen, P. "The Cognitivity of Moral Judgments." *Mind* 68 (January 1959): 57–72. Surveys some features of moral language that indicate its cognitive claim.

Goodman, Nelson. *Fact, Fiction, and Forest*. Cambridge, Mass., 1955. Chapter 3: Holds that rules of reasoning and individual arguments are justified by agreement with each other.

Hall, Everett. *Our Knowledge of Fact and Value*. Chapel Hill, N.C., 1961. Chapter 14: Suggests that our general evaluations are inductions based upon our particular emotions.

Hare, Richard M. *The Language of Morals*. Oxford, 192. Pages 45–55: Objects to the notion of nondeductive ethical reasoning.

——. Review of *An Examination of the Place of Reason in Ethics*, by Stephen Toulmin. *Philosophical Quarterly* 1 (July 1951): 372–75. Tries to refute Toulmin's attempt to get moral conclusions from factual premises.

Harrison, Bernard. "Category Mistakes and Rules of Language." *Mind* 74 (July 1965): 309–25. Explores both the use and misuse of the notion of a category mistake.

Harrison, Jonathan. "Can Ethics Do Without Propositions?" *Mind* 59 (July 1950): 358–71. Shows how the emotive theory can explain many features of ethical language that seem to require a cognitive analysis.

————. "Empiricism in Ethics." *Philosophical Quarterly* 2 (October 1952): 289–306. Claims that thought experiments do not give a priori knowledge in ethics.

Henderson, G. P. " 'Ought' Implies 'Can'." *Philosophy* 41 (April 1966): 101–12. Reveals some of the unclarities in the maxim that "ought" implies "can."

Hoffman, Robert. "Do We Ever Validate Moral Statements?" *Australasian Journal of Philosophy* 37 (May 1959): 57–61. Objects to the view that we can justify our conclusions only if we also justify our premises.

Hungerland, Isabel. "The Logic of Aesthetic Concepts." *Proceedings of the American Philosophical Association* 36 (October 1963): 43–66. Claims that aesthetic concepts are supported by nonaesthetic ones in a way that is neither deductive nor inductive.

Jackson, Reginald. "Practical Reason." *Philosophy* 17 (November 1942): 351–67. Claims that conclusion of practical reasoning is a choice.

Jarvis, Judith. "In Defense of Moral Absolutes." *Journal of Philosophy* 55 (November 20, 1958): 1043–53. Claims that a speaker who refuses to apply the word "right" or "wrong" to a paradigm case does not understand the meaning of the word.

————. "Practical Reasoning." *Philosophical Quarterly* 12 (October 1962): 316–28. Denies that there is any practical reasoning that is neither deductive nor inductive.

Kerner, George. "Approvals, Reasons, and Moral Argument." *Mind* 71 (October 1962): 474–86. Claims that the most basic way to justify moral judgments is by showing that the speaker is competent.

Kneale, William. "Objectivity in Morals." *Philosophy* 25 (April 1950): 149–66. One version of the ideal-observer theory of ethics.

Ladd, John. "The Distinctive Features of Obligation Statements." *Journal of Philosophy* 53 (October 25, 1956): 653–62. Develops a modified version of the practical syllogism that allows for exceptions in its application.

————. "The Issue of Relativism." *Monist* 46 (Summer 1963): 585–609. Argues that theoretical models do not apply to ethical judgments or arguments.

————. "The Place of Practical Reason in Judicial Decision." *Nomos* 7 (1964): 126–44. Argues that practical reasoning cannot be understood on the model of theoretical reasoning.

————. "Remarks on the Conflict of Obligations." *Journal of Philosophy* 55 (September 11, 1958): 811–19. Attempts to show

how the deductive model can account for the conflict of obligations.

Lewis, C. I. "Given Element in Empirical Knowledge." *Philosophical Review* 61 (April 1952): 168–75. Defends the argument that something must be certain if anything is to be probable.

———. *Mind and the World Order.* New York, 1929, Chapter 10: Argues that probable conclusions must rest on certain data.

Mackie, John. "A Refutation of Morals." *Australasian Journal of Psychology and Philosophy* 24 (September 1946): 77–90. Contends that all moral statements are false.

Mandelbaum, Maurice. "On the Use of Moral Principles." *Journal of Philosophy* 53 (October 25, 1956): 662–70. Argues against the view that moral principles function as premises from which we can deduce our obligations.

Moore, G. E. *Principia Ethica.* Cambridge, 1903. Pages 152–58. Discusses the difficulties in knowing what one ought to do arising from the fact that the consequences of any act are infinite.

Myers, C. M. "Thought Experiments and Secret Stores of Information." *International Philosophical Quarterly* 8 (June 1968): 180–92. A very interesting interpretation of thought experiments.

O'Connor, D. J. "Validity and Standards." *Proceedings of the Aristotelian Society* 57 (1956–57): 207–28. Argues that evaluative arguments can be "valid" in only an extended or figurative sense.

Odegard, Douglas. "Absurdity and Types." *Mind* 75 (January 1966): 97–113. Shows some of the problems in working out any theory of types to explain category mistakes.

Peirce, Charles Sanders. "The Criterion of Validity in Reasoning." In *The Philosophy of Peirce,* edited by Justus Buchler, pp. 120–28. New York, 1950. A classic pragmatic conception of reasoning.

———. "The Fixation of Belief." In *Collected Papers of Charles Sanders Peirce,* edited by Charles Hartshorne and Paul Weiss. Vol. 5, Cambridge, Mass., 1934. Pages 358–87: Criticism of the Cartesian demand for indubitables. Also suggests that the true belief is the one to which all scientific invetigators are fated to come in the end.

Pike, Nelson. "Rules of Inference in Moral Reasoning." *Mind* 70 (July 1961): 391–99. Suggests that no evidence can decide whether ethical reasoning requires special premises or special rules of reasoning.

Pitcher, George. "Emotion." *Mind* 74 (July 1965): 326–46. Tries to show how emotions can be reasonable or unreasonable.

Popper, K. R. *The Logic of Scientific Discovery.* London, 1959. Argues that falsification, which is deductive, is the only sort of reasoning needed in science.

Prichard, H. A. "Does Moral Philosophy Rest on a Mistake?" *Mind* 21 (January 1912): 21–37. Claims that it is a mistake to try to prove judgments of obligation.

Prior, A. N. "The Autonomy of Ethics." *Australasian Journal of Philosophy* 38 (December 1960): 199–206. Retracts his earlier claim that ethical conclusions cannot be deduced from factual premises.

Rawls, John. "Outline of a Decision Procedure for Ethics." *Philosophical Review* 60 (April 1951): 177–97. Another ideal-observer theory.

Reichenbach, Hans. "Are Phenomenal Reports Absolutely Certain?" *Philosophical Review* 61 (April 1952): 147–59. Argues that genuine probability does not require certain data.

Rice, P. B. *On the Knowledge of Good and Evil.* New York, 1955. Pages 209–10: Contends that thought experiments are not logical arguments.

Savery, William. "A Defense of Hedonism." *Ethics* 45 (October 1934): 1–26. Includes a fascinating collection of thought experiments.

Scheffler, Israel. "On Justification and Commitment." *Journal of Philosophy* 51 (March 18, 1954): 180–90. Develops a theory of justification in contrast with proving the truth of a proposition.

Schlick, Moritz. "Meaning and Verification." *Philosophical Review* 45 (July 1936): 339–69. Classic statement of a modified verifiability theory of meaningfulness.

Sharp, F. C. *Good Will and Ill Will.* Chicago, 1950. Pages 156–62: An ideal-observer analysis of "right."

Smart, J. J. C. "Reason and Conduct." *Philosophy* 25 (July 1950): 209–24. Argues that conduct can be rational in a sense analogous to deduction or empirical judgment.

Smith, James. "Impossibility and Morals." *Mind* 70 (July 1961): 362–75. Argues that "cannot" modifies rather than rules out "ought."

Sprigge, T. L. S. "A Utilitarian Reply to Dr. McCloskey." *Inquiry* 8 (Autumn 1965): 272–75. Contends that fanciful examples do not constitute valid thought experiments.

Stevenson, C. L. *Ethics and Language.* New Haven, 1944. Chapter 7: Argues that ultimate ethical arguments lack logical validity or anything analogous to validity. Chapters 5–7: Poses the problem of the relation of reasoning to persuading.

Strawson, P. F. *Introduction to Logical Theory.* London, 1952. Pages 173–79: Explains his conception of a presupposition.

―――. "On Referring." *Mind* 59 (July 1950): 320–44. Argues that referring expressions presuppose the existence of that to which they refer.

Stroud, Barry. "Wittgenstein and Logical Necessity." *Philosophical Review* 74 (October 1965): 504–18. Suggests how logical necessity might be grounded in human nature.

Toulmin, Stephen. *An Examination of the Place of Reason in Ethics.* Cambridge, 1950. Chapters 10 and 11: Explains how ethical conclusions can be derived from purely factual premises.

―――. *The Uses of Argument.* Cambridge, 1958. Chapter 3: Provides an alternative to the deductive model of reasoning.

Warnock, G. J. "Verification and the Use of Language." *Revue internationale de philosophie* 5 (1951): 307–22. Criticism of the verifiability criterion of meaningfulness and a defense of use as meaning.

Warrender, Howard. *The Political Philosophy of Hobbes.* Oxford, 1957. Chapter 2: Suggests various ways in which considerations bear on statements of obligation when he distinguishes the grounds, conditions, and instruments of obligation.

Wellman, Carl. "Emotivism and Ethical Objectivity." *American Philosophical Quarterly* 5 (April 1968): 90–99. Argues against emotivism that ethical sentences are objectively true or false.

―――. *The Language of Ethics.* Cambridge, Mass., 1961. Chapter 10: Discussion of critical meaning and our epistemic vocabulary; also an analysis of truth in terms of critical meaning.

―――. "Our Criteria for Third-Person Psychological Sentences." *Journal of Philosophy* 58 (May 25, 1961): 281–93. Reply to skepticism with respect to other minds.

Wright, G. H. von. "Deontic Logic." *Mind* 61 (January 1951): 1–15. A pioneer attempt to extend the bounds of deductive logic to cover some ethical arguments.

―――. "Practical Inference." *Philosophical Review* 72 (April 1963): 159–79. Discusses one sort of practical inference that seems to go from facts to an ought conclusion.